The Basics of Legal Writing

Revised First Edition

Mary Barnard Ray

Assistant Director, Legal Research and Writing Program
University of Wisconsin Law School

THOMSON

WEST

Mat #40738247

© 2008 Thomson/West
    610 Opperman Drive
    St Paul, MN 55123
    1–800–313–9378

Printed in the United States of America

ISBN: 978–0–314–19146–5

 TEXT IS PRINTED ON 10% POST
CONSUMER RECYCLED PAPER

DEDICATION

To my parents, H. Virgil Barnard and Catherine Wilson Barnard,
who taught me the basics of so many things.

ACKNOWLEDGEMENTS

NOTHING IS MORE HUMBLING than realizing you owe so much of a book to so many others. A thorough list of acknowledgments for this book would include every student I have taught, every teacher I have studied under, every colleague I have talked to about legal writing, and every book or article I have ever read about teaching, English, or legal writing. Most of all, it would include everyone who has worked in Wisconsin's Legal Research and Writing program. Barring that possibility, I'll limit myself to the most recent contributors. At West, thanks go to Bonnie Karlen, Heidi Hellekson, and Justin Hummel. Special thanks go to Carol Logie, who conquered the multiple formatting challenges this book presented.

At the University of Wisconsin Law School, thanks go to Christopher Benigni and Annie Hank for production assistance and for coping cheerfully with numerous details, to Robert Hugh Ellis and Kathryn Ray for careful proofreading, and to Mary Ann Polewski, my personal citation guru and editor of difficult passages. Thanks also to Tom Veith for logistic help that sped the revision along. I must also thank Susan Steingass, who challenged me to write this book now and who provided a judge's view of the content; Betty Karweick, who knows more about legal research than anyone I know; Julia Belt, who provided honest and thoughtful practitioner feedback whenever I asked; Margaret Baumgartner, who generously provided stellar answers to all my questions, even when busy with her own projects, and Virginia Hayes, who kept pushing me to add more opportunities for practice and who shared the understanding she has gained from years of teaching 1Ls. Thanks also to Sunil Rao for his research help.

Thanks also to the teachers who tested these materials on their students and provided invaluable feedback: Kristine Anderson, Mullen Dowdal, Laura Dunek, Tim Edwards, Judge Michael Gibbs, Robert Kasieta, Nancy Kiefer, Jason Knutson, Emily Kokie, Jaime Levine, Deborah Moritz, Peggy Nowicki, Edward Parson, Scott Petersen, Kim Peterson, Hillary Schwab, Michael Simpson, Travis Stieren, Debra Spector, and Annie Walljasper. Thanks are also due to teachers and staff members from previous years, who contributed to the development of Wisconsin's program. This book is an outgrowth of that development.

Thanks especially to all the students who told me what worked or did not work in earlier versions of the book, providing a true reader's viewpoint. Thanks finally, to my family, who kept me in touch with the rest of life during those necessary obsessive stages of writing: Dennis, Kathryn, William, Mark, and Marissa Ray.

TABLE OF CONTENTS

Preface

AS ITS NAME IMPLIES, this book presents the basic information you need to adapt your current writing skills to the challenges of legal writing and to understand why legal writing requires this adaptation. The first three chapters explain how your writing, reading, and research techniques will change to greater or lesser degrees as you enter your new discipline. Chapter Seven introduces the ways that persuasion strategies and writing techniques must be adapted for persuasion in the legal context.

This book introduces you to legal writing through legal research memos, a specialized research report that lawyers commonly write. Chapter Four shows you the parts that may appear in these legal research memos and how those parts are commonly constructed. As you learn about these research memos, you will also come to understand how lawyers analyze and structure information—how lawyers think.

Later the book shifts its focus to persuasive legal writing. Chapter Eight introduces you to persuasive briefs written to trial courts. That chapter explains all the parts of the brief to a trial court and shows you how all the parts of these briefs work together to convince a judge to rule in your client's favor.

This book also presents the basics in the sense of providing a foundation upon which you can build your writing process. It provides foundational skills for the sophisticated communication and structural techniques you will use to explain complex legal concepts. It also provides the foundational skills needed to persuade readers that your understanding is sound and reliable. For example, Chapter Five outlines clarity techniques you can use to enhance all your legal writing; Chapter Nine shows you how to make your persuasive writing more effective. As you master these writing techniques, you will learn how to communicate reliability, credibility, and professionalism in every document you write.

Because legal writing is often inextricably intertwined with oral presentations, this book also presents fundamental components of oral presentations of the law. Chapter Six provides you with strategies for working with your supervising attorney. Chapter Ten introduces you to oral arguments in the court room.

Although this book focuses on the basic foundational techniques of legal writing, the book is not limited to basic applications of these techniques. The later chapters show you how to apply those components and techniques to an ever widening array of documents. Chapter Eleven applies these techniques to the many kinds of correspondence you may write, ranging from letters to e-mail. Chapter Twelve applies these basics in three kinds of legal documents that represent the range of writing tasks you may face in your career: jury instructions, legal pleadings, and statutes.

The text is also basic in that it focuses on the core of the legal writing task at hand. Although particular details of format are often important to legal readers, those particular details can vary from state to state and court to court. This book explains when and how those rules are important to follow. But it seeks to avoid inundating you with many small details that can obscure more important points. Instead, it leaves those specifics to your legal writing professor or your employer. This should minimize the chance of giving you specific rules or techniques that contradict the particular practices in your law school or your court.

This book is organized to accommodate different learning and writing styles. All the major points made in the book are not only explained in the text, but also illustrated in the examples, explained in the commentary accompanying the examples, applied in writing exercises, and included in the checklists that pull all the techniques into a whole process. Thus, whether you learn best by having the general principle explained, by seeing concrete examples, by practicing, or by visual aids, this book presents the information in a way that is accessible to you. Additionally, the main points are all listed in the checklists included in each chapter. These checklists can help you remember to incorporate all that you have learned in your writing process. As a result, you will notice some intentional overlap of content: each major point is explained in the text, illustrated in the examples, and included in the lists describing the overall writing process. The book also accommodates different personal writing styles and different professional customs. Each sample legal research memo and each legal brief employs a slightly different format from the others, and each exhibits different personal writing styles.

By showing you the range of possible structures and styles, this book strives to show you which components of legal writing are fundamental and common to most documents and which components can vary. This information should send you out into the legal world with a broader sense of your options and your readers' expectations.

The Basics of
Legal Writing

1

Writing in a Legal Context

As a beginning law student, you already have writing experience that is unique to you. That experience may be extensive. You may have written many papers and essay exams as a political science or sociology major. You may be familiar with the syllogism through your work in philosophy, or with different learning styles though your work in education. Perhaps you have written fiction or professional articles in another field. You may have worked as a paralegal and therefore have first-hand experience with many specialized legal documents. Perhaps your previous experience was in a medical or physical science discipline, where you learned the importance of careful, thorough reporting of details. Or you may come from a background in business, where you learned to be concise, or engineering, where you learned to work systematically to get the job done. Perhaps you had a major where writing was seldom required.

Your experience, whether extensive or minimal, will in part determine what you need to learn about legal writing. Even if you did little or no writing in either your undergraduate curriculum or your work experience, you probably have ideas about what constitutes good writing. You have some ideas about what writing should do and what your reader expects from that writing. For example, you may work hard to create an interesting introductory paragraph, to put content into new words to avoid plagiarism, or to vary your sentence length to add interest. You may be careful to include enough examples. You may edit your text for passive voice and wordiness. Most college graduates have some ideas about what constitutes good writing, ideas based on their previous writing experience and on comments they have received.

Why Learn about Legal Writing?

No matter what your previous writing experience has been, you will have to adapt to write successfully in law school and as a lawyer. Although all good writing is effective because it communicates its message to the reader, the factors that make writing effective change whenever the nature of the message or the reader changes. Legal writing differs noticeably in both these areas. Those differences are the reason you need to learn about legal writing, even if you have extensive writing experience, even if you have written a dissertation, and even if you have been a paralegal.

To adapt effectively, you need to accept the differences legal writing presents. Learning effective legal writing is somewhat like learning a new language. Learning a new language does not require you to repudiate your first language. It does, however, require you to focus on understanding and respecting the new language and its related culture. Just as you would not be offended if someone corrected your grammar when you were learning a new language, you need not be offended when a law professor teaches you to organize differently, use words differently, or even think differently. Neither do you need to abandon your previous writing values. Although you need to adapt to the differences of legal writing, you do not need to change your writing style in other aspects of your life.

— *Figure 1-1* —
COMMON WRITING SITUATION FOR AN UNDERGRADUATE

WRITER:
Student

Effective
Writing
Decisions

READER:
Academic Professor

PURPOSE:
Getting an excellent grade

COMMON WRITING SITUATION FOR A BEGINNING LAW CLERK

WRITER:
Law Clerk

Effective
LEGAL
Writing
Decisions

READER:
**Senior Attorney,
Client, Others**

PURPOSE:
**Reliable analysis and
answer to a legal question**

Why is Legal Writing Different?

Decisions made by all writers are driven by three factors: the reader, the purpose, and the writer. All of those factors change in legal writing; the reader and purpose change substantially. Just as changing the vertices of a triangle changes the area the triangle covers, changing factors in writing changes the writing techniques that will be effective.

Accepting the difference is easier when you understand why the difference exists. Helping you understand these differences is the focus of this book. Because each student approaches legal writing from his or her own individual perspective, this book focuses on explaining what good legal writing is, allowing you to interpret for yourself how this writing fits into the context of your previous experience. At some points, you will read something that you already know, finding similarities between legal writing and your previous writing experience. But you will also encounter information about legal writing that may surprise you. Enjoy your individual reactions; they will make the process of learning about legal writing more interesting.

What is Legal Writing?

One important difference legal writing presents is that it affects people's lives. The written law that governs our lives is as varied as an amendment to the U.S. Constitution, a statute for the State of Georgia, an ordinance for the City of Sioux Falls, or a regulation for the Arizona Department of Transportation. Similarly, thousands of court decisions are written each year by hundreds of judges across the nation. When published, these legal decisions become a part of legal precedent. This precedent is then used to help judges decide similar cases in the future. Attorneys representing their clients may write legal memoranda or briefs to the courts that decide their clients' cases, and this writing helps the judge decide its outcome. All these types of writing affect the lives of the people involved in the case.

Other kinds of legal writing also have substantial effects on people's lives. Contracts create legal obligations for those who sign the document. Legal ownership is transferred from one person to another through deeds to property, wills, trusts, and bills of sale. Within the legal system, many other documents create legal steps within the larger process. Specialized legal documents called complaints set out the legal theory and facts that justify taking another party to court. Notices provide proof that the other party knows that he or she is being sued. Legal orders issued by the court can require people to give information to the other side or stay away from another person. In the course of any legal action brought before the court, numerous specific documents move the litigation process along and create a record of what was done.

Even documents commonly written in other fields take on legal significance when written by attorneys. When an attorney writes a letter to a client giving an opinion on a legal matter, that attorney takes on the responsibility of providing reasonably reliable information. If the attorney fails to do so, he or she can be liable for malpractice. When a first-year law clerk writes a legal research memorandum to a senior attorney, that attorney relies on the memorandum to provide reliable information. When a judicial clerk writes a bench memorandum or decision draft for a judge, that judge relies upon that document's information in writing the decision.

A second difference between writing in general and legal writing is the value legal writing places on thoroughness and accuracy. Legal writing must cover all the law that a court is required to consider when deciding the issue at hand. Although failing to find a relevant legal opinion might be unfortunate in a given research problem, failing to find a governing statute or opinion on point will make the answer wrong. That can lead to disastrous consequences in either the case's outcome or the lawyer's employment, or both.

Legal writing also differs in how it values clarity. Legal writing is good when it is easy to read. Although this quality of good legal writing may be described as simplicity, readability, clarity, or some other term, the goal is the same. You may find this goal ironic in light of the opinions you read in your first weeks of law school. Although clarity is valued, it is not always practiced in the field. Many judicial decisions are far from clear. Nevertheless, your reader will want you to write clearly. If you have written previously in other academic fields, you are likely to find that legal writing requires shorter sentences, more obvious transitions, and a smaller vocabulary. If you have done little writing before law school, you can relax a bit. You do not need to learn the complex sentence structures you will read in opinions. Think carefully, then state your points clearly, one at a time, and you will be off to a good start.

Legal writing also places a high value on conciseness. Legal writing is considered better if it is more concise. While an essay written for an undergraduate class might be considered too short, a legal memo cannot be considered too short. It may be insufficiently thorough or unclear in its presentation of the reasoning behind the answer, but length alone is not considered a plus. If you added quotes, flourishes, or other padding to your writing in your previous work or academic training, do not do it in legal writing. It does not help.

Legal writing requires the writer to follow more format and organization requirements than most other forms of writing. Legal readers are strict about format rules. For example, each court usually has a set of required rules that dictate the maximum length of briefs, the size of the typeface, the size of the margins, and even the color of the cover. If the legal writer fails to follow even one of these rules, the clerk of the court is likely to reject the document. The clerk will not accept a document with flawed formatting even if the document is submitted close to a deadline, and the document's rejection can mean that the client loses a chance to proceed in a legal action. Although law firms vary greatly in their preferences for in-house documents, they often have requirements about the format of document headings, the tone of letters, and other writing concerns.

Legal readers also require accuracy. Legal writers cite legal authorities for every sentence that relies on that source, and legal readers expect those citations to conform in all details to the required citation rules. Legal citation rules are rather complex; they differ from the rules for dissertations (the *MLA Style Book*), for books (*The Chicago Manual of Style*) and for newspapers (the *Associated Press Style Manual*). It will take you some time and effort to master the legal citation rules, no matter which guide your reader uses. You may find the details of the rules frustrating and wonder why they are so particular. The reason behind each of the rules is almost always efficiency or accuracy. For example, legal readers require citations after each sentence about the law so they can know accurately just how much comes from the cited source and how much is the writer's own reasoning. They require pinpoint citations because they want to be able to go right to the page or paragraph and check to see that the source is being used accurately. They require standard abbreviations so they can identify a source quickly without using more space than is necessary. Therefore, if you become frustrated with the details about citation rules, you can take some comfort in knowing that there is some goal behind the rule, and that in the years to come these rules will save you time and effort. *(Fig. 1-2, page 8.)*

The quality of legal writing is always important, even when the writing will not be a literary masterpiece. Legal writing affects the welfare of the client paying for the research. It matters to the attorney who requested the memo and entrusted his or her professional reputation to the clerk writing the memo. It matters to your success as an attorney. Well-written briefs increase your chances of winning in court. Well-written letters to clients increase the clients' respect for you, and hence their loyalty. Well-written research memos impress your employer and increase your chances for promotion. For good or ill, much of your reputation as an attorney will rest on the quality of your writing.

— *FIGURE 1-2* —
HOW LEGAL WRITING IS DIFFERENT

General College Writing	Legal Writing
• The document often affects no one other than the reader and writer, and primarily the writer.	• The document usually affects other people as well.
• The reader does not expect the text to cover every possibility. Cohesion is more important.	• The reader needs the document to cover all relevant possibilities. Thoroughness is more important.
• The reader usually wants sophisticated writing. Using a wide vocabulary and more complex sentences is considered better writing.	• The reader prefers clarity and readability over sophistication. Using precise words and shorter, simpler sentences is considered better writing.
• The reader is often impressed by description and length. The reader is not primarily concerned with finishing the document quickly. The document often has a page requirement.	• The reader wants a document that is concise yet thorough. The reader wants to finish the document quickly. The document often has a page limit.
• The writer often chooses the organization and format for documents.	• The court or senior attorney usually has rules about the organization and format, which the writer must follow.
• The reader usually values originality.	• The reader values accuracy.

What Does Legal Writing Look Like?[1]

While some legal documents look like general business documents, others differ substantially. Letters follow the usual format, although they are more likely to include subject lines and subheadings. Legal research memos similarly follow a memo format but have particular subsections. Contracts, wills, and other private legal documents have no required format, although particular law firms often have their own ways of setting up these documents. All litigation documents filed with a court begin with a caption naming the parties, the court, the case number, and the kind of document it is. They are set up in the format required by the particular court or law. These documents often include citations to other legal authorities, and those citations also follow a required format.

The format and appearance of all these documents, however, must conform to established rules particular to their legal context. This context may be a particular court system, agency requirements, a law firm's rules, or the requirements of your particular readers. Thus one member of a legislative committee may require a detailed comparison of a current draft with previous drafts, while another may require more detail about broader policy issues. Similarly, as a law clerk, you might have to write for two or more lawyers, each of whom has slightly different preferences for the memos you submit.

If your legal reader does have rules about writing, conform to those rules. If an attorney bothers to lay out particular rules, he or she is doing so in response to problems that occurred previously, to avoid ambiguity, inaccuracy, or inefficiency for the reader. Do not consider those rules as optional or advisory. Every little rule is important. If you submitted a document that did not conform to the requirements, the reader would see the document as carelessly constructed, and would question the validity of the content.

If your reader does not have particular rules, use your best judgment. Contrary to some popular opinion, everything about legal writing is not covered by specific and rigid rules. Most often, you will organize your content based on the logic of the content rather than based on any rule set down by your reader. Although there may be ineffective ways of organizing a particular document, there is often no one right way to organize. Legal writing requires you to make thoughtful choices.

When exercising your judgment, consider first what will be most efficient and clear to your reader. Also consider what is most logical given your content.

---

1. A sample Notice of Motion, legal research memo, and letter are included in Figures 1-4, 1-5, and 1-6.

Do not allow your own convenience to override these concerns. One hard truth about legal writing is that your reader's time is more valuable than yours. If you are writing a research memo for your senior partner, that partner's work is billed at an hourly rate substantially higher than yours. If you are writing for a judge, that judge is deciding your case amid a never ending pile of other important cases. If you are writing for a client, that client needs to believe that your work is focused on helping with the client's problem, not focused on some other reader. Meeting your readers' specific needs is a prominent concern in legal writing.

In summary, legal writing varies in keeping with the varying demands of its content and readers. All legal writing needs to be completed with attention to the readers' needs and preferences, to the content itself, and to accuracy and clarity. All legal writing matters. As you learn more about specific legal writing genres in the following chapters, you will see how the requirements of legal documents may vary, but accuracy and clarity are always valued.

— *FIGURE 1-3* —
GENERAL CHECKLIST FOR LEGAL WRITING

- **BASICS REGARDING LEGAL WRITING**
  1. Legal documents are written to prevent or solve problems.
  2. Legal documents usually discuss the law in the context of the particular situation in which the problem arose.

- **BASICS REGARDING LEGAL READERS**
  1. They are reading to get a job done, not for entertainment.
  2. They are under pressure to get the job done quickly.
  3. Their work matters. If they make mistakes, real people suffer real harm.
  4. Therefore, they are always checking your work to be sure it is reliable.

- **BASICS TO REMEMBER WHEN WRITING LEGAL DOCUMENTS**
  1. **Focus on the job.** Work within the parameters of the job you are being paid to do. Doing the job well is the best way to impress the reader, not sounding impressive.

  2. **Consider all the possibilities.** Within the parameters of the job, be thorough in research and in reasoning, thinking about the possible problems with your answer and considering alternatives that exist.

  3. **Be reliable.** Cite legal authorities accurately and whenever you use those authorities. Check your reasoning and make sure you have explained your logic thoroughly.

4. **Say exactly what you mean.** Do not overstate a point. Legal writing needs to be literally true. Do not use flowery or vague words.

5. **Follow the rules.** Be sure to follow any directions you receive about content, deadlines, and format of the document. Your reader expects no less than perfect compliance

— *FIGURE 1-4* —
SAMPLE COURT DOCUMENT

Court rules dictate the format and content of this legal document. The heading, commonly called the Caption, must follow this same form and include the same information. In the Captions on other documents filed regarding the same case, the name of the document will change, but the other information in the Caption will remain the same. The content and form of the body of the document are also governed by particular court rules. For example, a Notice like this one must include specific content to be valid. At a minimum, the Notice must include the date and time of the motion, as well as the kind of motion that the motion maker is presenting to the court. Other requirements include place, attorney's state bar number, phone number, and other contact information.

STATE OF WISCONSIN   CIRCUIT COURT   DANE COUNTY

PETROV SULLIVAN, LLC,
Plaintiff,

v.   Case No. 09999

DAPHNE DOMINSKI,
Defendant.

NOTICE

    PLEASE TAKE NOTICE that on September 27, 2007, at 1:00 p.m., Plaintiff will move the Court to set this action for trial because issues of fact exist.

    Dated September 13, 2007

             By_____
             Jared Jerdee, Attorney for Plaintiff
             2001 Williamson St.
             Madison, WI 53705
             State Bar #1234

— *FIGURE 1-5* —
SAMPLE LEGAL MEMO
Note: This legal research memo follows Bluebook citation format, using italics.

EXPLANATION

1. *This heading looks much like the heading for any office memo. It would usually follow the form preferred by the employer. This format includes lines for the client name and the file number, which facilitate consistent filing of information.*

2. *The Question Presented focuses the legal question that the legal research memo addresses. It includes three important groups of information: the relevant law (Wisconsin's Lemon Law), the question itself (did the purchaser provide sufficient notice), and the facts that will be relevant to answering that question (requesting a refund, citing the Lemon Law, and not offering to transfer title).*

3. *The Brief Answer explains how the facts and law fit together to support that answer.*

4. *The Statement of Facts' opening sentence focuses the reader on the client's problem. This also underscores the significance of this document for people other than the reader and writer. Based on the writer's research, the reader will decide how to advise this client and help her out of a stressful situation.*

1 TO: Attorney Gena Bardwell
FROM: Carlotta Quiroz
CLIENT: Jane Maven
FILE: 67032-2005-4
DATE: September 23, 2007
SUBJECT: Sufficiency of notice under the Lemon Law

2 QUESTION PRESENTED

Under Wisconsin's Lemon Law, did a vehicle purchaser's letter to the vehicle manufacturer provide sufficient notice by requesting a refund and citing the Lemon Law, even though it did not specifically offer to transfer the vehicle's title?

3 BRIEF ANSWER

Probably yes. Wisconsin courts interpret the Lemon Law statute in light of the legislature's intent to provide a remedy for purchasers of defective vehicles. The letter to the manufacturer requested a refund under the statute. That request reasonably implies an intent to follow the law and transfer title.

4 STATEMENT OF FACTS

Jane Maven asked our firm for advice about getting a refund for her defective 2007 Zelta Roadster. Soon after Maven purchased the car, she found that it had persistent transmission problems. The problems were serious; the car stopped running without warning and would not restart. Over the following two months, Maven took the car to the dealer three times, leaving the car for repair for a total of forty-two days. In all this time, the dealer was unable to fix the problem.

5 Maven subsequently wrote to Zelta Motor Car Company stating that her car was a lemon and requesting a refund. She also suggested that it might still be possible for Zelta to repair the car: "I have zero faith in your ability to repair the car. If you see it otherwise, let me know . . . ." Zelta responded by offering further repair. Maven responded in a second letter: "The dealer has already gotten their advice, and they say it can't be fixed. I want a refund. . . . Wis. Stats. 218.0171 requires you to do this . . . ."

You asked me to determine whether either of Ms. Maven's letters constitutes adequate notice under the Lemon Law.

6   **APPLICABLE STATUTE**

Wisconsin Statute section 218.0171 Repair, replacement and refund under new motor vehicle warranties

(1) In this section:

   . . . .

   (f) "Nonconformity" means a condition or defect which substantially impairs the use, value or safety of a motor vehicle, and is covered by an express warranty . . . but does not include a condition or defect which is the result of abuse, neglect or unauthorized modification . . . by a consumer.

   (h) "Reasonable attempt to repair" means any of the following occurring within the term of the express warranty applicable to a new motor vehicle . . . :

      . . . .

      2. The motor vehicle is out of service for an aggregate of at least 30 days because of warranty nonconformities.

(2) (a) If a new motor vehicle does not conform to an applicable express warranty and the consumer reports the nonconformity to the manufacturer . . . or any of the manufacturer's authorized motor vehicle dealers and makes the motor vehicle available for repair before the expiration of the warranty . . . , the nonconformity shall be repaired.

    (b) 1. If after a reasonable attempt to repair the nonconformity is not repaired, the manufacturer shall carry out the requirement under subd. 2. . . .

2. At the direction of a consumer . . . do one of the following:

a. Accept return of the motor vehicle and replace the motor vehicle with a comparable new motor vehicle . . . .

b. Accept return of the motor vehicle and refund . . . the full purchase price . . . .

. . . .

(c) To receive a comparable new motor vehicle or a refund due under par. (b) 1. or 2., a consumer . . . shall offer to the manufacturer of the motor vehicle having the nonconformity to transfer title of that motor vehicle to that manufacturer. No later than 30 days after that offer, the manufacturer shall provide the consumer with the comparable new motor vehicle or refund. . . .

7 | **DISCUSSION**

7. *The citation after the first sentence in the Discussion tells the reader exactly where the writer got this information, down to the particular subsection of the statute. Similarly, the citations after subsequent sentences tell the reader precisely where to find the supporting law. The abbreviation "Id." means that the source of the information is the same as the previously cited document.*

This first paragraph provides an overview so the reader knows how the court will resolve this question and how the rest of the Discussion will be organized.

The Lemon Law requires a vehicle manufacturer to replace a defective vehicle or refund the purchase price when a consumer meets all the statutory requirements. Wis. Stat. § 218.0171(2) (2005-06). First, the new vehicle's defect must be covered by an express warranty and must have occurred before the warranty expires. *Id.* § 218.0171(1)(f). Second, the defect must remain even after the manufacturer's dealer made a reasonable attempt to repair it. *Id.* § 218.0171(2)(b). Third, the consumer must have stated whether he or she is requesting a replacement or a refund. *Id.* § 218.0171(2)(b)2. Finally, the consumer must provide sufficient notice to the manufacturer that the consumer is invoking the Lemon Law. *Garcia v. Mazda Motor of Am., Inc.*, 2004 WI 93, ¶ 10, 682 N.W.2d 365, 368. To provide this notice, the consumer must also offer to transfer the vehicle's title to the manufacturer. *Id.* § 218.0171(2)(c). When all of these requirements have been met, the manufacturer must provide the replacement or refund within thirty days. *Id.*

8. *The writer needs to address all the requirements of the law, but some are easily resolved. This paragraph covers requirements that are not at issue, so the reader can set those aside and focus on the remaining issue.*

8 In Maven's situation, the only question is whether Maven provided sufficient notice even though she did not explicitly offer to transfer title. All other requirements have been met: (1) the Roadster's transmission was covered by an express warranty, (2) the transmission remained defective even after the dealer worked on it for more than thirty days, and (3) her second letter to Zelta specifically requested a refund.

9. *Here the writer synthesizes an explanation of the relevant law, using a combination of two precedent cases to explain how the law works. Later chapters include more examples of this synthesis.*

9 Although sufficient notice does not require the consumer to use explicit language about transferring title, it must be unambiguous. If a consumer requests something other than one of the statute's options, then the consumer has not provided the manufacturer with sufficient notice. *Berends v. Mack Truck, Inc.*, 2002 WI Ct. App. 69, ¶ 11, 643 N.W.2d 158, 162. But if a consumer unambiguously requests one of the statutory options, then the consumer may have provided adequate notice without explicitly offering to transfer title. *Garcia*, 2004 WI 93, ¶ 15.

A consumer's notice is too ambiguous when the consumer requests a remedy that is not listed in the Lemon Law. *Berends*, 2002 WI Ct. App. 69, ¶ 14. Berends purchased a new truck and subsequently had problems covered by the warranty. *Id.* ¶ 2. The dealer failed to repair the problem even after multiple attempts. *Id.* Berends then wrote a letter to the manufacturer asking for repair, replacement, or a refund. *Id.* After the manufacturer failed to respond, Berends filed a complaint under the Lemon Law. *Id.* ¶ 3. The manufacturer moved for summary judgment based on defective notice, and the trial court granted the motion. *Id.* ¶¶ 4-5. The supreme court affirmed the summary judgment because Berends did not specify a remedy and also asked for a non-statutory remedy. *Id.* ¶ 11-15. Because Berends offered the option of repair, the letter did not provide sufficient notice. *Id.* ¶ 14.

Although sufficient notice requires the consumer to offer to transfer title, a consumer may imply that offer by requesting a replacement under the Lemon Law. *Garcia*, 2004 WI 93, ¶ 15. Garcia's new Mazda exhibited problems, which the dealer was unable to repair after several attempts. *Id.* ¶ 4. Garcia wrote to Mazda requesting a replacement under Wisconsin's Lemon Law. *Id.* Mazda did not replace the car, Garcia sued, and Mazda filed a motion for summary judgment. *Id.* ¶ 6. Mazda successfully argued that Garcia's letter did not explicitly offer to transfer title. *Id.* But the supreme court reversed the trial court and court of appeals' decisions and found in Garcia's favor, reasoning that Garcia's request for a replacement under the Lemon Law logically implied an offer to transfer title. *Id.* ¶ 15.

10. *In this paragraph in particular, the writer uses short sentences to explain the precedent case's reasoning step by step, making it easy for the reader to follow. Although the sentence structure is simple, the writing will not bore the legal reader. That reader wants accuracy and efficiency rather than elegance or variety.*

10 The court may infer an offer to transfer title because it construes consumer protection statutes liberally to "advance the remedy that the legislature intended." *Id.* ¶ 8. A literal interpretation of the requirement would be inconsistent with the Lemon Law's purpose. *Id.* ¶ 15. That purpose is to "protect purchasers of new vehicles that turn out to be defective (colloquially known as 'lemons')."

Id. ¶ 9. The Lemon Law "does not require the consumer to use any 'magic words'" to transfer title. *Id.* ¶ 18. Instead, the court considers whether a reasonable person would infer an offer to transfer title from the letter's wording. *Id.* ¶ 15. Garcia requested a replacement, and no reasonable person would expect to retain ownership of the item being replaced. *Id.* Furthermore, referring to the Lemon Law implies an attempt to follow that law. *Id.* ¶ 16. Because Garcia referred to the Lemon Law in her letter, it was logical to infer that she meant to comply with the law, including transferring title to the manufacturer. *Id.*

11. *The final paragraphs apply the law to the client's situation to show the reasoning behind the writer's answer. The paragraphs echo many terms presented in the previous synthesis and explanation of the law. This repetition is necessary, rather than redundant, because the reader needs to know precisely how these legal concepts apply to the facts. Citations are not needed in these paragraphs, however, because the ideas come from the writer's analysis.*

11 Maven's request in her first letter was ambiguous about her choice of remedy and offer to transfer title. The ambiguity was created by her suggestion that Zelta might be able to repair the car. This suggestion offered Zelta a non-statutory option, just as Berends' reference to repair offered Mazda a non-statutory option. Because repair was an option and because Maven did not specify a single remedy, an offer to transfer title could not be logically inferred.

Maven's second request, however, was not ambiguous about the remedy and did logically imply an offer to transfer title, thus providing notice. This second request, like Garcia's, specifically asked for one of the statutory remedies and referred to the Lemon Law. Because Garcia's request provided sufficient notice, a court is likely to reason that Maven's second letter similarly provides sufficient notice. Although Maven asked for a refund rather than a replacement, she still specified a remedy provided by the statute. A reasonable person would likely infer that "refund" implies an offer to transfer title when Zelta refunds the purchase price. Maven also referred to the Lemon Law, which should show that she intended to follow the law, just as Garcia's reference to the law showed his intent to do so. Thus her second letter provided sufficient notice to invoke the Lemon Law.

— *FIGURE 1-6* —
SAMPLE LEGAL LETTER

Weide, Ortiz, and Wehrle
Attorneys at Law
944 Anderson Avenue, West Bend, WI

Atty. Jessica Ortiz
January 6, 2008

Ms. Angela Elsmere
458 Stevens Court
West Bend, WI

RE: claim against Aunt Iona's Kitchen Restaurant

Dear Ms. Elsmere:

As I mentioned in our phone conversation on January 4, I am writing to you to explain the details of the settlement Aunt Iona's Kitchen is offering to compensate you for the food poisoning you suffered on November 28, 2007. Although it is a substantial offer, I recommend that you reject the offer for the reasons explained below.

Specifically, Aunt Iona's Kitchen is offering you . . . .

In summary, I recommend rejecting the offer at this time. The decision, of course, is yours to make. At your earliest convenience, please contact my office for an appointment. At that meeting, we can discuss the settlement offer, resolve any questions you have, and decide how to precede.

Sincerely,

Jessica Ortiz, Attorney at Law
Encl.

Who Reads Legal Writing?

Readers of legal writing are not reading for pleasure. Waiting rooms at the dentist's office do not offer the visitors sample wills, pleadings, or settlement letters for light reading. Nor do law offices. Unlike news articles, literary essays, or biographies, legal writing is generally read only out of necessity. The reader wants the legal document to convey needed information, not to entertain. Reading is not optional, so the writer has no need to write an introduction solely to spark the reader's interest.

Legal readers are seeking information that they need to answer their questions. Judges read complaints to determine whether they indeed present actions for which the court can grant relief. Clients read their wills to make sure all their wishes have been taken into account. Lawyers and non-lawyers alike read a letter from a lawyer with care, looking for important information. Few sit on the front porch and relax while reading a legal document.

When lawyers read legal documents, they focus on the particular job at hand. They need reliable information that they can understand quickly. Thus lawyers highly value accuracy and clarity, rather than long introductions, subtle allusions, or interesting digressions.

When reading any document, lawyers almost always feel the pressure of time. They may be rushing to meet a deadline, such as the time limit imposed by a trial date or a statute of limitations. They may want to complete the job at a reasonable cost to the client, and cost is determined by the hours a job takes. They may just want to finish the job in time to get to their softball game. Whatever the reason, lawyers value conciseness in writing. The less reading time your documents require, the more lawyers will look forward to reading those documents.

Although they are hurried, lawyers still read carefully, checking for any errors or omissions in the legal document. Clients and others depend on the lawyer's answers. In turn, the lawyer is depending on the document to be reliable. To make sure it is, the lawyer, while reading every sentence and paragraph, is also mentally critiquing the document, checking its logic and the merit of its content. Lawyers do not read with a blanket sense of trust in the writer's ability or thought. They cannot afford to do that.

When non-lawyers read legal documents, they are trying to understand what the legal information means to them. When reading letters from attorneys, clients want to know whether the news is good or bad. They want to know what they need to do. When reading a settlement agreement, they want to be assured that everything is as expected and agreed. When reading a document from an anonymous attorney, such as a form contract, the non-lawyer is reading to understand what the reader has to do. The reader wants to understand both parties' obligations and the risks, if any, that the reader is taking on by signing the contract. The non-lawyer values clarity above all; he or she is just trying to understand what the document says. Although clarity is the primary concern, the non-lawyer also values a respectful tone. When the legal document not only communicates clearly, but also speaks respectfully to the reader, the lawyer who wrote it has won some client loyalty.

Good legal writing, like any good writing, fulfills the readers' needs. It communicates the writer's message to the reader effectively. Unlike other forms of writing, however, readers of legal writing need answers to legal questions or solutions to legal problems. The legal writer's message must be accurate above all. The content of legal writing affects people's finances, peace of mind, and lives. Legal writing always matters; that is why it must always be of high quality.

Applying What You Have Learned

Exercise 1-1
Adjusting to Legal Writing

Either alone or in a group with other students who had the same undergraduate major that you did, make a list of all the things you did to get an A on a paper. Be honest; your previous teachers will never see this list. After you develop a common list, compare that list with the qualities noted in Figure 1-2. Highlight the differences you find and then share ideas about how you can adjust your writing to succeed in your new profession.

2

Reading Opinions and Statutes

YOUR STUDY OF LAW WILL REQUIRE YOU to adapt not only your writing, but also your reading techniques. This adaptation occurs mainly because in law you receive needed information from sources that differ radically from those you have used in the past. For example, textbooks in previous studies were written to explain a course's content. These texts are organized deductively, with chapter titles and sub-sections that state the main points and with the text filling in details and explanation. Often, you could take notes as you read and have those notes fall into an outline. In law classes, however, you will learn from legal opinions written in previous legal cases, collected in texts called casebooks. Rather than being a textbook written specifically for the student's use, a casebook is an amalgamation of information from many legal authorities, most of which were written to be read by people with substantial legal experience. None of these sources of authority has been written for the explicit purpose of teaching students the law, yet these sources are the ones you must use to learn the law.

Legal research will require even further adaptation of your reading techniques because research will lead you to unedited versions of the legal authorities. While casebook editors delete editorial additions by book publishers and irrelevant parts of the authorities they use, the original sources will include all that information. You will research many cases to find the ones with law relevant to your client's situation. Within those relevant cases, you will sift through quantities of detailed information to extract the details you need. You will wade through cumbersome statutes to find all the relevant legal requirements. You need to stay focused on the issue at hand and to discern what is relevant or irrelevant to that issue.

Reading Legal Opinions

To identify the information relevant to your issue, first focus on the court's opinion itself rather than the information added by publishers or editors. When an opinion is printed in a case reporter, the editors add information between the title of the case and the beginning of the actual opinion. They add summaries of the points of law addressed in a case, cross references, and other research aids. For example, Figure 2-1 below lists the information that appears in Thomson West's source for the case of *Garcia v. Mazda Motor of America*.[1] between the case name and the beginning of the actual court opinion. None of this information was written by the court; it was prepared by attorneys working for

---

1. *Garcia v. Mazda* is one of the legal authorities relied on in the legal reseach memo examples in Chapters 1 and 4.

Thomson West. While this information can aid you in your research process, you must never rely on it for your legal reasoning; you must not quote or cite it in place of the court's language. You may, however, scan this preliminary information to identify portions of the opinion that may be useful. But do not dwell on it too long. The opinion itself, the language written by the judge, should be your main focus.

— FIGURE 2-1 —

EXAMPLE OF PRINTED INFORMATION ADDED BY EDITORS TO AN OPINION

EXPLANATION

1. *Citation to another sources for this legal opinion.*

2. *Specifics about the court, the parties involved, the case identification information used by the court, and relevant dates.*

3. *Procedural information that explains how the case reached this point in the judicial process, written by anonymous attorneys working for the publisher.*

2003 WI App 208

1 Adele R. GARCIA, Plaintiff–Appellant–Cross–Respondent,

v.

2 MAZDA MOTOR OF AMERICA, INC., a foreign corporation, and Hall Imports, Inc., a Wisconsin corporation, Defendants–Respondents–Cross–Appellants.†

No. 02–2260.

Court of Appeals of Wisconsin.

Submitted on Briefs April 10, 2003.

Opinion Filed Sept. 25, 2003.

3 Purchaser brought action against car manufacturer, alleging that manufacturer violated Lemon Law because it had not provided a comparable new vehicle without imposing conditions not required by the Law. The Circuit Court, Waukesha County, Lee S. Dreyfus, J., granted summary judgment for manufacturer, and purchaser appealed. The Court of Appeals, Vergeront, J., held that: (1) under Lemon Law, the thirty days within which the manufacturer is obligated to provide a comparable new vehicle or a refund of the purchase price at the direction of the consumer does not begin to run until the consumer offers to transfer title of the vehicle to the manufacturer; and (2) purchaser's request for a replacement vehicle did not satisfy the requirement that she offer to transfer title to her vehicle to manufacturer, and thus, manufacturer did not violate the Lemon Law by failing to provide purchaser with a comparable new vehicle.

Affirmed.

Lundsten, J., filed dissenting opinion.

GARCIA v. MAZDA MOTOR OF AMERICA, INC.
Cite as 671 N.W.2d 317 (Wis.App. 2003)

1. Appeal and Error ☞893(1)

Appellate court reviews summary judgments de novo, employing the same methodology as the trial court.

4 **2. Statutes ☞181(1)**

The purpose of statutory interpretation is to discern the legislature's intent.

3. Statutes ☞188, 190, 191

When interpreting statute, court first considers the language of the statute, and if that clearly and unambiguously sets forth the legislature's intent, court does not look outside the statutory language to ascertain that intent; rather, court applies the plain language to the facts at hand.

4. Statutes ☞190

A statute is ambiguous when it is capable of being understood in two or more different senses by reasonably well-informed persons.

5 **5. Statutes ☞190**

Statutory language is not ambiguous merely because the parties disagree on its meaning.

6. Consumer Protection ☞9

Lemon Law is a remedial statute designed to rectify the problem a new car buyer has when that new vehicle is a lemon. W.S.A. 218.0171.

† Petition for review granted December 16, 2003.

7. Consumer Protection ☞9

Under Lemon Law, the thirty days within which the manufacturer is obligated to provide a comparable new vehicle or a refund of the purchase price at the direction of the consumer does not begin to run until the consumer offers to transfer title of the vehicle to the manufacturer. W.S.A. 218.0171(2)(c).

8. Consumer Protection ☞9 **6**

The purpose of the Lemon Law is to improve auto manufacturers' quality control and reduce the inconvenience, the expense, the frustration, the fear and emotional trauma that lemon owners endure. W.S.A. 218.0171.

9. Consumer Protection ☞9

Thirty days within which car manufacturer was obligated to provide purchaser with a comparable new vehicle did not begin to run under Lemon Law until purchaser offered to transfer title to her vehicle to manufacturer, and purchaser's request for a replacement vehicle did not **7** satisfy the requirement that she offer to transfer title to her vehicle to manufacturer, and thus, manufacturer did not violate the Lemon Law by failing to provide purchaser with a comparable new vehicle. W.S.A. 218.0171(2)(c).

---

4. Research finding tools created by the company that published the opinion. For example, ThomsonWest uses a key number system it developed to help people locate other opinions that address the same topic. This system includes a listing of topics and sub-topics, followed by a one-sentence summary of the point made in the opinion.

5. Never use these summary sentences to support your argument. *You must rely on the court's statements.*

6. As the topics listed here illustrate, this opinion addresses many issues, many of which will not be relevant to the particular issue you are researching. For efficiency, sift through this irrelevant information and focus only on the information relevant to your research question.

7. After all this added information, you will finally reach the actual court opinion. This opinion appears on page 27.

▪ Legal Opinions from the Reader's Perspective

When you read an opinion, you will need to read inductively, in contrast to the deductive approach that works with most textbooks. Legal opinions present preliminary information before stating the main point. Therefore, you must read all the text in an opinion, sift through its details, and determine which details are relevant to your issue. Often you must read all the way through the opinion before you can determine what information to include in your notes. As you read more opinions and develop a clearer understanding of the law you are researching, your note taking will become more focused and efficient.

Reading an opinion also requires looking up legal terms as you read. The law uses many words in precise ways; you need to understand that usage to understand how the law works. Often these words are obvious because they are unfamiliar or Latin terms, such as "a priori." Sometimes, however, they will seem like ordinary terms, such as "careless." As you read the rest of the opinion and see longer discussions of the terms, you will realize that the court is using this word in a special legal context.

As you encounter new legal terms, focus particularly on the terms the court uses to resolve the issue you are researching. You may use that term to categorize a group of facts, as the writer in the memo about Ms. Maven's situation used the term "sufficient notice." This legal term may become a component of the law you need to explain and then apply when you write your answer to that issue.

■ Legal Opinions from the Writer's Perspective

Published opinions are usually written by appellate judges rather than the judges of the original trials. Generally a case is tried first by a trial court that hears witnesses, listens to the arguments, and reviews the evidence presented by the attorneys. Throughout the trial, the judge makes numerous decisions about many legal questions, such as who can be called as a witness, what questions can be asked, what instructions should be given to the jury, and what law should be applied. At the end of the trial, either the judge or a jury decides the case's outcome. In most jurisdictions, the documents that record the outcome of the trial are filed but no written opinion is published. After the original trial, the losing party may argue that the judge erred in some way and that the error affected the case's outcome. An appellate court reviews and decides the appeal.[2] Appellate reviews do not involve retrying the facts of the case; the appellate court does not hear witnesses, for example. Instead the appellate court reviews the record to determine whether the law and legal procedures were applied correctly in the original trial. When the appellate court makes its decision, that decision is written in an opinion, and those opinions are often published. These appellate opinions are the ones that you read.

As you read an opinion, it helps to remember that the opinion was not written with the law student in mind, as a textbook would have been. When the court writes an opinion, it focuses on explaining to the parties in the case why the court made the decision it did. The winning party, of course, is interested in the

---

2. In most jurisdictions the supreme court is the highest appellate court, but there are also other appellate courts in both the federal and state systems. You will learn more about these courts and jurisdiction in your course work.

court's reasoning but is generally just happy about winning; the losing party will read that opinion much more closely, looking for errors in the court's reasoning that could perhaps be appealed to the jurisdiction's highest court. The judge writing the opinion is well aware of these two readers, and of the losing party's search for error. Therefore, the opinion often details the reasons the losing argument was incorrect or not persuasive. As a result, the court often writes about incorrect legal reasoning before presenting the law and reasoning the court believes is correct.

Appellate courts also write with other attorneys in mind because they know that their opinions can be used as precedent in future cases. While this focus does not shift the organization, it does lead the court to include other information about how the legal standard works, why it is applied this way, what the limits are on the court's authority, and what the court is not addressing in the case. This information usually deepens your understanding of the legal standard you are researching.[3]

Organization of a Legal Opinion

Although judges are not required to follow a particular organizational format, many opinions fall into the following pattern. They begin by summarizing the legal procedure that happened leading up to this opinion. Next, the opinions include an explanation of the facts that lead up to the legal problem. After the factual situation has been explained, the opinions often address the arguments one party raised, usually the losing party. The opinions then explain why and how those arguments did not prevail. Finally, the opinion explains the legal standard that the court is using to resolve the issue and applies that standard to the facts.

The *Garcia v. Mazda Motor of America, Inc.* opinion illustrates this general organization, as explained below.

---

3. As you learn more about this, you will discern what is binding precedent and what is advisory but not binding. For example, when the court talks about a situation that is not the actual one facing the court, its comments on that situation are called "dicta" and are not binding authority.

— *FIGURE 2-2* —
SAMPLE 1, PARTS OF A LEGAL OPINION

EXPLANATION

1. *These three paragraphs provide **identification** of the attorneys for each party and the three appellate judges who together decided this case. These appellate judges are reviewing a decision made by a trial judge who first heard the case and decided in favor of Mazda. Thus this is the second time this case has been before a court. When reviewing a trial court's decision, an appellate court is checking to see if the trial court made any errors in interpreting the law or in procedure.*

2. *The opinion now summarizes the **procedural history** of the case. The first paragraph usually explains how the case reached this course and overviews the main legal question before the court. Often the procedural history is quite complex, and reading this paragraph entails understanding many legal terms. In this opinion, the procedural details are included later, within the explanation of the facts. In case you were wondering, the "J" at the beginning of the opinion stands for "judge" or "justice," preceded by the name of the judge who drafted the opinion. Sometimes, as here, the opening paragraph also states this court's decision. At other times, the conclusion is not stated until the end of the opinion.*

3. *This court has used headings to make the opinion's organization clearer. But even when the court does not insert headings, a summary of the facts usually follows the procedural history. When you become more experienced, you will begin to see how the court's statement of the facts reveals the court's view of the case. After you have read the opinion, you can identify the facts relevant to the court's decision. Relevant facts, or legally significant facts, occur when the case would not exist if those facts did not exist. For example, this case would not exist if Garcia's car had transmission problems, so the car's transmission defect is a material fact. Similarly, it is relevant that Garcia referred to the Lemon Law in her letter to Mazda.*

Wis. **319**

GARCIA v. MAZDA MOTOR OF AMERICA, INC.
Cite as 671 N.W.2d 317 (Wis.App. 2003)

1 On behalf of the plaintiff-appellant-cross-respondent, the cause was submitted on the briefs of William S. Pocan, Vincent P. Megna, and Susan M. Grzeskowiak, Jastroch & LaBarge, S.C. of Waukesha.

On behalf of the defendants-respondents-cross-appellants, the cause was submitted on the briefs of Jeffrey S. Fertl, Hinshaw & Culbertson of Milwaukee.

Before DYKMAN, VERGERONT and LUNDSTEN, JJ.

2 ¶1 VERGERONT, J.

This appeal concerns Wisconsin's Lemon Law, WIS. STAT. § 218.0171 (2001-02).[1] The trial court granted summary judgment in favor of Mazda Motor of America, Inc. and Hall Imports, Inc. on Adele Garcia's Lemon Law claim, concluding that the thirty days for Mazda to provide Garcia with a comparable new vehicle had not begun to run because she did not offer to transfer title of her motor vehicle to Mazda as required by § 218.0171(2)(c). We agree with the trial court. We conclude the plain meaning of this subsection is that the thirty days within which the manufac-

turer is obligated to provide a comparable new vehicle or a refund of the purchase price at the direction of the consumer does not begin to run until the consumer offers to transfer title of the vehicle to the manufacturer. Based on the undisputed facts, we conclude Garcia did not offer to transfer title of her vehicle to Mazda. Accordingly, we affirm the summary judgment.[2]

BACKGROUND **3**
¶2 The relevant background facts are not disputed. In February 2001, Garcia purchased and took delivery of a 2001 Mazda Tribute from Hall Imports. Within a few weeks of delivery, she experienced problems with the transmission/gear shifter when trying to shift out of park. Garcia brought the vehicle to Hall Imports for repairs on April 4, 2001, and again on August 1 and August 8 because the problem with the gear shift continued. During Garcia's trip to Billings, Montana, in early September 2001, she once again experienced shifting problems with the vehicle, and she left her vehicle at a Mazda dealership in Billings for repairs on September 5.

¶3 On September 20, while her vehicle was still being repaired in Billings, Garcia sent a letter by certified mail to Mazda's consumer compliance department. She explained the problems she had had with the vehicle, her attempts to repair it, and stated:

It is my understanding that the Lemon Law in the State of Wisconsin is that after a reasonable number of unsuccessful repair attempts by Mazda or its authorized dealers, or that the vehicle has been out of service for a specific number

1. All references to the Wisconsin Statutes are to the 2001-02 version unless otherwise noted.

2. Our disposition of the appeal makes it unnecessary for us to decide the issue Mazda

and Hall Imports raise on their cross-appeal: whether the trial court erred in concluding that, as a matter of law, Garcia and Mazda had not reached an enforceable settlement agreement before Garcia filed this action.

4. *Here the court provides **more detail** about the procedural history, quotes the portion of the statute relevant to this case, and states the decision of the lower court that this appellate court is now reviewing. This information is particularly important because this appellate court is reviewing the lower court's interpretation of this law.*

5. *As the court begins explaining its reasoning, it often summarizes the losing party's arguments. Although this organization would not make sense if the writer were focusing on teaching law students, it does make sense to the writer's primary audience: the losing party. The court writes the opinion to explain the decision to both parties, but the losing party is the one most likely to scrutinize the opinion looking for errors. The opinion writer tries to convince the losing party that the decision is reasonable. Although you may be tempted to write down this list of issues, it will be best to wait, just as you wait before taking notes on the facts. The court may very likely explain why these are not, in fact the real issues.*

6. *Appellate opinions usually include a paragraph explaining the **standard of review** that court must use when reviewing a lower court's decision. Here the standard is de novo, as the court explains, but different standards are used in different situations. Understanding what standard is used when is important not only for judges, but also for trial attorneys. You must understand the criteria the court will be using so that you can shape an effective and relevant argument for your client. You'll be learning much more about the standard of review in your law classes and in your later work with persuasive writing. Notice how a citation appears after almost every sentence. This is necessary because the reader needs to know the source of every point stated. In your own legal writing, you will also need to cite legal authorities this extensively.*

of days, that I'm entitled to either a comparable replacement vehicle or a refund of the purchase price. At this time the automobile has been out of service for a period of 16 days and I would like to have a replacement.

The receipt card shows Mazda received this letter on September 24. Mazda's consumer compliance specialist responded by letter that she would review the matter and contact Garcia.

¶ 4 Meanwhile, on October 5 Garcia picked up her vehicle at Hall Imports. She continued to have trouble getting her vehicle out of park and brought the vehicle again to Hall Imports for repair on October 16. She was told then that it would need a new transmission.

¶ 5 Mazda responded on October 18 to Garcia's letters (she had written another on October 12) by offering her an extended warranty instead of a replacement. Garcia refused and reiterated that she wanted a replacement vehicle. On October 26, Mazda contacted Garcia and said Mazda would provide a replacement vehicle. Garcia went to Hall Imports and placed an order for a new Mazda Tribute. The parties dispute whether they had an agreement at that time that Garcia would accept the replacement vehicle as a resolution of her complaint with Mazda or whether there were unresolved issues concerning the payment of sales taxes and other charges. However, that dispute is not relevant to this appeal. In either case, Garcia did not have a new vehicle by the time she filed this action on November 21, 2001. The complaint alleged that Mazda violated Wis. Stat. § 218.0171 because it had not provided a comparable new vehicle without imposing conditions not required by the statute.

4 ¶ 6 The defendants moved for summary judgment on the ground that the thirty-day time period in Wis. Stat.

§ 218.0171(2)(c) for Mazda to respond to Garcia's request for a comparable new vehicle was never triggered because Garcia had not offered to transfer title to her vehicle to Mazda. This section provides:

(c) To receive a comparable new motor vehicle or a refund due under par. (b)1. or 2., a consumer described under sub. (1)(b)1., 2. or 3. shall offer to the manufacturer of the motor vehicle having the nonconformity to transfer title of that motor vehicle to that manufacturer. No later than 30 days after that offer, the manufacturer shall provide the consumer with the comparable new motor vehicle or refund. When the manufacturer provides the new motor vehicle or refund, the consumer shall return the motor vehicle having the nonconformity to the manufacturer and provide the manufacturer with the certificate of title and all endorsements necessary to transfer title to the manufacturer.

The trial court agreed with the defendants and granted summary judgment dismissing the complaint.

DISCUSSION   **5**

¶ 7 Garcia contends on appeal that the trial court erred in construing Wis. Stat. § 218.0171(2)(c) because the subsection does not require that a consumer explicitly offer to transfer title. Rather, she asserts, such an offer is implicit in a request for a replacement vehicle because "replacement" implies that the consumer will give back the nonconforming vehicle in exchange for the new vehicle. Therefore, according to Garcia, the thirty days for Mazda to provide Garcia with a comparable new vehicle began to run on September 24, 2001, and expired on October 24, 2001.

[1–5] ¶ 8 We review summary judgments de novo, employing the same methodology as the trial court. *Green Spring Farms v. Kersten*, 136 Wis.2d 304, 315, 401   **6**

7. *Now the opinion moves to setting out the* **relevant legal standard,** *or the legal rule that the court will use to decide the issue. Just as you would use a standard measure to determine the size of a room, law uses legal standards to determine cases. Some of these standards are well settled rules that are stated the same way in every case. Other rules are fuzzier, worded generally, or worded differently by different sources. Here the relevant language comes from a statute, which was quoted earlier.*

In this paragraph, the opinion begins to explain what that statute means by discussing how that statute has been interpreted in previous cases, or precedent cases. If the relevant legal standard has developed through common law, or through previously decided cases rather than written statutes, then the court will present the law by explaining how those cases fit together. This fusion of statutory law and case law to explain the legal standard is called a **synthesis** *of the law. A synthesis is needed whenever no one statute or one previous opinion presents all the legal standards the court needs to use to resolve the case. In fact, it is unusual for one statute or opinion to be sufficient to explain the legal standard, so a synthesis is usually needed.*

N.W.2d 816 (1987). Generally, summary judgment is proper where there are no genuine issues of material fact and the moving party is entitled to judgment as a matter of law. *Id.* In this case, which party is entitled to judgment depends upon the proper construction of Wis. Stat. § 218.0171(2)(c). This presents a question of law, which we review de novo. *State v. Setagord,* 211 Wis.2d 397, 405–06, 565 N.W.2d 506 (1997). The purpose of statutory interpretation is to discern the legislature's intent. *Id.* at 406, 565 N.W.2d 506. We first consider the language of the statute. *Id.* If that clearly and unambiguously sets forth the legislature's intent, we do not look outside the statutory language to ascertain that intent; rather, we apply the plain language to the facts at hand. *Id.* A statute is ambiguous when it is capable of being understood in two or more different senses by reasonably well-informed persons. *Id.* However, statutory language is not ambiguous merely because the parties disagree on its meaning. *Id.*

7 [6] ¶ 9 Wisconsin Stat. § 218.0171, the Lemon Law, is "a remedial statute designed to rectify the problem a new car buyer has when that new vehicle is a 'lemon.' " *Berends v. Mack Truck, Inc.,* 2002 WI App 69, ¶ 8, 252 Wis.2d 371, 643 N.W.2d 158. If a new motor vehicle does

not conform to an express warranty and the consumer reports the nonconformity and makes the vehicle available for repair before the expiration of the warranty or one year after delivery of the vehicle, "the nonconformity shall be repaired." Section 218.0171(2)(a). If the nonconformity is not repaired after a reasonable attempt to repair, the consumer's remedies under § 218.0171(2)(b) are as follows:

(b) 1. If after a reasonable attempt to repair the nonconformity is not repaired, the manufacturer shall carry out the requirement under subd. 2. or 3., whichever is appropriate.

2. At the direction of a consumer described under sub. (1)(b)1., 2. or 3., do one of the following:

a. Accept return of the motor vehicle and replace the motor vehicle with a comparable new motor vehicle and refund any collateral costs.

b. Accept return of the motor vehicle and refund to the consumer and to any holder of a perfected security interest in the consumer's motor vehicle, as their interest may appear, the full purchase price plus any sales tax, finance charge, amount paid by the consumer at the point of sale and collateral costs, less a reasonable allowance for use . . . . [3]

---

3. We held in *Berends v. Mack Truck, Inc.,* 2002 WI App 69, ¶¶ 11–13, 252 Wis.2d 371, 643 N.W.2d 158, that the plain language of Wis. Stat. § 218.0171(2)(b) required the consumer to choose one of the two remedies and communicate this choice to the manufacturers. Because the consumer there did not do so, but instead listed these as alternatives in a demand letter to the manufacturer, we concluded the notice was defective. *Id.* We expressly left open the issue of "whether a consumer must explicitly state an intention to transfer title or whether such an offer can be inferred from the consumer's offer to return the vehicle." *Id.,* at ¶ 1 n. 2. We added: "However, we note for the reader's benefit that the most prudent approach would be to

explicitly offer to transfer title of the motor vehicle to the manufacturer." *Id.* We observe that our statement of the issue in *Berends* differs somewhat from the argument Garcia makes because the consumer in *Berends* demanded that the manufacturer "accept the return of his vehicle" as well as providing a new vehicle. *Id.,* at ¶ 2.

In *Berends,* the applicable statute was Wis. Stat. § 218.015(2)(b) (1997–98). The Lemon Law was renumbered Wis. Stat. § 218.0171, effective April 19, 2000, but was not substantively amended in the course of renumbering. Therefore, our interpretation in *Berends* is equally applicable to Wis Stat. § 218.0171, and we refer to the current numbering system in this opinion.

322 Wis.   **671 NORTH WESTERN REPORTER, 2d SERIES**

8. *Notice how the opinion uses the same phrase, "mandatory language," for the same idea throughout this paragraph. While other academic disciplines may want different words for variety, legal readers want precision and tight organization. Thus you will repeat terms frequently because you want to use the same word for the same meaning. This repetition also aids clarity because the repeated term provides a logical transition between sentences.*

9. *The opinion now applies the statutory language to the facts. This* **application** *of law explains what the majority of the judges found incorrect in Garcia's reasoning. Often an opinion focuses on what is wrong with the losing party's arguments before, or in place of, focusing on the court's reading of the law. As a result, sometimes you must think carefully to understand what the opinion is saying about the law. This is why reading a case is a slower process than other reading.*

10. *Both of these paragraphs focus on Garcia's argument and explains why the court did not agree. Each paragraph follows a similar pattern. It first outlines Garcia's argument and then the court's reasoning. In each paragraph, the shift to the court's reasoning is signaled by the word "however."* ***More obvious organization patterns*** *like these are quite acceptable in legal writing. You will develop your own patterns with practice, and legal synthesis will become easier and faster.*

3.   [Applying to leased vehicles.]
(Footnote added.)

[7] ¶ 10 Turning to the language of WIS. STAT. § 218.0171(2)(c), we see, generally, that this paragraph establishes the process by which the consumer obtains the chosen remedy and the obligations of both the consumer and the manufacturer in that process. The first sentence says in mandatory language that the consumer "shall offer to the manufacturer ... to transfer title of that [nonconforming] motor vehicle." Section 218.0171(2)(c). The second sentence says, again in mandatory language, that "[n]o later than 30 days after that offer, the manufacturer shall provide the consumer with the comparable new motor vehicle or refund." *Id.* "That offer," which starts the thirty days running, can only refer to the "offer to the manufacturer ... to transfer title of that [nonconforming] motor vehicle" in the preceding sentence. The third sentence, again in mandatory language, imposes certain obligations on the consumer when the manufacturer provides the chosen remedy: the consumer shall return the nonconforming motor vehicle to the manufacturer and "the certificate of title and all endorsements necessary to transfer title to the manufacturer." *Id.*

¶ 11 We see no ambiguity in the first two sentences of WIS. STAT. § 218.0171(2)(c): the consumer must offer to the manufacturer to transfer title to the nonconforming vehicle and that offer triggers the start of the thirty-day period within which the manufacturer must provide the consumer with the chosen remedy. Garcia's reading—that the request for a replacement vehicle is implicitly an offer to transfer title that triggers the thirty days—is not a reasonable reading of the statutory language. Presumably, a request for a refund of the purchase price could also be construed as an implicit offer

to transfer title to the nonconforming vehicle. Thus, under Garcia's reading, the consumer's request for either remedy starts the thirty days running and a separate offer to transfer title is never necessary because it is implicit in the request for one or the other remedy. However, if that is what the legislature intended, it would not have used the words "thirty days from that offer."

¶ 12 Garcia points out that the last sentence in WIS. STAT. § 218.0171(2)(c) requires that the consumer actually deliver the certificate of title and the necessary endorsement to transfer title before obtaining a comparable new vehicle or a refund. According to Garcia, it is therefore unnecessary for the consumer to offer to transfer title to accomplish the goal of making sure the manufacturer gets title to the nonconforming vehicle along with the nonconforming vehicle. However, it is for the legislature to decide what process will facilitate that goal, and the legislature has plainly decided that a consumer's offer to transfer title, in addition to a request for either a comparable new vehicle or a refund, should be required to trigger the manufacturer's obligation to provide the consumer's chosen remedy.

[8] ¶ 13 Garcia also argues that, in view of the remedial purpose of the Lemon Law, we should construe the language of WIS. STAT. § 218.0171(2)(c) in favor of consumers and not require an explicit offer to transfer title in addition to a request for a comparable new vehicle. The purpose of the Lemon Law as expressed by the supreme court is to "improve auto manufacturers' quality control ... [and] reduce the inconvenience, the expense, the frustration, the fear and [the] emotional trauma that lemon owners endure." *Hughes v. Chrysler Motors Corp.,* 197 Wis.2d 973, 982, 542 N.W.2d 148 (1996) (alterations in original) (citation omitted). This is with-

11. *In this paragraph, the court lays out its reasoning step by step. The first sentence states Garcia's position based on Alberte and the second explains Alberte's reasoning. The third sentence then explains why the court disagrees with that reasoning. Although conciseness is important in legal writing, clear reasoning is also important. Just as the court lays out its reasoning step by step, you will lay out your reasoning step by step.*

Also notice how the court again uses careful wording to describe the law. In this paragraph and throughout this opinion, several terms are used repeatedly, including "unreasonable," "offering to transfer title," and "non-conforming vehicle." In law, you learn to use these words with their legal meanings, which sometimes differ from their everyday meanings.

12. *Here the court summarizes its decisions. You will often use a similar technique when including a conclusion section in longer legal research memos.*

13. *When reviewing a case that includes a concurring or dissenting opinion, study that opinion too. By understanding where and how another judge differed on an issue, you can sharpen your understanding of that issue and the related debate.*

*This dissent is particularly important because **ultimately the state supreme court agreed with the dissenting judge, reversing the majority opinion**. If you look carefully at the citations in the sample legal research memos at the end of Chapter 4, you will notice that those memos cite the supreme court case rather than this one. After Garcia lost in this court, she appealed to the state supreme court, who decided in her favor. In that opinion, the supreme court cited with favor the dissenting opinion you are now reading.*

14. *Here the dissenting judge begins his reasoning by presenting the statutory language that explains the **relevant legal standard**. This judge agrees with the majority opinion on some points,*

out doubt a significant remedial purpose. However, the rule of statutory construction on which Garcia relies applies only when statutory language is ambiguous; it does not permit a court to rewrite unambiguous terms of the Lemon Law. *See Smyser v. Western Star Trucks Corp.*, 2001 WI App 180, ¶ 15, 247 Wis.2d 281, 634 N.W.2d 134.

¶ 14 Garcia also relies on *Alberte v. Anew Health Care Services, Inc.*, 2000 WI 7, ¶ 10, 232 Wis.2d 587, 605 N.W.2d 515, for the proposition that courts have "some scope for adopting a restricted rather than a literal or usual meaning of [a statute's] words where acceptance of that meaning ... would thwart the obvious purpose of the statute." (Second alteration in original) (citations omitted). In *Alberte*, the court rejected a literal interpretation of certain words because the court concluded it produced unreasonable results in light of the entire statutory scheme at issue in that case. *Id.*, at ¶¶ 10–12. We do not see how reading WIS. STAT. § 218.0171(2)(c) to require the consumer to offer to transfer title in order to trigger the thirty-day period thwarts the legislative purpose of the Lemon Law or is unreasonable in light of the entire statutory scheme. It is a requirement that is plainly set forth in the statute and it is a requirement that is easy for a consumer who has title to a nonconforming motor vehicle to comply with. The fact that a particular consumer did not comply with this requirement and therefore is not entitled to the remedy she seeks in a court action is unfortunate, but it does not mean that the requirement itself thwarts the purpose of the Lemon Law or is unreasonable in light of the entire statutory scheme. If the requirement of offering to transfer title is a technicality that causes more harm to unwary consumers than it does facilitate the actual transfer of title to the manufacturer, as

Garcia contends, then the solution lies with the legislature.

[9] ¶ 15 In summary, we conclude that the thirty days within which Mazda was obligated to provide Garcia with a comparable new vehicle did not begin to run under WIS. STAT. § 218.0171(2)(c) until Garcia offered to transfer title to her vehicle to Mazda. We also conclude that her request for a replacement vehicle did not satisfy the requirement that she offer to transfer title to her vehicle to Mazda. Accordingly, Mazda did not violate the statute by failing to provide her with a comparable new vehicle.

Judgment affirmed.

¶ 16 LUNDSTEN, J. (dissenting).

The majority concludes that Adele Garcia did not offer to transfer title to her vehicle to Mazda, within the meaning of Wisconsin's Lemon Law. I respectfully dissent because I believe Garcia gave Mazda clear notice that she was offering to transfer title under the Lemon Law.

¶ 17 As the majority explains, when certain criteria are met, Wisconsin's Lemon Law gives car owners a choice of two remedies and requires that the owners communicate their choice of remedy to the manufacturer. The applicable subsection provides in part:

> To receive a comparable new motor vehicle or a refund ... a consumer ... shall offer to the manufacturer of the motor vehicle having the nonconformity to transfer title of that motor vehicle to that manufacturer.

WIS. STAT. § 218.0171(2)(c). An offer under this subsection triggers a thirty-day time period for compliance by the manufacturer.

¶ 18 I agree with the majority that WIS. STAT. § 218.0171(2) unambiguously requires that a "lemon" owner communicate

324 Wis.   671 NORTH WESTERN REPORTER, 2d SERIES

to the manufacturer the remedy the owner desires and offer to transfer title to their vehicle in exchange for a refund or a replacement vehicle. Under the statutory scheme, a manufacturer must receive clear notice of such a demand and offer so that the commencement date of the thirty-day time period for compliance is likewise clear.

¶ 19 I point out that the majority does not seem to require magic words. That is, the majority does not say that a valid offer must include the words "offer" and "transfer title." For example, I suspect the majority would find a valid offer if Garcia had written: "Pursuant to the Lemon Law, I want a replacement car and I am willing to sign any papers or tender any papers needed to switch ownership of my current car to Mazda." Thus, I do not interpret the majority as holding that the legislature has mandated magic words. It follows that our disagreement is over whether the particular words used by Garcia communicated the offer required by the statute.

¶ 20 Garcia wrote:

It is my understanding that the Lemon Law in the State of Wisconsin is that after a reasonable number of unsuccessful repair attempts by Mazda or its authorized dealers, or that the vehicle has been out of service for a specific number of days, that I'm entitled to either a comparable replacement vehicle or a refund of the purchase price. At this time the automobile has been out of service for a period of 16 days and I would like to have a replacement.

Thus, Garcia specified that she was making her request for replacement under Wisconsin's Lemon Law and she specified that she wanted a replacement vehicle. The majority says, in effect, "ah, but she did not actually offer to transfer title to her current car when she gets the replacement." I do not understand this thinking.

¶ 21 There can be no doubt that Mazda understood that Garcia was invoking her right to a replacement vehicle under WIS. STAT. § 218.0171(2)(c) and communicating to the company that she would transfer the title to her "lemon" to Mazda. Indeed, she was statutorily obligated to transfer title when Mazda gave her a replacement:

When the manufacturer provides the new motor vehicle ..., the consumer shall return the motor vehicle having the nonconformity to the manufacturer and provide the manufacturer with the certificate of title and all endorsements necessary to transfer title to the manufacturer.

WIS. STAT. § 218.0171(2)(c). It is nonsensical for the owner of a "lemon" to demand a replacement and not, at the same time, be offering to transfer title.

¶ 22 The plain language of the statute requires that the "lemon" owner communicate to the manufacturer his or her choice of remedy and a willingness to transfer title. Garcia did not simply demand a replacement. She specified that she was making her demand under the Wisconsin Lemon Law. The only reasonable way to read her letter is that she was notifying Mazda, pursuant to the Lemon Law, that she wanted a replacement car and would give up her car, including title, when Mazda supplied a replacement.

¶ 23 Did Mazda think Garcia was trying to trick it? Did Mazda think Garcia was asking for a replacement, but was not also offering to transfer title to her current car, so that she would end up with two cars? Of course not. And, just as plainly, she could not succeed in such trickery because the statute requires that she transfer title upon receiving the replacement vehicle. To repeat, the only reasonable reading of Garcia's letter is that she was notifying Mazda that she wanted a replacement car and would, necessarily, give up her car, including title, when Mazda supplied a replacement.

¶ 24 Accordingly, I respectfully dissent.[1]

— FIGURE 2-3 —
SAMPLE 2, PARTS OF A CASE

EXPLANATION	THE COURT'S OPINION

Washington v. Hicks, 109 Wis. 2d. 10, 325 N.W. 2d 68 (Ct. App. 1982)

1. *Name of judge and summary of legal process to this point*

1 WEDEMEYER, J. This is an appeal from a judgment awarding Sam Ella Washington (Washington) $10,800, plus accrued interest, and awarding Martha Hicks (Hicks) $26,200, plus accrued interest, from proceeds of a group life insurance policy insuring the life of LeRoy Washington (LeRoy). We affirm.

2. *Facts leading to the litigation and to this decision*

2 Washington and LeRoy were married on August 27, 1938. They were divorced on June 22, 1961. The divorce judgment required LeRoy to keep his life insurance in effect and to maintain Washington as the beneficiary of the policy. At the time of the divorce, the only life insurance policy LeRoy carried was a group life insurance policy provided by his employer, Allis-Chalmers. The death benefit at the time of the divorce was $5,400.

On January 2, 1977, LeRoy changed the beneficiary on this group life policy to Hicks, contrary to the divorce judgment. LeRoy died from a fall at work on October 24, 1980. At the time of LeRoy's death, the death benefit of the group life policy was $18,500. A double indemnity clause in the group life contract increased the benefit to $37,000. Washington appeals the trial court's conclusion that she was only entitled to the value of the group life benefit ($5,400) plus an equal amount from the double indemnity clause.

3. *Recap of arguments raised by the parties, usually the losing arguments*

3 Washington argues four issues: (1) whether res judicata barred the trial court from dividing the proceeds of the group life contract; (2) whether the increased value of the group life contract was distributed to Washington under the provisions of the divorce decree; (3) whether equity bars Hicks from receiving any share of the life insurance proceeds; and (4) whether Hicks failed to prove the existence of another life insurance contract.

4. *Court's explanation of why the argument did not prevail.*

4 Washington's first argument is not relevant to a logical disposition of this case. By union contract with Allison-Chalmers, the value of the life group contract was increased subsequent to the divorce judgment. The divorce judgment by its terms did not anticipate or provide for an increase in insurance benefits, and therefore, no rights to the enhanced value accrued to Washington.

███████████████████████████████

Washington's second argument attacks the trial court's reliance on *Bloomer v. Bloomer*, 84 Wis. 2d 124, 267 N.W.2d 235 (1978). Bloomer held that contributions to a pension fund made after a divorce would not be assets of the marital estate. Id. at 127-28 n. 1, 267 N.W.2d at 237 n. 1. The trial court found in the present case that the subsequent contributions to the group life policy would, as in Bloomer, not be assets of the marital estate. We find no error of law by the trial court in analogizing Bloomer to the present case.

In response to Washington's argument that equity bars Hicks from sharing in the life insurance proceeds, the Wisconsin Supreme Court has stated:

5. *Court's explanation of the relevant legal standard*

5   Where divorce judgments have required the husband to carry a stated amount of life insurance for the benefit of his wife and children but the only policy in existence at the time of the husband's death is in excess of that stated amount and payable to a third party, courts of other jurisdictions have directed the beneficiary to pay an amount from the proceeds equal to the amount set

6. *Citations to cases using that legal standard*

forth in the divorce agreement. **6** See, e.g., *White v. Michigan Life Insurance Company*, 43 Mich. App. 653, 204 N.W.2d 772 (1972); *Nielsen v. Nielsen*, 535 Pac. 2d 1939 (Utah 1975) In these cases what it is, in effect, a constructive trust, has been imposed on a larger fund to the extent required by the divorce judgment. *Prince v. Bryant*, 87 Wis. 2d 662, 673-74, 275 N.W.2d 676, 681 (1979) (dictum).

7. *Application of the standard to this case*

7   We are in accord with the reasoning in Prince and we agree with the trial court's finding that equity does not bar Hicks from retaining some of the proceeds.

8. *Additional legal points handled briefly*

8   Washington's last argument is that Hicks failed to prove an affirmative defense. The trial court found that Hicks had indeed not proved her affirmative defense. This argument is thus not relevant to the disposition of the case.

Hicks argues that the trial court erred by presuming the group life policy in 1961 contained a double indemnity clause. While the existence of this presumption is debatable, Hicks waived appellate review of this issue by failing to cross-appeal. Sec. 809.10, Stats. For the same reason, Hick's argument that she be allowed to seek contribution from the estate is likewise waived.

9. *Court's decision*

9   *By the Court .*— Judgment affirmed.

Learning to read the law is a little like learning to drive a car. You must master many particular skills individually and then coordinate them into one smooth process. And, just as beginning drivers need to learn where to look when they are driving, you need to learn where to look for specific information in the sources you are reading.

Taking Notes on Legal Opinions

As you build skill in reading opinions, you will also begin to develop your own system for taking notes on the opinion you are reading and analyzing. These notes, called case briefs, are for your own use; therefore, the format and organization is yours to choose. As you choose that organization, focus on the purpose of those case briefs, which is to help you understand the opinion, to provide quick access to the information you need, and to have reliable notes to use when you apply the opinion to a legal problem.

Generally you will need to include the following information in your case brief:

- the legally significant facts;

- the legal principle, or legal rule, that is relevant to the legal question you are using the opinion to resolve; and

- the court's reasoning that supports that legal principle.

You may, however, write these parts in a different order. For example, you may identify the reasoning or the principle first and then identify the facts that are legally significant to that principle and used in that reasoning.

You may also want to include a section for the issue, or the question that the opinion resolves. Crafting a concise, accurate, and thorough issue is an art in itself, and is discussed in more detail in Chapter 5. You can write a preliminary issue, however, by matching the relevant legal term with the facts relevant to that term and crafting these into one sentence, usually worded as a question. For example, the issue in *Garcia v. Mazda Motor of America, Inc.*, one of the example opinions you just read, would include "offer to transfer title" as a key legal term. The facts relevant to "offer to transfer title" include Maven's request for a refund, her reference to the Lemon Law, and her omission of an explicit offer to transfer title. Combining these into a sentence, you can develop an issue statement like the following.

Did Maven's letter meet the Lemon Law's requirement for an offer to transfer title when she did ask for a refund and refer to the Lemon Law, but she did not explicitly offer to transfer title to Mazda?

This structure works because the legal issue is often whether the requirements of the relevant legal standard have been met by the facts, and the facts can usually be stated as a list at the end of the question.

As your understanding of the relevant legal standard becomes clearer, you are likely to develop more specific questions that you want your case brief to address. Sometimes, when you need more detail for your analysis of an opinion, you may find it helpful to develop a kind of worksheet or questionnaire you can use to structure your case brief. The following Figure 2-4 provides a sample of such a worksheet.

— *FIGURE 2-4* —
SAMPLE WORKSHEET FOR BRIEFING A CASE

■ **GENERAL FACTS**

- What court issued this opinion?
- What is the date of this opinion?
- Who were the parties?
- What did each party want?
- What was the final outcome of the case?

■ **FACTS RELEVANT TO YOUR ISSUE**

- What facts were relevant to the court's decision on the issue you are researching?
- Which relevant facts were similar to your case?
- Which facts differed?
- What was the court's decision on the relevant issue?

■ **REASONING AND OUTCOME ON YOUR RELEVANT ISSUE**

- What legal terms were used to discuss this issue?
- What, if any, are the relevant statutes or regulations?
- What, if any, are the relevant cases cited in the opinion?
- What legal standard(s) did the court use to resolve this issue?
- How did the court apply the legal standard(s) to the relevant facts?
- What, if any, policies did the court offer to support its decision?

Exercise 2-1
Taking Notes on an Opinion

Using the worksheet in Figure 2-4 or a different form that you prefer, take notes on an opinion you have been assigned in your legal writing class.

— FIGURE 2-5 —
CHECKLIST OF GOALS FOR READING OPINIONS
AS PART OF YOUR RESEARCH

Your Goals are the following:	Your goals are **NOT** the following:
1. Understanding how this opinion identified and resolved the issue relevant to your assignment: • what caused the problem • what legal standard the court used to determine how to resolve the problem and • which party won	1. Getting just the general idea about what happened and who won
2. Identifying the legal terms critical to the relevant issue	2. Copying down all the terms the court used *or* Rephrasing the legal concepts in your own words
3. Understanding what was relevant to the court's reasoning	3. Copying down every detail *or* Ignoring the court's reasoning
4. Extracting an understanding of the relevant legal standard used in this opinion	4. Outlining the opinion as you would outline a textbook chapter

Reading Statutes

At best, reading statutes is hard work. It requires paying attention to every word and punctuation mark. It requires thinking about what was omitted as well as what was included. It often requires cross-checking definitions and other statutes. Finally, it requires wading through some truly horrible sentences, as the following two-sentence sample illustrates.

> Whenever a parcel of land in any town which is accessible, or provided with a right-of-way to a public highway, is subdivided and the owner transfers any part of the subdivided parcel by metes and bounds that would otherwise be shut out from all public highways by reason of being surrounded on all sides by real estate belonging to other persons or by water without an adequate right-of-way to a public highway, the seller shall provide a cleared right-of-way at least 50 feet in width that shall be continuous from the highway to the part of the subdivision sold. In case the seller fails to provide the required right-of-way, the town board may, pursuant to proceedings under this section, lay out a road from the inaccessible land to the public highway over the remaining lands of the seller without assessment of damages or compensation to the seller.

Reading statutes is somewhat easier, however, if you understand some common drafting traditions surrounding the drafting of statutes. When you understand these traditions, you can begin your reading by breaking the statute into pieces that separate the information along traditional drafting patterns.

■ Analyzing Sentences in Statutes

Three drafting traditions are often used in statutes. First, many statute drafters begin a sentence by defining the item, entity, or activity that this sentence covers. Then, after defining precisely what the statute covers, the drafters explain the obligation or permission that this applies to that entity. This structure often creates a big "if . . . then" statement. The order is logical, but it creates unreadable sentences. This poor readability occurs because it takes quite a few words to precisely define the "if" part, or the subject of the sentence, so the reader is lost by the time he or she finally reaches the verb, the "then" part. For example, the previous statute can be divided into the following pieces.

If

Whenever a parcel of land in any town which is accessible, or provided with a right-of-way to a public highway, is subdivided and the owner transfers any part of the subdivided parcel by metes and bounds that would otherwise be shut out from all public highways by reason of being surrounded on all sides by real estate belonging to other persons or by water without an adequate right-of-way to a public highway,

Then

the seller shall provide a cleared right-of-way at least 50 feet in width that shall be continuous from the highway to the part of the subdivision sold.

If

In case the seller fails to provide the required right-of-way,

Then

the town board may, pursuant to proceedings under this section, lay out a road from the inaccessible land to the public highway over the remaining lands of the seller without assessment of damages or compensation to the seller.

The remaining traditions affect how these two parts are worded. Under the second tradition, the statutory language either requires or allows certain actions when explaining the obligation or permission. If the statute says "shall," it requires the action. "Shall" in a statute works like "must" in everyday speech. If the statute uses other language, it often is providing permission. This language works like "may" in everyday speech.

Then

the seller must provide a cleared right-of-way at least 50 feet in width that must be continuous from the highway to the part of the subdivision sold.

Then

the town board may, pursuant to proceedings under this section, lay out a road from the inaccessible land to the public highway over the remaining lands of the seller without assessment of damages or compensation to the seller.

Finally, sentences in statutes use lists to define concepts, often using many lists within one sentence. These lists lose the average reader in a forest of detail, although they do present a large amount of information concisely. For example, the first "if" phrase in the previous statute functions as a series of lists within lists.

If

a parcel of land

- in any town which is

    o accessible, or

    o provided with a right-of-way to a public highway,

- is subdivided and

- the owner transfers any part of the subdivided parcel

    o by metes and bounds

    o that would otherwise be shut out from all public highways because

    o it is surrounded on all sides

        - by real estate belonging to other persons or

        - by water without an adequate right-of-way to a public highway

If you rewrite the statute so that you can see these lists and identify the "if" and "then," and "shall" or "may" parts of that statute, you are well on your way to understanding it.

— *Figure 2-7* —
ANALYSIS OF A STATUTE'S SENTENCE

Original Statute

Whenever a parcel of land in any town which is accessible, or provided with a right-of-way to a public highway, is subdivided and the owner transfers any part of the subdivided parcel by metes and bounds that would otherwise be shut out from all public highways by reason of being surrounded on all sides by real estate belonging to other persons or by real estate belonging to other persons or by water without an adequate right-of-way to a public highway, the seller shall provide a cleared right-of-way at least 50 feet in width that shall be continuous from the highway to the part of the subdivision sold. In case the seller fails to provide the required right-of-way, the town board may, pursuant to proceedings under this section, lay out a road from the inaccessible land to the public highway over the remaining lands of the seller without assessment of damages or compensation to the seller.

Divided into Identifiers (If's) & Obligations or Permissions (Then's)	**Structured into Lists and Lists Within Lists**
Identifier	
IF a parcel of land in any town which is accessible, or provided with a right-of-way to a public highway, is subdivided and the owner transfers any part of the subdivided parcel by metes and bounds that would otherwise be shut out from all public highways by reason of being surrounded on all sides by real estate belonging to other persons or by water without an adequate right of way to a public highway,	**IF** a parcel of land which is (1) in any town which is 　　(a) accessible OR 　　(b) has right of way to 　　　　public highway (2) is subdivided AND (3) the owner transfers part of parcel 　　(a) by metes and bounds 　　(b) that otherwise would be 　　　(i) shut out from all public 　　　　highways OR 　　　(ii) surrounded on all sides by 　　　　1. real estate belonging to 　　　　　other persons OR 　　　　2. water without adequate 　　　　　right of way to a public 　　　　　highway

IFS, THENS

Obligation

THEN the seller **SHALL** provide a cleared right-of-way at least 50 feet in width that must be continuous from the highway to the part of the subdivision sold.

Identifier

IF the seller fails to provide the required right-of-way,

Permission

THEN the town board **MAY**, pursuant to proceedings under this section, lay out a road from the inaccessible land to the public highway over the remaining lands of the seller without assessment of damages or compensation to the seller.

LISTS

THEN seller **MUST**
(1) provide a right of way
    (a) cleared AND
    (b) at least 50 feet wide AND
    (c) continuous from highway to part of the parcel sold

IF seller
(1) fails to provide right of way
    (a) cleared OR
    (b) at least 50 feet wide OR
    (c) continuous from highway to part of the parcel sold

THEN the town board **MAY**
(1) lay out a road
    (a) follow the proceedings required under this section
    (b) from the inaccessible parcel sold
    (c) to the public highway
    (d) over the seller's remaining land
(2) not pay assessment of damages or compensation to the seller.

Applying What You Have Learned

Exercise 2-2: Reading a Statute

Apply the statute reading techniques you just learned to the following subsection of a statute.

Any damages suffered by a landowner upon whose land any highway is or will be laid out, widened, altered or discontinued may be fixed by an agreement signed by the owner and the supervisors and be filed in the town clerk's office. In the event that any owner, other than this state or the United States, does not so agree with the supervisors as to damages or does not deliver to the supervisors a written release of all claims for damages, the supervisors shall, at the time of making the highway order, assess the damages which the owner will sustain by reason of laying out, widening, altering or discontinuing the highway and shall make a written award specifying the sum awarded by them to each owner; and if any owner of land is unknown, the supervisors shall specify the damages awarded to the owner, and describe the owner's land in their award. The award shall be signed by the supervisors and be filed in the town clerk's office with the order laying out, widening, altering or discontinuing the highway.

■ Understanding a Statute's Wording

After you have broken the statute into pieces and organized it, you need to check the meaning of the words in that statute. You cannot rely on your general understanding of the words as they are used in everyday conversation. In statutes, words are often specifically defined, sometimes with rather odd meanings. For example, the following definition is taken from Wisconsin Statute section 401.102.

(b) Words of the masculine gender include the feminine and the neuter, and when the sense so indicates words of the neuter gender may refer to any gender.

The next step in reading a statute is identifying the words that you need to look up. The need to look up some words is apparent because they are unfamiliar, such as "metes and bounds." Others, however, are quite familiar, but you may not know the exact legal meaning, such as "public highway." For example, to understand the statute we analyzed in Figure 2-6, you might need to look up all of the words listed below in Figure 2-7.

— FIGURE 2-7 —

WORDS FROM PREVIOUS STATUTE THAT
MAY HAVE SPECIFIC, UNIQUE MEANING

• parcel	• town	• transfers	• accessible
• real estate	• right of way	• seller	• metes and bounds
• public highway	• other persons	• subdivided	• water
• owner	• cleared	• continuous	• provide
• road	• proceedings	• inaccessible	• sale
			• assessment

Sometimes the statutory section you are reading includes the definitions you need. Often, however, the section you are reading is a part of a larger statute or a larger collection of statutes about a particular topic. In the beginning of your law studies, you may not be working with that larger unit. If you are, however, applicable definitions might appear either at the beginning or the end of the larger, complete statute. Statutes are amended and supplemented over the years, and often their organization becomes confusing over time. Thus it is often useful to scan a table of contents, which may reveal the location of other definitions. Sometimes you will need to consult definitions located elsewhere in the statutes of your jurisdiction. Sometimes you may look up words in a legal dictionary. Standard dictionary definitions are seldom used, and are not always reliable sources for your analysis of statutory language.

When you have finished analyzing the parts of the statute and defining the terms, you will be well on your way to understanding the statute, but you are not finished. Most statutes will have been discussed and interpreted in some previous opinions in your jurisdiction. Thus you will also locate those opinions and, using your skill at reading case law, read those opinions to complete your understanding of this statutory language.

— *FIGURE 2-8* —

CHECKLIST FOR READING A STATUTE

1. Organize the information into *if . . . then* clauses.

2. Identify the major parts: identifiers and either obligations or permissions.

3. Outline each part so you can see the lists within lists.

4. Identify terms that may be specially defined.

5. Look up relevant definitions for those terms in the statutes.

6. Read court opinions that have discussed and interpreted the meaning of this statutory language.

Even the basic language skill of reading takes on new dimensions and presents new challenges in the field of law. With an understanding of the most common organization patterns used in legal opinions and statutes, however, you can begin to develop strategies that speed you along your way. You can break these documents into discrete pieces, organize them to clarify the logical relationship between those pieces, identify and define any critical terms, and finally, recombine the information in light of your new understanding.

APPLYING WHAT YOU HAVE LEARNED

Exercise 2-3
Reading and Analyzing a Statute

Using the process described above and illustrated in Figure 2-6, read the statute that is included as part of your closed memo assignment. Come to class prepared to explain the statute and to discuss its application to your case. List your questions about that application and any issues that the statute suggests for your client.

3

Researching the Law[1]

1. This chapter provides a very basic introduction to the nature of legal research, to jurisdiction, and to its processes and sources. It is intended to support, not supplant, more specific and extensive information on research process and sources from your classroom teacher.

ONE COMMON WRITING TASK for lawyers is reporting their research on a legal question. This task is central to most entry–level positions for law students, whether those positions involve working for an administrative agency, for senior partners in a private law firm, or for supervisors in a legal aid office. Lawyers must be able to explain the law to others, and they must be reliable in both finding all the needed, relevant law (the mandatory authority) and explaining it.

Researching law differs from researching in other areas. In science, research focuses on developing and testing new hypotheses. In contrast, legal research often focuses on surveying many possible legal hypotheses and choosing the one most likely to be accepted by the court hearing the case. In law, the test of your hypothesis is whether it succeeds when used on behalf of a real person to solve a real life problem. When researching for a dissertation or article, researchers often need to find an innovative idea that has not yet been explored in the literature. The legal researcher who is searching for a solution to a client's problem, however, is happy to find that enacted or common law has already developed the idea that supports the client's case. The legal researcher wants an argument that has proven successful in precedential cases. The legal researcher uses an innovative argument only when no settled rule of law provides an answer that favors his or her client.

Legal research requires the researcher to find and apply the law currently in effect, or good law. Legal research is most often used to predict how a court is likely to rule on a particular legal question. Because the court will base its answer on the relevant law in a given jurisdiction, the legal researcher first needs to determine what that relevant law is. Because the law is a body of information that may change daily, this is a challenge. Over time, statutes and regulations may be revised or repealed. Cases may be reversed or distinguished from subsequent cases. The legal researcher needs to be careful that the law upon which he or she depends is good law.

Legal research also differs from research in other fields because it must take jurisdictional boundaries into account. In other fields, a researcher tries to cover all the sources relevant to a topic. For example, a historian researching the West Coast reaction to the bombing of Pearl Harbor might read the New York Times as well as West Coast newspaper accounts of the event because the Times would be read on the West Coast as well. A legal researcher working on a client's problem, however, focuses initially on the law within the particular legal jurisdiction that will decide the case. All legal authorities are not relevant in all court rooms. Authorities from another jurisdiction are not essential to the research, while authority from the governing jurisdiction is mandatory.

Sometimes several courts could have jurisdiction over a given legal situation. For example, a case may sometimes be brought in either a federal or a state court. When this concurrent jurisdiction exists, the attorney will make a strategic choice of courts. To make this decision, the attorney will consider multiple factors, such as the relevant statutes, the convenience of the court's location, and the potential sympathies of a jury in the jurisdiction.

— FIGURE 3-1 —

HOW LEGAL RESEARCH IS DIFFERENT

Researching in Other Areas	Researching Law
• Often develops and tests one new hypothesis	• Surveys all possible hypotheses and chooses the one most likely to prevail
• Often prefers innovation over previously established ideas	• Prefers settled law, or established precedent, over innovative argument
• Often focuses on general possibilities in the future	• Focuses on likely action taken by current court
• Covers all relevant sources, regardless of who wrote it	• Limits research to sources within the legal jurisdiction, at least initially
• May focus on all sources regardless of time when those sources originated	• Focuses on law currently in effect rather than law that is no longer followed

Understanding Legal Authority

To locate any relevant law from your jurisdiction, you will need to identify the relevant legal authorities, find them, and determine what they mean. Before you can find these authorities, you need to understand some basic concepts about legal authority and the sources of that legal authority.

To understand the legal questions raised by a client's situation, you will need to read multiple sources of law. These sources may be the legal authority itself. But the sources may also include a commentary on a statute or a case. When the source is the legal authority itself, it is called a primary source. These primary sources include, for example, constitutions, statutes, agency regulations, and court opinions in previous cases. You can use a primary source as support for your reasoning in a legal research memo to your employer or in an argument to the court. These primary sources are recognized as the law itself, as legal authorities, whether that law was written by a legislature (a statute), an executive agency (a regulation), or a judge (an opinion). When the source is a commentary on the law, it is called a secondary source. Secondary sources commonly include law review articles, scholarly commentaries on legal opinions, legal dictionaries, and legal encyclopedias. Since secondary authorities are other writers' commentary about the legal authority, secondary sources have less persuasive value.

Your research will focus on finding the most useful primary legal authorities that address and resolve your issue. You will use secondary sources, however, to find those primary legal authorities, and you may also use those secondary sources to help you understand an issue in general. When you find primary authorities, you will need to read each source carefully to extract the information that will help you resolve your issue.

Thorough legal research must cover all the law that a court is required to consider when deciding the issue at hand; this law is called the mandatory authority. Mandatory authority is circumscribed by jurisdiction. For example, each state has its own jurisdiction over matters that occurred in the state between citizens of that state. A California state court must consult relevant California statutes and relevant cases decided by the state's appellate and supreme courts. It does not, however, have to follow Illinois statutes or case law. Similarly, the federal court system is divided into different jurisdictions, each with its own mandatory authority but all are required to follow the decisions made by the United States Supreme Court. Jurisdiction can also be circumscribed by subject matter. Some courts have jurisdiction only over specific legal matters, such as bankruptcy, within the geographic jurisdiction.

Mandatory authority includes the relevant statutes enacted by the governing legislature. It also includes cases that were decided within the jurisdiction, applied the same law, and perhaps had similar facts. An appellate court creates mandatory authority for all the trial courts in its jurisdiction when it publishes an opinion. Thus a decision from either the Southern District of the Florida Appellate Court or the Florida Supreme Court would be mandatory authority for the juvenile court in Dade County, Florida, when that case dealt with the same issue and facts similar to those presented in a case before the juvenile court.

Understanding the Sources of Primary Legal Authority

In the United States, law can be created by any of the three branches of the government: legislative, executive, or judicial.

When the legislative branch creates law, it does so by enacting statutes. These statutes are then published in a unified code, and that code is one source of law for you to research. Statutory codes, whether federal or state law, are large, complex bodies of law. To find the particular statutes that apply to your situation, you may use the indices to the statutes or sometimes secondary authorities as research tools. One common tool is an annotated version of a statutory code, such as the United States Code Annotated. These annotated sources include not only the statutory language, but also explanations and references to cases that have interpreted those statutes.

When the executive branch creates law, it often does so by promulgating agency regulations. These regulations generally provide the details needed to implement legislative statutes. For example, the Environmental Protection Agency, the Department of Health and Welfare, and the Federal Communications Commission all promulgate rules. Although you may not work with agency rules much in your first year of law school, you will work with them later in your practice. These rules, published by the various agencies, are numerous, and that number grows every year.

Each agency will have its own rules published in its own agency code, and some of these codes are also available in annotated versions. When you begin exploring these agency codes, you will understand the need for areas of specialization in law. Fortunately, you can develop a sound foundation for any future specialization by learning how to negotiate your way through your jurisdiction's rules. Doing this will allow you to build skills that you can adapt and use when researching agency law.

— *FIGURE 3-2* —
KEY LEGAL CONCEPTS

- **JURISDICTION** = the areas of subject matter and the geographic area covered by a particular court and set of laws

  = part of the court system that hears the matter and can decide a given issue

- **LEGAL AUTHORITIES** = written statements about the law that can be used to make legal decisions

- **SECONDARY AUTHORITIES** = writings about the primary authorities

  = sources that explain, organize, or comment on the primary authorities

  = can sometimes be used as persuasive authority

- **PRIMARY AUTHORITIES** = written statements of the actual law from governmental entities

  - **STATUTE** = written statement of law enacted by a legislature

  - **REGULATION** = written statement of law promulgated by an executive agency

  - **OPINION** = the judges' written explanation of how the law resolves a case

- **MANDATORY AUTHORITY** = primary authority that is
  + on the same legal question
  + relevant given the facts
  + from the same court or the higher, appellate courts who have jurisdiction over the court

- **PERSUASIVE AUTHORITY** = primary authority that is
  + on the same legal question
  + related to similar facts
  + from a different court that does not have jurisdiction over this court

- **PRECEDENT** = cases that should be used to resolve an issue because they are mandatory authority.

- **COMMON LAW** = law applied by courts in written opinions that arises from established legal tradition rather than from any statutory source

- **GOOD LAW** = law still being followed in a jurisdiction

When the judicial branch creates law, it does so indirectly, as a byproduct of the decision made in a specific case. When the court writes an opinion to explain the reasons for its decision in a case, it is explaining how the law works and what the law is on a particular point. As that judicial opinion provides new information about how the law works, it adds to the law.

Almost all the state judicial opinions available to you focus on how the law should be applied to a set of facts, rather than about what the facts actually are. This is because most written opinions come from appellate courts. The opinions you read will usually have been written to resolve an appeal of some issue arising from the initial trial or trial court's decision. These appellate opinions are the ones usually published and thus available for your research. Opinions from state supreme courts are also published and available for your research; these opinions address state constitutional questions, make new common law, and correct errors made by appellate courts. In the federal court system, some trial court opinions are published, as are all federal appellate court and the United States Supreme Court opinions. The opinions are published in sets of reference books, called reporters, and in electronic databases.

The law interpreted within these judicial opinions may come from statutes, administrative regulations, or common law. Common law includes law that arose through the common practices of the people in resolving conflicts. This idea of a common law, imported from English law, is relied on predominately in some areas of law, such as torts. In other areas, such as criminal law, it is rarely used.

Considering the number of statutes and regulations enacted and the thousands of cases decided within each jurisdiction each year, the idea of finding the needed law seems daunting. The legal system, however, has developed extensive research tools to help you find that law.

— *FIGURE 3-3* —
SOURCES OF LEGAL AUTHORITY

Finding Legal Authority

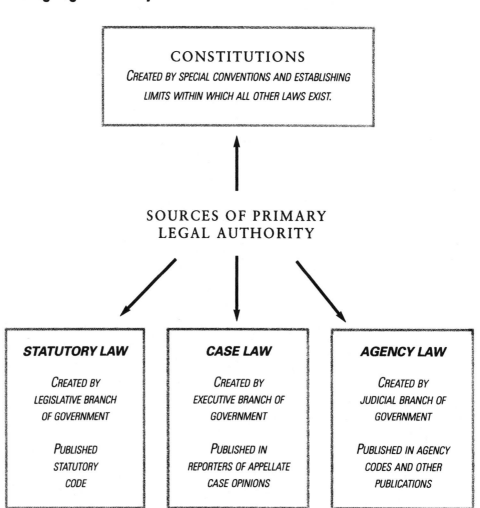

CONSTITUTIONS
CREATED BY SPECIAL CONVENTIONS AND ESTABLISHING
LIMITS WITHIN WHICH ALL OTHER LAWS EXIST.

SOURCES OF PRIMARY
LEGAL AUTHORITY

STATUTORY LAW

CREATED BY
LEGISLATIVE BRANCH
OF GOVERNMENT

PUBLISHED
STATUTORY
CODE

CASE LAW

CREATED BY
EXECUTIVE BRANCH OF
GOVERNMENT

PUBLISHED IN
REPORTERS OF APPELLATE
CASE OPINIONS

AGENCY LAW

CREATED BY
JUDICIAL BRANCH OF
GOVERNMENT

PUBLISHED IN AGENCY
CODES AND OTHER
PUBLICATIONS

To find and understand the primary authorities, you will often use secondary authorities and other specialized legal research tools. Lawyers have many secondary authorities and research tools at their disposal, such as legal dictionaries, legal periodicals, model jury instructions, legal encyclopedias, and treatises on areas of law, often called hornbooks. Specialized legal research tools include annotations, indexes, practitioner's guides, and computerized legal search engines.

Secondary authorities have various formats and uses. Legal dictionaries, as the name implies, provide you with definitions of different legal terms. While these definitions are not primary authority, they can help you understand what the primary authority is saying. For example, you may look up the dictionary's definition of a Latin term you encounter when reading a case. Legal periodicals range from law reviews, with long articles and lots of footnotes, to state bar magazines, with short articles providing advice or updates on changes in the law. Either source can be useful because it provides specific information on a particular legal area. These sources may also provide citations to cases or other materials relevant to your issue. Model jury instructions are published by individual jurisdictions primarily for use by judges within that jurisdiction. These instructions have been developed by committees to help the judge explain a particular point of law clearly while remaining legally accurate. As such, these instructions can provide you with a clear, legally accurate explanation of the law you are using in your research. Legal encyclopedias include entries on all sorts of specific legal concepts. These entries can be useful to give you an overall picture of an area of law that you are researching. Legal treatises are individual books that explain a particular area of the law, such as contracts or torts. They are often useful to give you an overall picture of an area of law that you are researching. Sometimes just studying the table of contents of a treatise can help you understand the particular sub-divisions of an area of law and help you focus on particular terms you need to research further.

— *FIGURE 3-4* —

SOURCES OF SECONDARY AUTHORITY

- annotated statutory codes
- legal encyclopedias
- legal treatises on areas of law
- legal periodicals

- head notes in a case reporter series
- legal dictionaries
- law reviews
- practitioner guides

Some secondary authorities are specialized research finding tools. These tools are impressive creations. They organize vast amounts of information into efficient indexes, searchable databases, and checklists. The annotated code books, such as the United States Code Annotated (USCA), provide not only the statutory language of the Code itself but also annotations about how a statute has been changed over the years. It can tell you whether a statute is still in effect or has been repealed, and it notes the cases that have applied the statute to a set of facts. Because they do refer to cases that have applied a particular statute, annotated codes can quickly lead you to the mandatory authority you need. Indexes, whether in paper or electronic form, can lead you to law review articles discussing a particular legal issue, and footnotes in those articles can also lead you to cases in your jurisdiction that address the issues you need to research. Practitioner's guides can provide you with advice on how to proceed in a particular area of law and can help you know what areas of law are well settled and which are still open to different interpretations.

Two major search engines for computer-assisted legal research (CALR) currently exist, each widely used in the profession: LexisNexis and Westlaw. While each system has its particular strengths and weaknesses, both systems provide you with electronic access to millions of cases, statutes, regulations, and secondary authorities. Each system includes searching tools that can tell you whether a case is still good law.[2] These tools can also link you quickly to any statute or other case cited within its text, and they can tell you the name of every subsequent case that mentions the case you are reading. The interconnections are mind boggling, and learning to use these search engines effectively is several steps beyond Googling to find a former classmate.

— *Figure 3-5* —

SAMPLES OF LEGAL RESEARCH FINDING TOOLS

- index to legal periodicals
- digests
- LexisNexis computer-assisted legal research
- WestLaw computer-assisted legal research
- Shepard's citations

2. Westlaw uses KeyCite and LexisNexis uses Shepard's Citator.

Secondary authority is useful to beginning researchers because it can help them avoid the pitfalls of researching the law solely via computerized search engines. Computerized search engines work by scanning all the documents in a data set for particular words. They are fast and thorough, but literal; computers do not look for the sense of the word, but for the word itself. Thus if you wanted to find dog bite cases involving St. Bernard's and you searched the database for "St. Bernard," you might get cases referring to an incident that happened in "St. Bernard's" church or parish. And you would not find references to dog bite cases that did not name your particular canine species. Their results, therefore, are only as valid as the search terms you enter. Secondary authorities, in contrast, are written and organized by experienced lawyers who are experts in the field. These writers understand the overall structure of this area of law, the legal terms commonly used in the area, and the essential components of the area of law. To create search terms that will retrieve the law you need accurately, you will need this kind of understanding. You, as a novice, however, do not have that understanding. A little background reading in a secondary source can make a computerized search with terms much more reliable.

Using These Sources and Tools as Part of a Research Process

After you understand how to use various legal research tools to retrieve the legal authority, you will begin combining this understanding into an overall research process. This process will enable you to find all the mandatory authority on a particular legal question.

One factor that will affect your research process is economics. Research costs money. Clients or someone must pay for the researcher's time, for the books in the legal library, and for the cost of CALR. A legal researcher must factor this cost into his or her research because the researcher cannot incur $10,000 of research expenses while researching a client's claim for $3,000. While these components can be expensive in legal practice, they are free while you are in law school when your mistakes will not incur cost for a client. Therefore learn as much as you can about using research tools efficiently while you are in school. Pay particular attention to sources that are free, such as books in the local law library and government databases that are available free of charge. Keep your notes on how to use these sources, and try to understand more than one way to find the information you need. If you become a cost effective researcher while in school, you will bring great value to your clients, your employers, and your profession.

Another factor that will affect your research process is time. Time pressures will exist in practice as well as in law school. They will exist because your time as a legal researcher is money. Time pressures will also appear when you need to find an answer to a legal question in a few hours or a day, rather than in a week or two. Thus, as you learn about the dizzying array of legal research authorities and finding tools, make note of which sources are the most efficient for completing particular tasks. This information will help you adjust your research process to accommodate different priorities. When speed is more important than expense, you may use more expensive CALR resources to find information quickly. When expense is a greater concern than speed, you can shift your research process toward using free on-line resources or hard copy resources at your local law library.

Although variations in economics and time affect research, several steps are essential in all situations. One essential step is to accurately identify the jurisdiction relevant to your legal problem. When you identify this, you narrow the database of statutes and cases upon which your search must focus, which helps you find the mandatory authority more easily. For example, if you were researching a contracts dispute in Minnesota, you would be able to focus your search on Minnesota statutes, regulations, and case law because those are the sources of the primary, mandatory authority that governs the situation you are researching. When you have identified an enacted law that governs your situation in your jurisdiction, you will also need to determine exactly how that law would apply to your situation. To do this, you have to find examples of how that law has been applied previously. This means you must research previous cases interpreting that authority.

Although each experienced lawyer has his or her individual approach to research, the various approaches fall into two broad categories: (1) starting with primary authority or (2) starting with secondary authority. Lawyers need to be able to research either way, since each works best in certain situations. For example, you may be able to start with primary authority if you are researching an issue in an area of law with which you are familiar. You are more likely to need to start with secondary authority, however, when researching an area of law that is newer to you. As a new student of law, this means that you may want to use secondary authorities to avoid gaps in your research and to help you identify relevant statutes, which can lead to relevant cases.

If no enacted law exists as a primary authority governing your situation, then you must find examples of cases that have resolved situations similar to yours and reason by analogy. To do this, you will need to choose effective search terms, a skill you will develop in your research classes. The cases you find will tell you how your jurisdiction has handled similar situations using common law.

This common law is not always clearly stated in one case or consistently stated in all the cases you find. Often, you must analyze the facts and the courts reasoning in each of several cases, compare and contrast that reasoning, and then synthesize that reasoning into your own statement that explains the law, drawing on your understanding of all the cases you have found. This synthesis of the law requires thorough, careful analysis, another skill you will be developing in your legal research and writing courses.

One final, essential step in your research is checking to make sure that the law you have found is still in effect in your jurisdiction, or is still good law. This process, called updating your sources, can be done quickly by using Shepard's Citations in book or electronic form or Westlaw's Keycite system.

Learning how to research the law thoroughly, accurately, and efficiently takes practice and experience. It requires both a clear sense of how law works in general and relentless attention to detail. It is not a skill that is completely mastered in a few days, or even a few months. Fortunately, it is a skill you will practice frequently, because researching the law is a component of almost every other legal task.

— FIGURE 3-6 —
GENERAL CHECKLIST FOR LEGAL RESEARCH

- KEEP A RECORD of your research, so you know what you have checked or not.

- IDENTIFY the correct jurisdiction for your issues and the parties involved.

- When you are unfamiliar with the area of law, use SECONDARY SOURCES to gain a broad understanding of the area of law and figure out where to look for your primary authority.

- Locate all STATUTES OR REGULATIONS that are mandatory authority for your issues.

- Locate all the MANDATORY CASE AUTHORITY in your jurisdiction.

- Rely on PRIMARY AUTHORITIES for the law.

- UPDATE all your authorities to be sure they are still good law.

4

Drafting Legal Research Memoranda

ONE KIND OF LEGAL WRITING document you will encounter early in your career is the legal research memorandum. Legal research memos are specialized variations of the internal office memo used in every organization. Like those memos, legal research memos communicate information from one employee to another. The difference in legal research memos lies in their specific purpose and their importance to the client. Legal research memos explain the law relevant to a particular question, often analyzing how a court is likely to apply that law to a client's particular facts. These legal research memos are often requested by a senior attorney, who will rely on the memo when deciding on a course of action.

Legal research memos can address a variety of questions. For example, if you were the in-house legal counsel for an insurance company, the CEO might ask you to determine how to revise the company's standard life insurance policy to conform to a new regulation from a state's Department of Insurance Examiners. If you were a staff attorney for a state appellate court, one of the judges might ask you to review the briefs from all sides of a case and evaluate the merits of their arguments, researching the relevant law to determine what law the judge should apply. If you are an associate in a law firm, another lawyer may ask you to analyze facts and law and recommend a course of action based on that analysis.

The Purpose of Legal Research Memos

Attorneys rely on legal research memos for important decisions. When a senior lawyer requests a research memo, that lawyer is requesting information he or she needs to decide what action to take or what action to recommend to a client: whether to sue or settle, to sign or reject a contract, to advocate for a proposed law or oppose it, to prosecute or not. To make a sound legal decision, the requesting lawyer needs to know the current law on the question and how a court would likely apply that law to the specific situation at hand. Although the attorney may not show the document to the client, he or she will read it to understand how the law works in this area and, trusting its research, will advise the client. In your own legal research memos, if your research is thorough and your answer is clear, then the attorney will advise the client wisely and your employer will come to rely on you more in the future. If, however, your legal research memo is incorrect or incomplete, then the client may suffer the consequences of a bad decision. Your employer's reputation may also suffer, as will yours.

Legal research memos are also important because attorneys may use them as a future resource. Although the research memo focuses on a particular situation at a particular point in time, someday it may be retrieved from the files and read as background information when a similar question arises. For this reason, the legal research memo needs to be complete enough to be understood outside a specific context.

Legal research memos differ in focus from general memos written in other kinds of business. Other businesses use memos to communicate about routine internal matters, such as arranging vacation times, new office policies, or updates on projects. But legal research memos focus on answering particular legal questions based on particular facts. Because the answer is so important and because future readers may consult the memo in different situations, the legal research memo must communicate the question addressed with great precision. It also must clarify the facts and law upon which the answer rests. Finally, because the readers are depending on this memo to be correct, the legal research memo must, with great precision, explain the reasoning that leads to the particular answer. Thus legal research memos are often more impersonal and more detailed in their explanations.

— *Figure 4-1* —

Why Legal Research Memos are Important

- Other attorneys rely on them when advising clients about decisions they must make.

- The attorney's reputation rests on the reliability of his or her advice.

- Legal decisions that clients must make affect their liberty and financial well being.

The Structure of Legal Research Memos

To accomplish their purposes, legal research memos often have subsections and are somewhat formally written. These subsections each have specific functions. Even though certain content is repeated in various subsections, the subsections themselves are not repetitious. Each subsection uses that content to provide a piece of the overall answer. Memo forms vary from firm to firm. Which components you include will also depend on your memo's length, its context, and your reader's preparation. Although few memos include all of the following components, memos may include the following parts: Heading, Introduction, Statement of Facts, Question Presented, Brief Answer, Applicable Statutes, Discussion, and Conclusion.

■ Heading

The Heading will probably look familiar to you, since it is similar to memos generally. It uses the same format and kind of content used in other memos in your firm; standardization of this format makes it much easier to keep the research memos accurately filed and therefore easily retrievable. The subject line identifies the legal question the document addresses and provides filing information.

■ Introduction

A legal research memo may or may not include an Introduction, depending on its length and the complexity of its content. The Introduction's purpose is to provide the reader with a general sense of the issue so he or she can read the Statement of Facts with a better understanding of its significance. The Introduction does this by summarizing the initial question that the memo addresses and the topics covered in answering the question. It may include an answer to the question, but often does not.

■ Statement of Facts

This section explains how and why this legal question arose. It does this by explaining the facts that gave rise to the particular legal issues at hand. It tells a story, but not simply the story of what happened to the client. It tells the story that created a legal question, one not obviously answered by the law. By the end of the Statement of Facts, the reader should not only understand what happened, but also understand how these events have created a legal question worth researching.

■ Question Presented

The Question Presented tells the reader, in one sentence, exactly what the problem is. It states the question that, when answered, gives the reader the information he or she needs to advise the client or decide what action to take.

The Question Presented is more informative than the original question given when the memo was assigned. For example, in the sample memos at the end of this chapter, the assigning attorney for Maven may have asked the writer to determine "whether Maven can recover under the Lemon Law." Or he may have said, "Maven is trying to get a refund for her defective new car—can she do that?" But the Questions Presented in the sample memos focus the law more precisely and include the facts relevant to this issue.

■ Brief Answer

This section of the memo answers the Question Presented and outlines the reasons behind the answer. When the Brief Answer lays out the reasons in the same order in which they will subsequently be discussed, it also foreshadows the organization of the coming Discussion.

■ Applicable Statute

This section, which may or may not be included, provides a convenient reference for the legal standard the court will use to determine the issue. It includes relevant excerpts of any statutes or regulations used to answer the question.

■ Discussion

The Discussion explains the reasoning that supports the writer's answer. Its content is crucial to the entire document. When the Discussion is written well, the reader can see the writer's reasoning and has confidence that the conclusion is valid, barring actual misstatement of the law used.

A well-written Discussion can also assist the writer. As a new employee on the lower rungs of the career ladder, you may find it difficult to commit yourself to a clear answer to a legal question. As you lay out your reasoning in the Discussion, you are able to check your work. If your Discussion explains the legal standard clearly and you can see your logic step by step, then you can submit the memo with confidence.

The Discussion includes three components: an opening paragraph, the applicable legal standard, and an application of that standard to the facts.

The Discussion's opening paragraph is not an introduction so much as an overview or a roadmap showing what is to come. This paragraph presents the big picture of the Discussion. It helps the reader avoid losing focus while reading the detailed reasoning that follows in this section. It introduces the applicable law by breaking it into components that will subsequently be discussed, by presenting those components in the order in which they will be discussed, and by structuring that presentation so the reader sees how the components fit together.

The paragraphs that follow the opening paragraph explain the legal standard, or legal rule, the court will use to resolve the problem. These paragraphs must provide the reader with sufficient information to determine whether the writer's understanding of the law is accurate. Although the relevant legal standard may be clearly stated in one statute, regulation, or court decision, often it is not. In these situations, the writer must synthesize that legal standard, or the legal rule, from various legal authorities.

At the beginning of each paragraph, a thesis sentence states the paragraph's main point. This structure allows the reader to understand the point being made, which makes it easier for the reader to check the writer's logic. It also allows the reader to scan the Discussion and focus on the paragraphs he or she most wants to check. Rather than being boring, thesis sentences are favored by the legal reader because they make the most efficient use of the reader's time. When the reader is convinced that the writer is correct in his or her understanding of this component of the law, then he or she is ready to see the application of this component to the facts.

After the relevant legal standard has been sufficiently explained and supported, the Discussion applies that legal standard to the facts this memo addresses. Although it uses the same facts stated in the Statement of Facts, the Discussion puts those facts to a different purpose. The Discussion's application section compares the facts to the legal standard. If the standard comes from case law, the application may compare the legal research memo's facts to the facts from those opinions. Its purpose, however, is not to compare the memo's facts to those of a previous opinion, but rather to explain how the facts measure up against the legal standard used in the previous opinion.

The Discussion proceeds similarly, step by step, until all the relevant law has been presented and applied with enough support to convince the reader of its reliability. For each component of that law, the Discussion includes the relevant legal standards and an explanation of how the court is likely to apply those legal standards to the relevant facts.

■ Conclusion

This section summarizes the main points made in the Discussion, giving a capsule of the reasoning that led to the Brief Answer. Just as the introductory paragraph provided an overview of the law and how it fits together, the Conclusion can provide an overview of the application of that law and how it fits together to provide the answer to the reader's original question. The reader, having just finished a careful review of the detail of each logical step, is reminded of the big picture.

— *FIGURE 4-2* —
PARTS OF A LEGAL MEMO

PART & PURPOSE	COMPONENTS	STRUCTURE
Heading • Identifies subject and provides filing information	• Names • Date • Legal topic • File number	TO: FROM: DATE: SUBJECT:
Introduction *[often omitted]* • Provides sense of legal issue so the facts can be better understood in longer memos	• Overview of the legal problem • General statement of the question the memo addresses • The answer, sometimes	• One paragraph
Question Presented (QP) *[sometimes omitted]* • Shows the reader the exact legal problem: the question that, when answered, will tell you what the outcome must be	• Introduction of relevant law • Legal question • List of significant facts	• Explains why this question matters legally • Establishes general legal context. • Identifies a key legal concept in question • Explains the facts that make a difference in the answer • Includes the facts that show how this question is debatable • Usually written as one sentence, often in question form

PART & PURPOSE	COMPONENTS	STRUCTURE
Brief Answer *[sometimes omitted]* • Shows the reader what the answer is and foreshadows the organization of the reasoning	• Answer to QP • Answers regarding each component • Preview of components of the legal standard	• Includes a yes or no decision, modified as needed, such as "probably no" or "yes if . . . ," but avoids "maybe." • Includes the information from the Discussion's overview paragraph and the Conclusion, combined and condensed into a few sentences at most • Discusses components in the same order used in the overview paragraph and the Conclusion
Statement of Facts *[occasionally omitted]* • Shows the reader how this legal problem arose	• Legally significant facts, even if unfavorable • Needed background	• Tells story related to the legal problem but not everything that happened • Groups content around themes, time sequence, or location relevant to the story
Applicable Statutes *[sometimes omitted]* • Shows the reader the legal language that the court would apply to the question	• Excerpts of any statutes or regulations used in analysis	• Quotes statute or regulation; does not paraphrase • Is edited to omit irrelevant information and make relevant point more apparent • Is not edited so much that the context of the relevant part is lost

PART & PURPOSE	COMPONENTS	STRUCTURE
Discussion • Shows the reader your reasoning and legal support, step by step, so the reader can double-check your work • Communicates organization clearly, consistently, and completely • Helps the writer double check the validity of the reasoning	• Overview • Applicable legal standard • Application of standard to facts	• Introduces the law a court would apply to solve the problem • Explains how that law breaks into components, each of which must be discussed • Shows the reader what parts to expect in the coming discussion • Sometimes overviews both the legal standard and the application; sometimes only the legal standard • Explains each component introduced in the overview, in the same order • Gives the reader enough information to check the writer's analysis and be assured that the writer is correct • Includes citations after most sentences to inform reader of all legal authorities • Sums up each paragraph's point in a thesis sentence, so the reader has the option of scanning the Discussion, stopping only to check the parts that concern the reader • Applies each component to the facts in the same order

PART & PURPOSE	COMPONENTS	STRUCTURE
Conclusion [often omitted] • Reminds the reader of the big picture after all the detail of the Discussion	• Summary of application	• summarizes application on each point of law • moves through the components in the same order used in the overview paragraph at the beginning of the Discussion. • with the overview paragraph in the Discussion, book-ends the discussion by summarizing how the law introduced in the overview has applied to the client's facts

The Process of Writing a Legal Research Memo

Although the parts of a legal research memo often appear in the order listed above, you do not need to write the parts in that same order. In fact, if one part of a memo is difficult to write, one solution is to shift to writing another part of the memo. Later, after other parts are written, you may find the remaining part no longer presents a difficulty.

You may find it most efficient to start with either the Question Presented or the Discussion. Drafting a preliminary Question Presented is a good place to start because it provides a sense of the question, and this can help you plan your remaining research. Drafting a preliminary Discussion can help when your research has clarified the relevant law but has left you unsure of the main issue needed in the Question Presented. As you write your explanation of the relevant legal standard for your reader, you will come to understand it better yourself. At some point in this process, you will probably see where your issue lies. If neither of these approaches is working, you can try writing quick drafts of easier parts, such as the Heading or Statement of Facts, but realize that you are warming up rather than getting to the heart of the matter.

■ Writing the Question Presented

While drafting the Question Presented is a useful beginning step, you will probably not arrive at your final version of that Question Presented before drafting the Discussion. Questions Presented are difficult to get right before you have completed your research and have drafted the rest of the document. Therefore, expect to return to the Question Presented throughout the writing process, refining it as your understanding of the law and application is refined.

Questions Presented are complex, efficient sentences. Questions Presented coordinate two discrete bodies of information, the relevant law and the relevant facts, around the precise legal question to be answered. To begin constructing this sentence, you can begin by stating these two bodies of information separately and concisely, as is done in the following three samples, all drawn from the situation addressed in the sample legal research memo at the end of Chapter 1.

Examples: Chosen Law and Relevant Facts

Law: Wisconsin's Lemon law

Facts:
- The car had a defective transmission that makes the vehicle unusable.
- The defect was in the transmission, which was covered by warranty.
- The manufacturer did have a reasonable chance to repair the car.
- The car was out of service for a total of 44 days (April 4-11, April 18-May 9, May 9-26).
- Maven wrote two letters to the manufacturer.
- Maven's first letter said she wanted her $75,000 back and "I have zero faith in your ability to repair the care. If you see it otherwise, let me know . . . ."
- Maven's second letter said "I want a refund. Send me the check right now. Wis. Stats. 218.0171 requires you to do this within 30 days."
- Neither of Maven's letters specifically said that she offered to transfer title of her car to the manufacturer.

After narrowing the facts and law as much as possible, you can develop your research plan. In the sample given, that research would entail learning what the Lemon Law requires and find case law that explains how that law has been interpreted in previous cases.

After you have completed your research, you will be able to state the law and facts more specifically. As the following three examples illustrate, valid Questions Presented can differ depending on how the writer interprets the law. You often cannot create one right statement of law or facts that is above all debate, but you can create a Question Presented that is within the range of accurate choices.

Examples: Chosen Law and Relevant Facts

Law: To invoke Wisconsin's Lemon Law, a consumer must specify the relief the consumer is requesting, either a refund or a replacement vehicle.

Facts: • Maven wrote two letters to the manufacturer.

• Maven's first letter said she wanted her $75,000 back and "I have zero faith in your ability to repair the care. If you see it otherwise, let me know . . . ."

• Maven's second letter said "I want a refund. Send me the check right now. Wis. Stats. 218.0171 requires you to do this within 30 days."

Law: Wisconsin's Lemon Law requires a vehicle manufacturer to provide a consumer with a replacement vehicle or a full refund

• when the vehicle sold to the consumer is defective in a way that substantially impairs use of the vehicle,

• when that defect is in a part covered by a warranty,

• when the manufacturer has had reasonable opportunity to repair the vehicle but has failed to do so, and

• when the consumer has asked for one of the remedies provided under the statute.

Facts: The car has a defective transmission.

• The transmission is covered by warranty.

• The manufacturer did have a reasonable chance to repair the car.

• Maven sent two letters asking for a refund.

• Maven's first letter also referred to the possibility of repair.

Law: Wisconsin's Lemon law requires a consumer to offer to transfer title of the defective car to the manufacturer when requesting a refund or replacement, and then the manufacturer must comply within 30 days.

Facts: Maven wrote two letters to the manufacturer.

- Maven's second letter referred to the Lemon Law statute.

- Neither of Maven's letters specifically said that she offered to transfer title of her car to the manufacturer.

The next challenge in crafting your Question Presented is determining exactly what question logically links these two bodies of information. To do this, look for a term in the law that functions like a label. Often the question is whether these facts fit under that label. For example, consider the following questions to link the previous three examples.

Examples: General Issues

- Did either of Maven's letters invoke the Lemon Law?

- Did Maven fulfill all the requirements of the statute, so that Zelta is required to refund her money?

- Was the information in Maven's second letter enough to meet the requirement to offer to transfer title, even though she didn't explicitly say that?

Although all of these questions will need some revision, they provide a starting point for the reader. With this question, you now have the three parts of the Question Presented. At this point, you may stop revising the Question Presented and draft your Discussion or other parts of the memo.

The final challenge in writing the Question Presented is organizing all the needed information into one readable sentence. The clearest way to do this is to present one body of information before the question and one after, so that you keep your subject and verb together. Usually the law comes before the question because that is the broader context that makes the facts relevant. Figure 4-3 illustrates common patterns for the Question Presented.

— *FIGURE 4-3* —

STRUCTURE OF QUESTION PRESENTED

General pattern

1	**2**	**3**
introduction of law	legal question	list of facts

Sample applications of general pattern

1. Under [law], did [question] when [facts]?

2. Applying [name of law], which [key point about law], does [fact term] constitute [legal term] when [facts]?

3. Under [name of law] requiring [legal criteria], is [fact term] a [legal term] if [facts]?

Sample 1

Under Wisconsin Statute Section 218.0171(2)(2005-06), covering refunds for defective new cars, did either of Maven's letters provide Zelta Motor Car Company with the statutorily required notice that obligates the Company to refund the price of her Zelta Roadster?

Sample 2

Applying the Wisconsin Supreme Court's past broad interpretation of the requirement to offer to transfer title, did either of Maven's letters imply an offer to transfer title when both letters requested a refund and the second letter also cited Wisconsin's Lemon Law?

Sample 3

Under Wisconsin's Lemon Law Statute Section 218.0171(2)(c) (2005-06), did a vehicle purchaser provide the vehicle manufacturer with adequate notice when the purchaser sent the manufacturer a letter requesting a refund under the statute but not specifically offering to transfer the vehicle's title?

__Sample 4__

Under the Lemon Law's requirement that the consumer must request either a replacement or a refund to provide notice to the manufacturer, did either of Maven's letters provide notice when the first included a reference to her lack of faith in their ability to repair followed by "if you see it otherwise, let me know," but the second only requested a refund?

These samples all present the law in a way that helps the reader see the general standard for punitive damages, although they select different ways to express that law. They all present the facts relevant to the law, although they include different details and organize those facts differently. And all four focus the question on the central issue to be determined.

Sometimes your reader will not require a Question Presented in your memo, or will want a less complete, formal sentence. If a less formal Question Presented is needed, try omitting the introductory phrase about the law, keeping only the major facts, and perhaps summarizing those facts, as in the following example.

Example, Informal, Short Question

Did a consumer provide adequate notice to invoke the Lemon Law statute when she requested a refund and referred specifically to the statute, even though she did not explicitly to transfer title to the manufacturer?

When drafting an informal question, be wary of conclusory statements. Do not make such a statement if the fact is at all debatable.

You are likely to return to the Question Presented throughout the writing process. It is often both the first and the last part of the memo that you will write.

■ Organizing the Statement of Facts

To know what facts to include in this section, you need to know something about the law regarding this legal question. Yet knowing the law involves knowing the facts. You face a chicken-or-egg situation; you are not quite sure what comes first. As a legal writer, you will have to develop your discernment of relevant facts and law relevant to your issue in tandem. Work out each part as much as you can, then begin your research. As you learn more about the law, refine your understanding of the relevant facts. By the time you have fully refined your understanding of the facts to have a clear focus of which facts are relevant, you will be further along in your analysis.

To tell the reader the story behind the legal question, select and organize your facts with care. When selecting the facts to include, first select only the facts that gave rise to the legal issue, the key facts or legally significant facts. Key facts are relevant facts: facts which in some way relate to the legal issue presented. You can identify these key facts by asking whether the legal issue would still exist if the facts did not. For example, in Maven's situation, you can see initially that the issue would not exist (1) if the transmission had not been defective, (2) if the transmission were not covered by the warranty, (3) if the dealer had not had a chance to repair the transmission, (4) if the dealer had been able to repair the transmission, or (4) if Maven had never written to the manufacturer asking for a refund. Therefore you would include all of these facts in the Statement of Facts. You could begin creating your Statement of Facts by writing out your description of those facts or by simply listing them, as we did for the issue above.

The Statement of Facts must include these key facts even if they are unfavorable to the client you are representing. Your reader needs to be fully informed of the situation, including the weaknesses in the case. In no circumstances do you want your reader to learn about weaknesses in the case from the opposing attorney in that attorney's brief to the court.

After you have included the key facts, include enough background information to make the situation clear to the reader. This background information needs to be sufficient, yet concise.

The organization of the Statement of Facts will vary, but generally it is governed by one of the following: legal relevance, chronology, or location. Sometimes it may work to keep the facts grouped by their legal relevance. For example, if you were writing a Statement of Facts about a convenience store robbery, you might group facts from various conversations before the robbery because all those facts are relevant to the issue of intent. Sometimes, however, such a grouping would be too confusing to the reader. For example, if the facts relevant to intent occurred at events both before and after the robbery, then your story might be clearer if told in a chronological order. In that situation, you would organize all the facts chronologically and group them into paragraphs that function like scenes in a movie.

Occasionally you will organize facts by the location of the events. This approach might be best, for example, if you need to explain what happened inside the convenience store and what happened in the getaway car outside the store. In this situation, your reader would become confused if you skipped back and forth between the car and the store, just to maintain chronological order. A more likely organization would be to describe what happened in the convenience store and then what happened in the car, clarifying your transition to the reader with a phrase that signals the change in time and location, such as "While the robbery was occurring, Anthony Soper was waiting in his car in the parking lot outside the store." By considering various possible organizations, you will be better able to select the one organization that tells your story most effectively. Depending on the organization you choose, you may find yourself adding or subtracting various background facts. That is part of the writing process.

Expect to revise the Statement of Facts after you finish the Discussion. You may begin drafting a Statement of Facts after you have begun your Question Presented. But do so with the understanding that you will revise. Alternatively, you may simply list the facts that seem important to you and begin your research, waiting to draft the Statement of Facts until after you have drafted the Discussion. After you have completed your Discussion, you can draft the Statement of Facts and make sure it includes all the needed information. Also check to see that unneeded information is removed. This will take a little extra time, but it will save your reader time, which your reader will appreciate.

■ Organizing the Discussion

The structure of the Discussion arises from the logical structure of the legal standard. Thus as you come to understand the law you are researching, you will begin to see how to organize this section. Sometimes the law may contain various elements, each of which must be considered and applied to the facts. If so, you may find it most logical to organize around those elements. For example, if you found that a particular law used a three-part test to determine when that law applied, then you would need to cover all three parts of that test. You would introduce those elements in your overview paragraph and discuss each one of them individually in subsequent paragraphs.

When your law is composed of discrete elements, you may use those as your organizing structure. If so, try varying the order of those elements. By experimenting with order, you can see which order works best for your overall organization. Then you can use that order throughout the Discussion, including in your overview paragraph. You want the overview to present the elements in the same order in which they are subsequently addressed. Keeping the order consistent makes the organization easier to see and makes the overall Discussion clearer.

Sometimes a historical approach is the most workable option for organization. A historical approach may be needed when the law derives from common law or when the history is significant to the court's interpretation of that law. This historical approach is similar to the chronological approach you might use in your Statement of Facts, although that similarity is not obvious as you read most Discussions. In this approach, you may begin with some background about the development of the law you are explaining, such as a description of the problem that this law was created to solve. This background may include information about legislative history, previous opinions that were reversed, or other historical factors. After providing sufficient background, you may then explain the law that was created, reaction to it, subsequent adjustments to the law, and end with the law as it is currently being applied. Sometimes you may need to include information from some dissenting opinions or other information that suggests future adjustments that may occur. This is especially important if the adjustment is needed to resolve your client's situation.

When your Discussion needs to address more than one legal standard or needs to address a question of which law to apply, you may find that the most workable option is to organize around the various laws that may apply. This organization roughly parallels the process of organizing a Statement of Facts by location. If you choose this organization, your overview paragraph should introduce the reason the relevant law is in question and should list the various laws that may be applied. The synthesis then explains each of those legal standards one by one, explaining its elements or history, as applicable. After the Discussion has presented each legal standard, it addresses the question of which law should govern the situation.

Whenever you subdivide your explanation of the legal standard, you also have other choices about how you group the application of that legal standard. For example, if you had three subdivisions of the legal standard, you might decide to organize your Discussion around those three subdivisions. Thus if your legal standard involved a three-part test, your preliminary organization might look like this.

Example, Possible Organization of a Subdivided Legal Standard

1. Explain that the law has a three-part test and that all three parts must be met. *(overview)*

2. Insert a subheading about part one.

3. Explain part one. *(legal standard)*
4. Explain that part one is met. *(application)*

5. Insert a subheading about part two.
6. Explain part two. *(legal standard)*
7. Explain that part two may or may not be met. *(application)*

8. Insert a subheading about part three.
9. Explain part three. *(legal standard)*
10. Explain that part three is met. *(application)*

This organization has the advantage of keeping the application close to the law, so the reader has the law fresh in his or her mind while reading the application. It has the disadvantage, however, of making it harder to see how the law fits together as a whole. Thus this organization is more useful when the law you are using has discrete components with little overlap.

Alternatively, it might make more sense to you to organize around a presentation of the law and then the application, which gives you two main parts. Your preliminary outline might look like the following.

Example, Possible Organization of a Subdivided Legal Standard

1. Explain that the law has a three-part test and that all three parts must be met. *(overview)*

2. Insert a subheading about the law.
3. Explain part one. *(legal standard)*
4. Explain part two. *(legal standard)*
5. Explain part three. *(legal standard)*

6. Insert a subheading about the application.
7. Explain that part one is met. *(application)*
8. Explain that part two may or may not be met. *(application)*
9 . Explain that part three is met. *(application)*

This organization has the advantage of unifying the law so the reader can understand how it works together. It has the disadvantage, however, of delaying the application of the law, so that the reader has to keep all the law in mind and then apply it all later in the reading process. This organization is more useful when you have law that cannot be applied in discrete parts, but must be applied as components of a whole.

Finally, you might decide to organize the law around the outcome of your application. Your preliminary outline might then look like the following.

Example, Possible Organization of a Subdivided Legal Standard

1. Explain that the law has a three-part test and that all three parts must be met. But change the order in which you list the parts to 1, 3, and 2. (overview)

2. Insert a subheading about two parts being met.

3. Explain part one. *(legal standard)*
4. Explain part three. *(legal standard)*
5. Explain that part one is met. *(application)*
6. Explain that part three is met. *(application)*

7. Insert a subheading about one part being in question.
8. Explain part two. *(legal standard)*
9. Explain that part two may or may not be met. *(application)*

This organization can be used only when the components of the law logically do not need to be discussed in a particular order. It has the advantage of helping the reader understand the outcome more readily. It has the disadvantage, however, of simply being different, so it is less useful for common areas of law where the reader expects the elements to appear in a certain order.

Working out your organization before you write the Discussion is helpful, but not essential. Sometimes with very complex areas of law, you may have to begin by writing out an explanation of the law, as best you can. Step back and read what you have written. Identify the points you have made and extract those into a list. From this list, see if you can develop an organization. Occasionally it takes several tries before you find the organization that makes sense to you. But, when you have a sense of your organization, you are ready to begin writing an organized draft.

Writing the Discussion

Even if you have your organization clearly in mind, the writing task may seem daunting. It can be hard to know where to start explaining a complex issue. Often the writer finds it most logical to write out the legal standard first, then the application, and finally the overview paragraph. No particular writing order is required, however, so start wherever you can. The important goal is to have a good Discussion when you finish, rather than to follow any particular process.

■ Presenting The Legal Standard

After the overview paragraph, which you can write later, the Discussion explains the legal standard, the logical formula for resolving the question step by step.

If a statute or administrative rule establishes components of your legal standard, this explanation begins with that statute or rule; it is your logical starting point because it is the mandatory authority, the point where the court would begin its reasoning. Each paragraph presents a point about one of those components of the law in its thesis sentence. The paragraph following each of those thesis sentences provides the reader with enough information to determine that this component is correct.

Example, Paragraph on Legal Standard

Wisconsin enforces covenants not to compete only when they meet specific statutory requirements.

A covenant by an assistant, servant or agent not to compete with his or her employer or principal . . . after the termination of that employment or agency, within a specified territory and during a specified time is lawful and enforceable only if the restrictions imposed are reasonably necessary for the protection of the employer or principal.

Wis. Stat. § 103.456.

As you write the explanation of each component of the law, focus on both accuracy and clarity. For example, do not just cut and paste entire statutes or

---

regulations into the memo. That would be accurate, but not clear, because it would leave to the reader the task of sorting relevant language from all the irrelevant details. But do not paraphrase the law so broadly that it becomes inaccurate. Similarly, if your law comes from an opinion, avoid quoting long passages or paragraphs. Quote only the central language; often this will be a word or short phrase, rather than a whole paragraph.

To find a workable balance of accuracy and clarity, identify the phrases or components of the statute that are relevant to your issue and quote those. Delete irrelevant sections of the statute, marking any changes within quotes with ellipses or brackets as needed. Paraphrase background aspects of the law. You may also attach a copy of the portion of the statute that you are explaining. When explaining an opinion, do not lose your focus and begin writing a book report. Rather, focus on using the opinion to explain the relevant legal standard. Include the detail needed from the opinion to explain the legal standard, whether it is facts, reasoning, or policy. Explain the significance of those facts. Omit any details that may have been important to the original opinion but that are not relevant to the legal standard you are discussing.

For further accuracy, identify the source of every point you make about the law. Generally, every sentence in an explanation of a statute includes content drawn from that statute, from case law interpreting that statute, or other legal authority. Therefore every sentence is usually followed by a citation to its source.[1] If two sentences are based on the same source, each sentence will still be followed by its own citation.

Example, Paragraph Using Case Law

To be reasonable, a covenant must be limited to the geographic area in which the employee has served customers. *Wis. Ice & Coal v. Leuth*, 250 N.W. 819, 820 (Wisc.1933). In *Leuth*, the court found Wisconsin Ice and Coal's covenant not to compete to be overly broad because its restricted territory included not only the area covered by the employee, but also the areas covered by forty-five similar workers. *Id.* Covenants not to compete are allowed only to provide the employers with protection that they reasonably need. *Id.* Wisconsin Ice and Coal did not need protection from an employee's influence with customers the employee has not met, and therefore the broad restriction in its employee contract was unneeded and invalid. *Id.*

---

1. You will learn the particular form used for legal citations later. For now, it is enough to know that you need to identify your source.

This repeated citation is not redundant; it is needed for accuracy. Without a citation after the first sentence, the reader cannot be sure if the source for that sentence is the same as the source for the second sentence. The legal reader wants to be confident that your work is accurate and is accurately based on legal authority. Occasionally, the context makes it clear that both sentences come from the same source, and in that situation the legal reader may not require a citation after every sentence. To be safe, though, err on the side of including citations rather than omitting them.

As you explain the reasoning behind the legal standard, you usually need to characterize the facts from the present case in a way that shows their significance to the issue. You explain the quality of the fact that makes it meet the legal standard. That characterization of the facts creates a "middle term," which is often a crucial component of your reasoning. You often find courts creating these middle terms in the reasoning underlying an opinion. The courts also often explain how the facts meet this middle term. The middle terms created by the courts and included in the passage below are marked in bold italics.

Example, Use of Middle Terms to Explain the Legal Standard

Non-compete covenants are unreasonable as to the territory when they cover an ***area larger than the one actually served by the employee***. *Union Cent. Life Ins. Co. v. Balistrieri*, 120 N.W.2d 126, 129 (Wis. 1963); *Behnke v. Hertz Corp.*, 235 N.W.2d 690, 694 (Wis. 1975). Under facts similar to this case, the court found a non-compete covenant covered an unreasonable territory when it restricted an insurance salesperson from working in any state where his employer was licensed to operate, even though he had sold insurance only in Milwaukee County. *Union Cent. Life*, 120 N.W.2d at 130. The court reasoned that the employer did not need protection from the employee's influence over customers with whom he had never worked. *Id.* Because the covenant imposed unnecessary territorial limitations on the employee, it was stricken completely. *Id.* Similarly, you need to use these middle terms to explain how the courts would view the facts in your situation.

████████████████████████████████████

Example, Use of a Definition as the Middle Term to Explain the Legal Standard

> [I]f a word is not defined in a statute, we look next to recognized dictionary definitions to determine the common and ordinary meaning of a word. . . . Garcia demanded a "replacement" vehicle from Mazda. The dictionary definition of "replacement" is . . . . *"one that takes the place of another. . . ."*

■ Applying the Legal Standard

After presenting the legal standard, the Discussion applies that standard to the facts. In the application, the writer retraces his or her steps, applying each point of the legal standard in the same order used in the presentation of the legal standard. This parallel order helps the reader remember the points more easily and makes the application more logical.

In these application paragraphs, the reader learns which facts are relevant to this particular component and how they are relevant. Although the supporting facts have been stated in the Statement of Facts, the Discussion now puts those facts to a different use.

Just as you did not just cut and paste the statute or long quotations into the paragraphs presenting the legal standard, you do not just cut and paste facts into the application. Doing that would leave all the work of reasoning out the application for the reader. Instead, select those facts that are relevant to the particular point at hand and state them concisely. For example, when applying the legal standard regarding the common meaning of a word to Maven's situation, the writer would include references to the words Maven used and the dictionary definitions of those words.

The first sentence of each paragraph about the application makes a statement about how the law will apply given the client's facts. The body of the paragraph then explains why or how that point of law is or is not established by the facts. Each paragraph needs to have enough facts for the reader to be able to check the accuracy of the writer's application, just as he or she checked the law.

The application also explains the court's reasoning as it relates to these facts and this law. This explanation of how the law applies to the facts is a key part of legal reasoning, and it is the part that expresses the writer's thinking. While all the previous components of the memo have been drawn from other sources, the reasoning comes from the writer's own thoughts.

A middle term is needed to explain the reasoning behind the application, just as it was used to explain the legal standard previously. Because that middle term explains the legal standard, the writer of the application needs to explain how the facts do or do not fit under that characterization. See how the writer in the following example uses the middle terms in the application of the legal standard.

Example, Use of a Middle Term to Apply the Legal Standard

> Quinn's restriction, covering "anywhere east of the Mississippi," is unreasonable because it is much larger than Dane County, the area Ms. Ellerkamp actually served. Just as Behnke's covenant applied to a geographical territory that exceeded the area actually served by the employee, Quinn's covenant applies to a territory that exceeds the area Ms. Ellerkamp actually served. Furthermore, Quinn's covenant exceeds the territory served by the entire company; Quinn has offices only in the Midwest but none in the Eastern U.S.

The application section explains how components of the law apply to the facts, point by point. Although writing all this may seem tedious and sometimes obvious at first, discipline yourself to show this logical work. Remember that your reader needs to be able to check your work, and you need to check it too. By the time you finish writing out a thorough Discussion, you should either find the logical errors in your reasoning or you will have confidence that your information is reliable.

■ **Writing the Overview Paragraph**

One way to start drafting the overview paragraph is to address the question on the reader's mind. Your reader most often is an attorney who understands that the first step in predicting how a court will resolve an issue is determining what legal standards the court will use. Thus the legal reader's first question naturally is, "What is the governing law on this?" You can begin the Discussion by addressing that question. For example, Maven's attorney, reading the memo, might be asking what the law is on punitive damages. So you might use any of the following as your opening sentence.

- To recover under Wisconsin's Lemon Law, a consumer must meet eligibility requirements and provide sufficient notice to the manufacturer. Wis. Stat. § 218.0171 (2)(a) (2005-06).

- In Wisconsin, a consumer may recover the full purchase price of a new vehicle by meeting all the requirements under a statute known as the Lemon Law. Wis. Stat. § 218.0171 (2005-06).

- Recovery of a vehicle's purchase price is possible under Wisconsin's Lemon law, which "protect[s] purchasers of new vehicles that turn out to be defective." *Garcia v. Mazda Motor of Am.*, Inc. 2004 WI 93 ¶ 9, 682 N.W.2d 365, 368 (2002).

When you think of the question in your reader's mind as he or she turns to this section of the memo, your opening sentence often comes naturally.

After the opening sentence, the overview paragraph presents the components of the legal standard so the reader can understand how all these components are relevant to the issue and to each other. It presents those components in the same order in which they appear in the body of the Discussion. Generally the overview paragraph contains no more than one sentence about each legal standard to be explained in the subsequent paragraphs. It usually indicates how those legal standards fit together logically by using lists, parallel structure, and clear and accurate transitions. Because the overview mirrors the organization of the legal standard and the application, writing it is fairly easy after those two sections have been drafted.

Preparing the Memo's Other Parts

For efficiency, consider writing the following sections last, even though all but the Conclusion will appear early in the finished memo. All these parts provide clear, concise overviews of parts of the memo, and it is much easier to write a concise overview after all the other pieces are completed. If you choose to write these parts early in the process, draft them quickly. Use them to help you focus on the task at hand, but do not spend time polishing every word or detail. You are likely to need to revise them later.

■ **Introduction**

The Introduction reminds the reader why this memo was requested. It states the general situation, although not in the detail found in the Statement of Facts.

Example, Opening to Introduction

Our client, Mary Maven, wants to return her 2007 Roadster for a refund under Wisconsin's Lemon Law.

It then states the question, although much more generally than in the Questions Presented.

Example, Second Sentence in Introduction

She has come to us to determine whether she can successfully sue the manufacturer, Zelta Motor Car Company (Zelta) for that refund.

This version of the question is often similar to your preliminary Question Presented, the one you drafted at the beginning of your research. Here is the complete sample Introduction.

Example, Complete Introduction

Our client, Mary Maven, wants to return her 2007 Roadster for a refund under Wisconsin's Lemon Law. She has come to us to determine whether she can successfully sue the manufacturer, Zelta Motor Car Company (Zelta) for that refund. Maven has written two letters to the manufacturer requesting a refund. In her first letter, Maven asked for refund, but also referred to the possibility of repairing the Roadster. Zelta responded to the first letter by offering to repair the car. In her second letter, she asked only for a refund, not offering a further opportunity to repair. She also specifically referred to the Lemon Law statute. She did not, however, offer to transfer title of the vehicle, which is statutorily required. Zelta has not yet responded to her second letter.

■ Conclusion

The Conclusion unites the applications of all components of the law and shows how they combine to answer the question. You can draft the Conclusion by simply reflecting on the answer and stating it, making sure you touch on all the major points made in the document.

The Conclusion roughly parallels the Discussion's overview paragraph. While the opening paragraph gives an overview of the law and how it fits together with the facts, the Conclusion gives an overview of its application to those facts. Therefore, another way to draft the Conclusion is to copy the introductory paragraph into this section. Then, where the Introduction stated a component of the law, insert a statement about the result of your application of that component.

Similarly, the Conclusion reminds the reader of all the points of your application and explains how they add up to answer the question the reader asked. Thus, a third way to draft the Conclusion is to copy each of the thesis sentences from the application paragraphs and then condense that content into a few summary sentences. For example, if the law you were discussing had three elements, you might write one sentence summarizing the outcome on each element. You might then write a fourth sentence that states the overall outcome, given the outcome on those elements. This summarizing sentence may come before or after the sentences summarizing the elements.

■ Brief Answer

The Brief Answer tells the reader the answer to the particular Question Presented in one or two sentences. It usually suggests the Discussion's structure because the Answer introduces the components of the law. Sometimes a Brief Answer is somewhat longer than two sentences, but it should not be more than one paragraph. Often a longer Brief Answer is useful with a less detailed Question Presented, because a more detailed Brief Answer can present the background information that has been omitted from the less detailed Question Presented.

In essence, the Brief Answer takes the information from the Discussion's overview paragraph, which summarized the law, and combines it with the information from the Conclusion, which summarized the application of that law. So one way to write this is to copy in those two sections, combine each component of the law with the outcome of its application, and get one sentence on each component of the law. If you then condense that information into fewer sentences, you can create a concise, clear, congruent Brief Answer.

Another way to write Brief Answers is to recombine the components used in the Question Presented. For example, see how the Brief Answers below use many of the same legal terms that were used in the corresponding Questions Presented. See also how the descriptions in the Brief Answer characterize the specific facts listed in the Question Presented.

Example 1, Question Presented and Brief Answer

Under Wisconsin's **Lemon Law** statute section 218.0171(2)(c), did a **vehicle purchaser** provide the vehicle manufacturer with **sufficient notice** when the purchaser sent the manufacturer a letter **requesting a refund** under the statute but not specifically offering to transfer the vehicle's title?

Probably yes. Wisconsin courts generally interpret Wisconsin's consumer protection laws, such as the **Lemon Law**, liberally in light of the legislature's intent. The legislative intent behind the Lemon Law was to provide consumers with the option of returning a faulty vehicle and getting a refund. The **vehicle purchaser**, Maven, **requested a refund** in her second letter, and this **request** implies her intent to return the car. Thus her letter would likely be interpreted to provide **sufficient notice**.

Example 2, Question Presented and Brief Answer

Under Wisconsin **Statute** section 218.0171(2) (2005-06), covering **refunds** for **nonconforming vehicles,** did either of Maven's **letters** provide Zelta Motor Car Company with the **statutorily required notice** that obligates the Company to **refund** the price of her Zelta Roadster?

Yes. Maven's second letter provides the **statutorily required notice.** When a car buyer has a vehicle that meets the **statutory** qualifications of a **nonconforming vehicle,** that car buyer may request a **refund** of the full purchase price by notifying the manufacturer that the buyer wants a **refund** and by offering to transfer title of the vehicle. Maven's first **letter** did not provide adequate **notice** because it referred to the option of repair, and so it is not clear that she specifically wanted a **refund.** Maven's second letter, however, does specify that she wants a **refund.** Although her second letter does not state that she offers to transfer title to the manufacturer, a court will probably infer that transfer from her request for a **refund**. The Wisconsin Supreme Court has inferred an offer to transfer title from a request for a replacement vehicle, and that logic would apply to a request for a **refund.**

Example 3, Question Presented and Brief Answer

Applying the Supreme Court's past broad interpretation of the requirement to **offer to transfer title**, did either of Maven's letters **imply an offer to transfer title** when both letters requested a refund and the **second letter** also **referred to** Wisconsin's **Lemon Law?**

Probably yes. The Supreme Court has interpreted a request for a replacement vehicle as logically implying an **offer to transfer title** of the defective vehicle, and it has interpreted a **reference to the Lemon Law** as **implying an offer to transfer title** because that reference shows an attempt to follow the law. Under this reasoning, the court could infer an offer to transfer title based on either of Maven's two requests for a refund. Additionally, Maven's **second letter** included a reference to the **Lemon Law**, which would likely be interpreted to be an attempt to follow the law.

Viewed as a group, the Introduction, Brief Answer, and Conclusion appear congruent rather than repetitious. They provide the reader and the writer with a reminder of the purpose behind the legal research memo.

■ **Applicable Statutes**

The statute or regulation may be edited to remove unneeded information, but otherwise it is quoted, not paraphrased. When editing a statute, be careful to keep enough language so that the context is clear. You may delete irrelevant portions of the statute, as long as you mark any deletions accurately with ellipses. You may change the case of a letter or make other small grammatical changes to make your edited quotation grammatical, but be sure to enclose those changes in brackets.

■ Heading

The Heading is one part of the memo that will look familiar to you. It includes the standard content, often in a standard memo format.

Example, Heading

To:	Dean C. Short, II
From:	Denise Kampmeier
Date:	November 24, 2007
Re:	Maven request for refund from Zelta Motors, File Number 04-187

The main thing to remember when writing the heading is to use the same format and kind of content used in other memos in your firm; standardization of this format makes it much easier to keep the research memos accurately filed and easily retrievable.

— FIGURE 4-4 —

ASSIGNING MEMO FOR FOLLOWING SAMPLE MEMORANDA

TO: Law Clerk
FROM: Gena Bardwell
DATE: Sept. 5, 2007
RE: Maven request under Lemon Law, File Number 04-187

Please research whether Ms. Maven is in a position to sue Zelta Motors under Wisconsin's Lemon Law. I'm specifically concerned about whether Maven's two letters constitute legally sufficient notice to invoke the thirty day time limit the law gives companies to respond. If the first letter does provide enough notice, then she can proceed now to sue Zelta for the refund plus damages. If the first letter doesn't provide notice, then she'll have to wait until the thirty day limit passes. If neither letter provides notice, then she'll have to write one that does provide notice and wait for thirty days after the date of that letter.

In the attached file[2], you'll find the statute, several cases to consider, copies of the correspondence between Maven and Zelta, the definition of "refund" from the dictionary I would cite in court, and a transcript of my interview with the Service Manager at Ross Motors, who sold her the car.

---

2. The file is omitted here for brevity.

— *FIGURE 4-5* —
LEGAL MEMORANDUM—PARNELL

Note: This legal research memo follows Bluebook citation format, using underscoring.

1. *This subject line includes a file number, one way some firms file their documents. It also includes a general description of the issue the legal research memo will address. Often your employer will have a prescribed format for headings.*

1 To: Gena Bardwell
From: Richard Parnell
File#: 67032-2005-4
Client: Jane Maven
Date: September 23, 2007
Re: **Sufficiency of Notice to Manufacturer to Enforce Wisconsin's Lemon Law**

QUESTION PRESENTED

2. *This Question Presented (QP) provides a lot of information, but it remains readable because (1) it keeps the subject, verb, and direct object together ("did a vehicle purchaser provide adequate notice"); (2) it states the relevant law before the subject; and (3) it organizes the facts about the letter into a list at the end of the sentence. Notice how background information is stated generally ("vehicle") while key facts are given in more detail ("did not specifically offer to transfer the vehicle's title"). The subject, verb, and object state the legal question itself ("did a vehicle purchaser provide adequate notice").*

2 I. Under Wisconsin's Lemon Law statute, subsection 218.0171(2)(c), did a vehicle purchaser provide adequate notice to the manufacturer in her second letter when she requested a refund and referred to the Lemon Law, but did not specifically offer to transfer the vehicle's title?

3. *The second QP uses the same structure as the first and also uses many of the same words. This helps the reader compare the two, seeing what is different about the second QP. Parallel structure and repetition of key terms are writing techniques that are useful in legal writing, and you will see them used more frequently here than in other kinds of writing.*

3 II. Under Wisconsin's Lemon Law statute, subsection 218.0171(2)(b), did the purchaser's first letter provide adequate notice when it asked for a refund but also offered the non-statutory option of repair?

BRIEF ANSWER

4. *Each Brief Answer (BA) answers the question directly, explains the legal standard, and then explains how the facts in the QP, when measured against that standard, lead to the resulting answer. This provides the reader with a quick answer, although the Discussion is needed to fully support and explain that answer.*

4 I. Probably yes. Wisconsin courts interpret Wisconsin's consumer protection laws, such as the Lemon Law, liberally in light of the legislature's intent. The legislative intent behind the Lemon Law was to provide consumers with the option of returning a faulty vehicle and getting a refund. The vehicle purchaser requested a refund in her second letter. This request implies her intent to return the car and transfer title to the manufacturer. Under this reasoning, her letter provided adequate notice.

II. No. A consumer fails to provide adequate notice under the statute when that consumer offers a non-statutory option. The purchaser's first letter offered the option of repair. Thus it did not provide sufficient notice.

5   **APPLICABLE STATUTE**

Wisconsin Statute section 218.0171 Repair, replacement and refund under new motor vehicle warranties

(1) In this section:

   . . . .

(f) "Nonconformity" means a condition or defect which substantially impairs the use, value or safety of a motor vehicle, and is covered by an express warranty . . . but does not include a condition or defect which is the result of abuse, neglect or unauthorized modification . . . by a consumer.

(h) "Reasonable attempt to repair" means any of the following occurring within the term of the express warranty applicable to a new motor vehicle . . . :

   . . . .

2. The motor vehicle is out of service for an aggregate of at least 30 days because of warranty nonconformities.

(2) (a) If a new motor vehicle does not conform to an applicable express warranty and the consumer reports the nonconformity to the manufacturer . . . or any of the manufacturer's authorized motor vehicle dealers and makes the motor vehicle available for repair before the expiration of the warranty . . . , the nonconformity shall be repaired.

(b) 1. If after a reasonable attempt to repair the nonconformity is not repaired, the manufacturer shall carry out the requirement under subd. 2. . . .

5. The Applicable Statute section is included when you are using statutory language that cannot be easily quoted within the Discussion itself. Sometimes a copy of the statute is attached with the relevant language highlighted, rather than being re-typed into the research memo itself.

2. At the direction of a consumer . . . do one of the following:

    a. Accept return of the motor vehicle and replace the motor vehicle with a comparable new motor vehicle . . . .

    b. Accept return of the motor vehicle and refund . . . the full purchase price . . . .

    . . . .

(c) To receive a comparable new motor vehicle or a refund due under par. (b) 1. or 2., a consumer . . . shall offer to the manufacturer of the motor vehicle having the nonconformity to transfer title of that motor vehicle to that manufacturer. No later than 30 days after that offer, the manufacturer shall provide the consumer with the comparable new motor vehicle or refund. . . .

STATEMENT OF FACTS

6. *This Statement of Facts begins with a quick summary of the situation, identifying the client, the other parties, and the general question at hand. After that overview, it begins the chronology of events. It has omitted unneeded detail, such as the specifics of the repairs. But it retained the facts important to the relevant legal standard, such as the number of days that the car was out of service. Some other facts, such as the price of the car, are included to clarify the situation, even though they are not legally significant. Each paragraph in the chronology contains a logical group of information. The second paragraph explains the problems with the car. The third explains the first letter and response, and the last explains the relevant details of the second letter and Maven's subsequent action. Thus organized, the facts read quickly and clearly.*

6   Our client, Jane Maven, has asked us to advise her about getting a refund from Zelta Motor Car Company (Zelta) for her 2007 Roadster. Ever since she purchased the car, the transmission has not operated properly and the dealer has been unable to fix it.

Maven purchased a Zelta Roadster for $75,000 from Ross Motors, Inc., (the dealer) on March 1, 2007. Within a week, she experienced problems with the car. It stopped running without warning and would not restart, forcing Maven to have the car towed. During the subsequent two months, Maven had the Roadster towed to the dealer three times. Each time she left it with the dealer for repairs for a week or more. In total, her Roadster was out of commission for forty-two days while the dealer attempted to repair it. Finally, on May 26, 2007, the dealer said it could not fix the problem.

7 Maven sent a letter to the Roadster's manufacturer, Zelta, on June 20, 2007. The letter stated, "This car is a LEMON . . . . [W]hat I want most is my $75,000 back." However, it also included the option of repairing the vehicle: "I have zero faith in your ability to repair the car. If you see it otherwise, let me know . . . ." On July 10, Zelta's attorney responded in a letter saying that Zelta had asked the dealer to contact specialists at Zelta's factory for repair advice.

Maven responded on July 15 in a second letter in which she specifically cited Wisconsin's Lemon Law and restated her demand for a refund: "I want a refund. . . . Wis. Stats. 2180171 requires you to do this within 30 days." Maven has not yet received a response to this letter. You asked me to determine whether either of these letters provided adequate notice under the Wisconsin Lemon Law.

DISCUSSION

8 To recover under the Lemon Law, a consumer must meet eligibility requirements and provide adequate notice to the manufacturer. Wis. Stat. § 218.0171(2) (2005-06). When a consumer is eligible and has provided notice, the Lemon Law requires the manufacturer to provide the consumer's chosen remedy. Id. § 218.0171 (2)(b). To be eligible under the Lemon Law, the consumer's vehicle must first fail to conform to an express warranty. Id. § 218.0171(2)(f). Then the consumer must make the vehicle available for repair before the warranty expires or before the end of one year of ownership. Id. § 218.0171(2)(a). If the nonconformity remains after reasonable attempts to repair, then the consumer must notify the manufacturer. The consumer must also specify whether the consumer wants a replacement vehicle or a refund of the full purchase price. Id. § 218.0171(2)(b). To provide adequate notice, the consumer must also offer to transfer the vehicle's title to the manufacturer. Id. § 218.0171(2)(c). After the consumer has provided adequate notice, the law requires the manufacturer to comply within thirty days. Id. Maven has met these requirements and will be able to recover.

9. *The second paragraph clarifies which elements are at issue and which are not. Sometimes a paragraph like this is unneeded, and sometimes this information can be handled in the body of the opening paragraph. Here, however, the opening paragraph is complex enough that the writer has chosen to set this information off in a separate paragraph.*

10. *In this paragraph, the writer synthesizes the law from various sources into one unified explanation. The first sentence states the paragraph's thesis, which is an overview of the legal reasoning, and then explains and supports that thesis. This paragraph structure is particularly useful in legal writing. The reader is checking your logic, and that is easier to do when the conclusion is stated at the beginning.*

You might be wondering about the "Id." appearing after many of the sentences. These citations tell the reader that the source of the information in the sentence is the same as the source for the previous sentence. When all the information comes from the same source, you might think all these citations are unnecessary, and some attorneys might agree. The citations after each sentence, however, are more precise because the avoid making the reader guess how much comes from one source. When in doubt about your reader's preferences, err on the side of citing more often, not less.

11. *Here and in the following paragraphs, the writer begins with a thesis sentence stating another point about the law. In fact, if you read the first sentence of every paragraph in the Discussion, you will have a useful summary of the writer's logic and main points. A legal reader needs this kind of clear summary and direct organization because the reader uses the Discussion to check the writer's logic and to understand how the law will work in the client's situation.*

9 The issues that remain are whether either of Maven's letters to Zelta provided adequate notice. Maven's Roadster did fail to conform to an express warranty, meeting the first requirement. The requirement for a reasonable attempt to repair was met; the dealer spent more than thirty days attempting to repair the Roadster.

10 When notifying a manufacturer of a request for relief under Wisconsin's Lemon Law, a consumer must fulfill two requirements. Id. § 218.0171(2). First, the consumer must choose the statutory remedy of either a replacement vehicle or a refund. Id. § 218.0171(2)(b)(2). Second, the consumer must offer to transfer title of the nonconforming vehicle to the manufacturer. Id. § 218.0171(2)(c). The consumer implies this offer to transfer title by requesting a replacement vehicle under the Lemon Law. Garcia v. Mazda Motor of Am., Inc., 2004 WI 93, ¶ 15, 682 N.W.2d 365, 369-70. Therefore a request for a replacement satisfies the notice requirement. If a consumer offers a non-statutory option, however, then the consumer has not provided sufficient notice. Berends v. Mack Truck., Inc., 2002 WI Ct. App. 69, ¶ 14, 643 N.W.2d 158, 162-63.

11 A consumer's letter can provide adequate notice without explicitly offering to transfer title. Garcia, 2004 WI 93, ¶ 15. Garcia purchased a new Mazda but experienced problems with the car soon after the purchase. Id. ¶ 4. She then took the car in for repairs. Id. The Mazda dealer was unable to repair the car, even after multiple attempts. Id. After the repair attempts failed, Garcia wrote to Mazda requesting a replacement under Wisconsin's Lemon Law. Id. Mazda failed to comply; Garcia subsequently filed suit. Id. ¶ 6. Mazda moved for summary judgment because Garcia's letter did not explicitly offer to transfer title to the vehicle. Id. The trial court granted the motion and the court of appeals affirmed. Id. The supreme court, however, inferred an offer to transfer title in Garcia's letter and reversed the lower courts' decisions. Id. ¶ 3.

When determining whether a consumer has fulfilled the statute's notice requirements, the Wisconsin Supreme

Court considered the legislative intent behind the statute. Id. ¶ 8. It "construe[s] remedial, consumer protection statutes like the Wisconsin Lemon Law 'with a view towards the social problem which the legislature was addressing when enacting the law.'" Id. (quoting Dieter v. Chrysler Corp., 2005 WI 45, ¶ 19, 610 N.W.2d 832, 837). Because the statute does not define "offer to transfer title," the court applied the plain meaning rule, using recognized dictionary definitions. Id. ¶ 14. The word "replacement," which Garcia used in her letter, is defined as "substitution." Id. ¶ 15 (citation omitted). In turn, "substitute" is defined as "one that takes place of another." Id. (citation omitted). Using these definitions, the court determined that Garcia's letter implied an offer to transfer title because a literal interpretation would be inconsistent with the purpose of the Lemon Law. Id. Furthermore, Garcia's letter specifically referenced the Lemon Law, which implied an attempt to comply with the requirements of that law. Id. ¶ 16.

12   When a consumer offers a non-statutory remedy, however, the notice is inadequate because the consumer has not followed the statute's unambiguous language. Berends, 2002 WI Ct. App. 69, ¶ 14. Berends purchased a new vehicle and subsequently had problems covered by the warranty. Id. ¶ 2. After the dealer made numerous unsuccessful attempts to repair the vehicle, Berends wrote to the manufacturer requesting relief under the Lemon Law. Id. The letter also included the option of repairing the defects within "seven business days." Id. The manufacturer did not repair the vehicle and Berends filed a complaint. Id. ¶ 3. The manufacturer filed for summary judgment based on defective notice and the trial court granted the motion. Id. ¶ 5. The court of appeals affirmed the summary judgment. Id. ¶ 10. The statute's language provides only two remedies: refund or replacement of the vehicle. Id. ¶ 14. When any remedy is offered that is not included in the Lemon Law, the manufacturer does not have proper notice. Id. Without proper notice, the letter does not trigger the thirty-day period in which the manufacturer must provide the requested remedy. Id. ¶ 15.

12. *So far the paragraphs in this Discussion have been focused on explaining what a consumer must do to invoke the Lemon Law. To explain this, the writer has used information from the statute itself, but also from two cases that interpreted the statute. Notice how the sentences focus on the main points about the law, rather than the sources of that law. This helps unify, or synthesize, the explanation of the law. For example, this paragraph begins with "When a consumer offers a non-standard remedy." rather than "In* Berends, *the court held that . . . ." Beginning with the name of the case would make the explanation of the law read more like a book report. By beginning with a focus on the problem at hand, a consumer offering another remedy, the writer focuses on how the law works, not the source of the law.*

13. *In this paragraph, the writer begins explaining how the law applies to Maven's situation. This transition is clearly signaled by the opening words of the thesis sentence: "Maven's second letter." In the third sentence, notice how the writer uses parallel sentence structure and repetition of terms to present logically parallel facts: "Just as Garcia's letter specifically requested a replacement, Maven's specifically requested a refund." This use of repetition is not boring or redundant. Instead, it is a kind of transition that clarifies the comparison. Repetition of legal phrases is necessary for accuracy because those words represent the legal concept itself. If the writer used different terms, the legal reader would not see the connection as readily and the writer's legal conclusion would not be as accurate.*

13 Maven's second letter probably provided adequate notice even though it did not explicitly offer to transfer title. Like Garcia, Maven requested a specific remedy. Just as Garcia's letter specifically requested a replacement, Maven's specifically requested a refund. Although Maven chose a different remedy than Garcia, that choice probably would not change the reasoning. Under the plain meaning rule and in light of the legislative intent, the word "refund" implies an offer to transfer title. "Refund" is defined as "to give back" or "repayment or balancing of accounts." Websters Third New International Dictionary, Unabridged, 1910 (2002). Under this reasoning, Maven's request implies an offer to transfer title.

14. *The writer takes the time to explain his reasoning fully. Although you might think this point is too obvious to explain, most legal readers would disagree. Just as you would work out the math in a complicated formula to reach your result, you need to work out the logical steps to make sure your application is correct. Your reader wants to see that logic laid out in sufficient detail so the reader can, in turn, check that logic.*

14 Inferring notice based on a request for a refund is appropriate in light of the legislative intent behind the statute. Garcia, 2004 WI 93, ¶ 8. It "would be 'nonsensical' for a consumer to demand a replacement without offering to transfer title." Id. ¶ 15. Similarly, it would be nonsensical for Maven to demand a full refund without transferring title of the Roadster. Furthermore, like Garcia, Maven referred to the Lemon Law specifically in her second letter. Under the same reasoning used in Garcia, this reference implies an attempt to comply with the requirements of the Lemon Law.

15. *The writer uses clear transitions to show how this paragraph relates logically to the paragraph at 12. The writer uses numbers, "Maven's first letter," and the transitional phrase "in contrast." Like using turn signals when changing lanes, using these transitions helps the reader know where you are going.*

15 Maven's first letter, in contrast, did not provide adequate notice. That letter offered a non-statutory remedy. Maven's first letter included the phrase, "Unless you can repair this car right away," along with her request for a refund. Like Berends' reference to the option of repairing the defects, Maven's language offered a remedy not included in the Lemon Law. Therefore, as with Berends' letter, Maven's first letter did not provide adequate notice.

— *FIGURE 4-6* —

LEGAL MEMORANDUM—VU

Note: This legal research memo follows Bluebook citation format, using italics.

EXPLANATION

Kuphal, Walz and Johns, S.C.

5200 West Deming Way
Kewaunee, WI 54216

To: Gena Bardwell
From: Donald Vu
Date: September 23, 2007
Re: Maven Lemon Law Claim

1. *This research memo organizes the material differently, organizing around one Question Presented (QP) rather than two. The organization of a memo is mainly governed by the logical structure of the law used to answer the question. Sometimes, as in this situation, several different organizations are possible.*

This QP uses the same general structure as the QPs in the previous research memo. However, this one includes some explanation about the Lemon Law to help the reader see the relevance of the facts to the issue, but presents the facts more generally, merging information about the two letters.

2. *This Brief Answer (BA) uses several shorter sentences to provide the answer. The first sentence answers the question directly. The second explains the relevant legal standard. The following sentences explain how the facts in the QP lead to the resulting answer under that standard. The legal terms that appeared in the QP now reappear in the answer, combined with facts to explain the reasoning. This research memo includes the Statement of Facts after the QP and BA. When this order is used, it is not as important to have an overview of the legal situation at the beginning of the facts.*

QUESTION PRESENTED

1   Under Wisconsin Statutes section 218.0171(2), covering refunds for defective new vehicles, did either of Maven's letters provide Zelta Motor Car Company with the statutorily required notice that obligates Zelta to refund the price of her defective car?

BRIEF ANSWER

2   Yes. Maven's second letter provides the statutorily required notice. When a consumer buys a vehicle that is nonconforming under the statute, that consumer may obtain a refund by notifying the manufacturer that the buyer wants a refund and by offering to transfer title of the vehicle. Maven's first letter did not provide adequate notice because it included repair as an option, and so it was not clear that she wanted a refund. But Maven's second letter did specify that she wanted a refund. Although her second letter did not directly offer to transfer title, that offer may be implied. Precedent has inferred an offer to transfer title from a request for a replacement vehicle, and that logic would apply to a request for a refund.

3. *The first paragraph of the Statement of Facts describes the car's problems. This opening might leave the reader wondering what the legal issue will be, but the QP and BA have already clarified that, so this paragraph will not be confusing to the reader.*

This Statement of Facts is organized chronologically, with each paragraph explaining the events at a different time or location, like scenes in a movie. This organization can be the clearest choice when you have only one series of events, or when the sequence of events is itself important.

4. *The writer states the facts objectively by providing non-debatable facts. The writer avoids making judgments about those facts, such as "Maven was angry" or "Zelta dodged the issue." Objective facts are particularly important in a research memo because even a small change in the facts can change the outcome.*

As in the previous sample's Statement of Facts, this writer omits unneeded details. For example, we do not know the details of Maven's conversation with the mechanics or the detail of the repairs done on the car. If you compare these facts to those in the previous sample, you will see slightly different choices about what is included. Both versions, however, include all the facts that will be used in the following Discussion.

STATEMENT OF FACTS

3   Maven purchased a new Zelta sports car on March 1, 2007. Within a few days, the car began vibrating and making whining noises at high speeds. A few days later, the car began popping out of gear unpredictably. On April 4, she took the car to the dealer, who tried to fix the problem. Maven picked up her car on April 11, but was back at the dealer's on April 18 with the same problem. On May 9, she again picked up the car, but she was back in three days with the same problem. On May 26, she picked up the car a third time. The dealer's mechanic explained that they were unable to fix the transmission problems, even though they had replaced the transmission.

4   Maven then wrote to Zelta Motor Car Company requesting a refund but also asking them to let her know of other repair steps they could suggest. Zelta responded by asking the dealer to contact factory specialists for advice. Maven wrote a second letter in response. In this letter, she cited the Lemon Law statute by number, asked for a refund, and did not offer other alternatives. Zelta has yet to respond to this letter.

Maven has come to us to determine whether she can obtain a refund from Zelta.

APPLICABLE STATUTE

Wisconsin Statute section 218.0171 Repair, replacement and refund under new motor vehicle warranties

(1) In this section:

. . . .

(f) "Nonconformity" means a condition or defect which substantially impairs the use, value or safety of a motor vehicle, and is covered by an express warranty . . . but does not include a condition or defect which is the result of abuse, neglect or unauthorized modification . . . by a consumer.

(h) "Reasonable attempt to repair" means any of the following occurring within the term of the express warranty applicable to a new motor vehicle . . . :

    . . . .

    2. The motor vehicle is out of service for an aggregate of at least 30 days because of warranty nonconformities.

(2) (a) If a new motor vehicle does not conform to an applicable express warranty and the consumer reports the nonconformity to the manufacturer . . . or any of the manufacturer's authorized motor vehicle dealers and makes the motor vehicle available for repair before the expiration of the warranty . . . , the nonconformity shall be repaired.

    (b) 1. If after a reasonable attempt to repair the nonconformity is not repaired, the manufacturer shall carry out the requirement under subd. 2. . . .

    2. At the direction of a consumer . . . do one of the following:

        a. Accept return of the motor vehicle and replace the motor vehicle with a comparable new motor vehicle . . . .

        b. Accept return of the motor vehi-

cle and refund . . . the full purchase price . . . .

. . . .

   (c) To receive a comparable new motor
       vehicle or a refund due under par. (b) 1.
       or 2., a consumer . . . shall offer to the
       manufacturer of the motor vehicle hav-
       ing the nonconformity to transfer title
       of that motor vehicle to that manufac-
       turer. No later than 30 days after that
       offer, the manufacturer shall provide
       the consumer with the comparable new
       motor vehicle or refund. . . .

DISCUSSION

5. *Although its wording differs from the previous sample, this Discussion also starts by addressing the reader's question about Wisconsin's Lemon Law.*

5 Wisconsin enacted its Lemon Law "to protect purchasers of new vehicles that turn out to be defective."
Garcia v. Mazda Motor of Am., Inc., 2004 WI 93, ¶ 9, 682
N.W.2d 365, 368. The Lemon Law requires the vehicle's
manufacturer to either replace a vehicle or refund the full
purchase price within thirty days when the consumer has
met all the requirements under the statute. Wis. Stat.
§ 218.017(2) (2005-06). Those statutory requirements are

6. *Legal writing makes frequent use of lists. Here the list is enumerated and set off from the text because each element in the list
is relatively long. Setting it off this way makes it easier for the
reader to see the overall structure of the elements.*

6   (1) the vehicle must fail to conform to an express
           warranty,

      (2) the consumer must make the vehicle available
           for repair before the warranty expires or within
           one year of purchase,

      (3) the nonconformity must still be present after
           reasonable attempt to repair, and

      (4) the consumer must provide sufficient notice to
           the manufacturer of the remedy the consumer
           wants and the consumer's willingness to trans-
           fer title of the non-conforming vehicle.

7. *When a citation follows indented text, that citation appears at the beginning of the first line after the indention. This placement shows that the citation is the source of the indented material, not part of the quotation.*

8. *In this paragraph, the writer has taken care to keep subjects and verbs close together. For example, the first three sentences could have been worded as follows.*

> *The consumer's notice to the manufacturer, to invoke a remedy under the Lemon Law, must specify the remedy the consumer wants. Two possible remedies, getting a replacement vehicle or a full refund of the purchase price, are provided by the statute. A notice that includes options other than these two statutory remedies does not provide sufficient notice.*

These sentences are not awful, but taken together they make the reader work harder to understand the content. Over the course of the Discussion, this kind of writing would make the research memo much more difficult to read.

9. *This Discussion presents all the relevant law before moving to application. It also applies all the points of law to the first letter, then to the second. In contrast, the Discussion in the previous sample research memo presented the law regarding election of a remedy separately and then applied it to the second letter, then to the first letter. It then presented the law regarding inferring notice and applied that to each letter.*

When presenting the explanation of the relevant legal standard, or the synthesis, in one larger unit, the writer needs to divide that explanation into sub-points, each stated in a thesis sentence at the beginning of the paragraph. The writer may need to insert subheadings to further clarify the organization. Dividing a longer synthesis requires making these narrow distinctions, which can be difficult. But you must make these distinctions to divide the explanation into clear, manageable pieces for the reader. This makes it much easier for the reader to understand your reasoning.

10. *Here the writer uses quotations effectively. Quotations are short, with irrelevant details not being quoted. They are also worked smoothly into the logic of the overall paragraph. Use of quotations can be a stylistic choice. Some legal readers prefer to see the actual quotes, while other prefer a paraphrase, which usually fits more smoothly into the overall explanation of the law.*

7 *Id.* Maven's situation met the first three elements. The only question remaining is whether she provided sufficient notice.

8 Under the Lemon Law, the consumer's notice must specify the remedy the consumer wants. The two possible statutory remedies are a replacement vehicle or a full refund. *Id.* (2)(b)(2). If the notice includes options other than these, it does not provide sufficient notice. *Berends v. Mack Truck. Inc.*, 2002 WI Ct. App. 69, ¶ 14, 643 N.W.2d 158, 162-63. An offer to repair the vehicle would be inconsistent with the statute. *Id.* When Berends wrote to the manufacturer of his nonconforming truck and asked for relief under the Lemon Law, he included the option of repairing the truck's defects. *Id.* ¶ 2. When the manufacturer failed to comply, Berends sued. *Id.* ¶ 3. The circuit court, however, granted summary judgment in the manufacturer's favor. *Id.* ¶ 5. The court of appeals upheld the ruling because "[b]y providing Mack Truck a third option, Berends failed to follow the unambiguous language of [the statute], rendering his notice defective." *Id.* ¶ 14.

9 Sufficient notice also includes an offer to transfer title of the nonconforming vehicle to the manufacturer. Wis. Stat. § 218.0171 (2)(c). The statute does not allow the consumer to retain the nonconforming vehicle and still get a refund or replacement. *Id.*

10 An offer to transfer title, however, need not be stated explicitly. *Garcia*, 2004 WI 93, ¶ 15. In reversing the lower courts' rulings, the Wisconsin Supreme Court stated that "[t]he statute does not require the consumer to use any 'magic words.'" *Id.* ¶ 18. Rather, the court looks to the sense of the statutory requirements: "One enduring principle of statutory interpretation is that statutes are to be interpreted reasonably to give effect to the textually manifest statutory purpose." *Id.* ¶ 15 (citing *Kalah v. Circuit Ct.*, 2004 WI 58, ¶¶ 44, 46, 49, 681 N.W.2d 110, 123-25). Therefore Garcia's "demand for a replacement vehicle adequately implied an offer to transfer title." *Id.* ¶ 18.

To determine whether a consumer's request for a replacement included an implicit offer to transfer title, the supreme court looked to "the common and ordinary meaning of a word." *Id.* ¶ 14. The common meaning of "replacement" implies "substitution," which in turn implies giving up ownership of the original vehicle. *Id.* ¶ 15 (citation omitted.). Giving up ownership implied an offer to transfer title. *Id.* "[I]t would be 'nonsensical' for a consumer to demand a replacement without offering to transfer title to the original vehicle." *Id.* Furthermore, because Garcia's letter referred to the Lemon Law after detailing her problems with her vehicle. *Id.* ¶ 16. Although the manufacturer argued that the offer to transfer title was unclear unless explicitly stated, the court rejected that reasoning: "when a consumer demands a replacement vehicle under the Wisconsin Lemon Law, the consumer impliedly offers to transfer title to the old vehicle." *Id.* ¶ 19.

11 Maven's first letter did not invoke the Lemon Law because she did not specify the remedy she wanted. The letter included an option that was not specified in the statute: she asked the manufacturer to inform her of repair steps they suggested. Like Berends' offer of repair, Maven's offer of another opportunity to repair the vehicle is inconsistent with a demand for relief under the Lemon Law. Therefore, her first letter did not unambiguously imply an offer to transfer title.

Her second letter, however, did specify a remedy and imply an offer to transfer title, providing sufficient notice. Maven requested a refund, which logically implies returning the non-conforming vehicle to the manufacturer and transferring title. Although Maven requested a refund rather than a replacement, that difference is immaterial. It would have been nonsensical to conclude that Garcia would demand a replacement without offering to transfer title to the original vehicle. Similarly, it would be nonsensical to conclude that Maven would request a refund without offering to transfer title to her vehicle. Maven's reference to the Lemon Law further supports inferring an offer

11. *In this application, the writer compares Maven's situation and the facts of Berends. To do this, the writer uses parallel wording and structure. For example, "Berends' offer of repair" parallels "Maven's offer of another opportunity to repair." That phrase is repeated in the concluding sentence to link these facts to the paragraph's conclusion. This repetition of terms should not be confused with being repetitive. Repeating terms here links ideas and shows the similarity of the facts. This repetition is adding clarity, rather than wasting the reader's time.*

to transfer title. Garcia's reference to the Lemon Law established an implied offer because "no reasonable person could confuse the letter as something other than an attempt to invoke and comply with the law." *Garcia*, 2004 WI 93, ¶ 16. Similarly, Maven's reference to the Lemon Law should not be reasonably viewed as anything other than an attempt to comply with the law.

12. *This research memo's conclusion is not set off from the rest of the Discussion, but otherwise includes the same summarizing information.*

12 In summary, Maven probably can succeed in recovering a refund under the Lemon Law. Although her first letter did not provide sufficient notice, her second letter specified one statutory remedy, meeting the first notice requirement. Assuming the court would apply the reasoning in *Garcia* to Maven's situation, Maven's second letter would also imply an offer to transfer title of the vehicle, thus meeting the second notice requirement. Therefore the second letter provided sufficient notice to invoke the statute and obligate Zelta to pay a refund.

— *FIGURE 4-7* —
LEGAL MEMORANDUM—KAMPMEIER

Note: This legal research memo follows
ALWD citation format.

EXPLANATION

Gallagher & Kennedy, P.A.

4200 Old Sauk Road
Madison, WI 53709

1. *This Heading includes the briefest subject line of the examples here, placing the content overview in the Introduction.*

1 To: Dean C Short, II
From: Denise Kampmeier
Date: September 23, 2007
Re: Maven v. Zelta Motors,
       File Number 04-187

INTRODUCTION

2 Client Jane Maven came to us for advice about getting a refund from Zelta Motor Car Company for her defective Zelta Roadster. She wrote to Zelta asking for a refund or advice about repair, and Zelta responded with an offer of repair. She wrote again asking only for a refund, but Zelta has not yet responded to that letter. This memo addresses whether these letters provided adequate notice to invoke Wisconsin's Lemon Law.

STATEMENT OF FACTS

3 Ms. Maven bought a Zelta Roadster on March 1, 2007. The car had transition problems, so she returned it to the dealer for repair, which took one week. Within a week of picking up the car, she had to return it for the same reason. The dealer kept the car for three weeks, replacing the transmission. Nevertheless, Ms. Maven experienced the same problems three days after picking up the car. This time, she returned the car and asked them to take "this piece of junk" off her hands. Maven intake notes (Sept. 13, 2007). After talking to the technicians, she agreed to let them try once more to fix the problem, but they were unable to do so. Two weeks later, Ms. Maven picked up the car from the dealer.

After learning about Wisconsin's Lemon Law, Ms. Maven wrote to the manufacturer, Zelta Motor Car Company, stating the following.

> This car is a LEMON under any definition. I am so disgusted that what I most want is my $75,000 back.

> Based on my experience with Zelta and Ross Motors, I have zero faith in your ability to repair the car. If you see it otherwise, let me know . . . .

Letter from Jane Maven, client, to Juanita Esposito, Pres., Zelta Motor Car Co., First Letter about Nonconforming Vehicle (June 20, 2007). Zelta responded with an offer to

2. *This Introduction helps the reader understand the general situation. The following information can then be understood in that context. Introductions are often omitted in shorter legal research memos.*

3. *This Statement of Facts covers the facts concisely but makes some different choices about which facts to include or omit. When deciding what facts to include, you will make some judgment calls; however, always include all the facts you will be using in the Discussion. While the Discussion explains the legal significance of those facts, the Statement of Facts explains how the facts fit into the overall story that leads up to the legal question. For example, all of the sample research memos include information about the content of Maven's two letters, the dealer's efforts to fix the car, and the manufacturer's response.*

█████████████████████████

pay all repair cost and a suggestion that she take the car to a larger dealership for repair. Ltr. from Joseph Anderson, Vice Pres., Zelta Motor Car Co., to Jane Maven, client, Response to First Letter (July 10, 2007). Ms. Maven responded with a second letter including the following.

> I want a refund. Send me the check right now. Wis. Stats. 218.0171 requires you to do this within 30 days.

Ltr. from Jane Maven, client, to Joseph Anderson, Vice Pres., Zelta Motor Car. Co., Second Letter about Nonconforming Vehicle (July 15, 2007). Zelta has not yet responded to this letter.

4. *This writer uses two Questions Presented and organizes the Discussion around those two issues. The first question is about specifying a remedy, while the second addresses the offer to transfer title.*

4 **QUESTIONS PRESENTED**

1. Wisconsin's Lemon Law requires a consumer to specify a remedy to provide notice to the manufacturer. Did Maven provide notice by stating, "I want a refund"?

2. The supreme court has implied an offer to transfer title from a consumer's request for a replacement vehicle. Did Maven imply an offer to transfer title by requesting a refund and citing Wisconsin's Lemon Law?

5. *The first question is resolved more easily than the second, and this is reflected in the relative length of the two Brief Answers and of the corresponding sub-sections of the Discussion. Do cover all the issues, but do not use more words than you need.*

5 **BRIEF ANSWERS**

1. Yes. Maven's second letter provided adequate notice to invoke the Lemon Law because it specifically requested a refund, which is one of the two statutory options.

2. Probably yes. A request for a replacement has been held to imply an offer to transfer title. Under this reasoning, a request for a refund would logically imply an offer to transfer title. Additionally, Maven's reference to the Lemon Law would likely be interpreted to show her attempt to follow the law.

APPLICABLE STATUTE

Wisconsin Statute section 218.0171 Repair, replacement and refund under new motor vehicle warranties

(1) In this section:

> . . . .

> (f) "Nonconformity" means a condition or defect which substantially impairs the use, value or safety of a motor vehicle, and is covered by an express warranty . . . but does not include a condition or defect which is the result of abuse, neglect or unauthorized modification . . . by a consumer.

> (h) "Reasonable attempt to repair" means any of the following occurring within the term of the express warranty applicable to a new motor vehicle . . . :

> > . . . .

> > 2. The motor vehicle is out of service for an aggregate of at least 30 days because of warranty nonconformities.

(2) (a) If a new motor vehicle does not conform to an applicable express warranty and the consumer reports the nonconformity to the manufacturer . . . or any of the manufacturer's authorized motor vehicle dealers and makes the motor vehicle available for repair before the expiration of the warranty . . . , the nonconformity shall be repaired.

(b) 1. If after a reasonable attempt to repair the nonconformity is not repaired, the manufacturer shall carry out the requirement under subd. 2. . . .

2. At the direction of a consumer . . . do one of the following:

   a. Accept return of the motor vehicle and replace the motor vehicle with a comparable new motor vehicle . . . .

   b. Accept return of the motor vehicle and refund . . . the full purchase price . . . .

. . . .

(c) To receive a comparable new motor vehicle or a refund due under par. (b) 1. or 2., a consumer . . . shall offer to the manufacturer of the motor vehicle having the nonconformity to transfer title of that motor vehicle to that manufacturer. No later than 30 days after that offer, the manufacturer shall provide the consumer with the comparable new motor vehicle or refund. . . .

DISCUSSION

6. *This opening paragraph overviews the legal standard in the first few paragraphs and then states the outcome of the application of that law. The writer uses careful repetition of terms to connect the sentences logically. For example, "provide with notice" links the end of the first sentence and the beginning of the second. The end of the second sentence is linked with the beginning of the third by the phrases "the manufacturer must" and "if the manufacturer fails." This kind of repetition is not a problem. Instead, it is a logical outgrowth of clear reasoning when you use the same term for the same idea, as the legal reader expects you to do.*

6 To qualify for a refund under the Lemon Law, a consumer (1) must have a vehicle under warranty that remains defective after reasonable efforts to repair and (2) must provide the manufacturer with notice that is sufficiently clear. Wis. Stat. § 218.0171(2) (2005-06). After the consumer has provided this notice, the manufacturer must replace the vehicle or provide a full refund within thirty days. *Id.* at § 218.0171(2)(c). If the manufacturer fails to do this, then the consumer may bring an action to recover damages. *Id.* at § 218.0171(7). Ms. Maven's vehicle qualifies under the Lemon Law. Her second letter to Zelta provided the notice required to invoke the Lemon Law when viewed under the broad interpretation used in precedent cases.

Under Wisconsin's Lemon Law, a consumer may return a vehicle for the full purchase price when that consumer meets all the conditions required by the statute. *Id.* at § 218.0171(2)(b). First, the vehicle must have a defect that substantially impairs its use, and that defect must not be caused by the consumer. *Id.* at § 218.0171(1)(f). The defect must also be in something covered by an express warranty. *Id.* Second, the consumer must tell the dealer about the defect within the warranty period and must make the vehicle available for repair. *Id.* at § 218.0171(2)(a). Third, the defect must still be present after reasonable attempts to repair. *Id.* at § 218.0171(2)(b). This reasonable attempt requirement is met when the vehicle has been in for repair at least four times or for a total of at least thirty days. *Id.* at § 218.0171(1)(h).

7 Maven's vehicle meets all the required conditions. The car has a defective transmission that substantially impairs the vehicle's use. Maven did not cause the defect, and the car's warranty expressly covers transmission problems. Maven also reported the problem and took it in for repair three times. Finally, the car was in the shop for seven days the first time, twenty-one days the second, and fourteen days the third, for a total of forty-two days.

8

1. Specifying a Statutory Remedy

9 After meeting all of the statutorily required conditions, the consumer must provide the manufacturer with adequate notice. Adequate notice occurs when the consumer (1) specifies which statutory remedy he or she is choosing and (2) offers to transfer the vehicle's title to the manufacturer. *Id.* at § 218.0171(2).

10 The statute requires the consumer to specify unambiguously whether the consumer is requesting a refund or a

7. *Here the writer applies the previous law to the client's case. Again, parallel structure and repetition of terms help the reader see the logical relationship of this application to the previous synthesis.*

8. *This writer uses headings to divide parts of the Discussion. Although sub-headings are more commonly used in longer memos, they can be helpful any time the Discussion breaks into sub-issues. When these subheadings reflect the logical relationship and organization of the Discussion's parts, they reinforce and clarify the writing.*

9. *This writer uses enumerated lists to present the elements of notice. Writers often find a few organizational structures that they prefer and then use those frequently. Thus, with experimentation and practice, legal writing gets easier and faster.*

10. *Here the writer includes several sentences explaining the facts of the precedent case and the reasoning behind the court's decision. When explaining precedent, give your reader the information he or she needs to check your reasoning. The information you need to include will vary depending on that reasoning.*

replacement. *Berends v. Mack Truck, Inc.*, 643 N.W.2d 158, 162 (Wis. App. 2002). Offering the manufacturer the choice of further repair is inconsistent with the statutory remedies. *Id.* at 162-63. "For purposes of triggering the thirty-day time limit established by [the statute], the consumer must either demand that the manufacturer provide a new vehicle or demand that the manufacturer refund the purchase price." *Id.* at 163. Under this reasoning, Mr. Berends' letter failed to provide sufficient notice because he offered the option to "repair these defects within seven business days" when asking for a replacement. *Id.* at 160. Including the repair option created an ambiguity about whether the statute was being invoked. *Id.* at 163.

11 Ms. Maven's first request is ambiguous about the remedy and thus fails to qualify as notice. Her first request implied an option for repair when it stated, "I have zero faith in your ability to repair the car. If you see it otherwise, let me know . . . ." Although her reference to repair is not as specific as Berends', she does ask them to inform her if they think they can repair the vehicle. That possible reading is confirmed by Zelta's response, which suggested further repair.

Ms. Maven's second request, however, is not ambiguous because it did not include the option of repair. She stated only, "I want a refund," which is unambiguous.

2. Offering to Transfer Title

12 Although the statute requires the consumer to offer to transfer title to the manufacturer, the court interprets this requirement in light of the statute's purpose. "As we have repeatedly stated, we construe remedial, consumer protection statutes like the Wisconsin Lemon Law 'with a view towards the social problem which the legislature was addressing when enacting the law.'" *Garcia v. Mazda Motor of Am., Inc.*, 682 N.W.2d 365, 368 (Wis. 2004) (*citing Dieter v. Chrysler Corp.*, 610 N.W.2d 832 (Wis. 2000)). The legislature created the Lemon Law to protect consumers who purchase defective vehicles. *Id.* While the

11. *Here the writer begins applying the law to the client's situation. The application moves in the same order in which the law was presented. This parallel structure adds clarity and helps both reader and writer be sure that every point has been addressed. Sometimes, as you write the application, you may find that you need to say some additional points. In that situation, parallel structure may not work. When that happens, write the application you need, but then go back and check the presentation of the law to see if it needs to be reorganized or revised. Working back and forth between the two parts like this often helps you write a better Discussion.*

12. *Rather than including a transition sentence or paragraph here, the writer lets the headings and structure of the Discussion's overview prepare the reader for the new topic.*

Lemon Law does require a consumer to offer to transfer title of the vehicle, it "does not require the consumer to use any 'magic words.'" *Id.* at 370.

An offer to transfer title may be inferred based on reasonable interpretation rather than an explicit statement. *Id.* at 370. To determine what constitutes an "offer to transfer title," the court has looked at the dictionary definitions of the consumer's words. *Id.* at 369. For example, Garcia's demand for a "replacement" vehicle implied an offer to transfer title. *Id.* at 369-70. "[I]t would be 'nonsensical' for a consumer to demand a replacement without offering to transfer title to the original vehicle." *Id.* at 370. "A literalistic interpretation of the Wisconsin Lemon Law on these facts would not be consistent with the statute's remedial purpose." *Id.*

13. *The thesis sentence of this paragraph and subsequent ones state the point each paragraph supports, providing an easy way to skim the Discussion and understand its main points.*

13 When the consumer also refers to Wisconsin's Lemon Law, the inference of an offer to transfer title is strengthened. *Id.* The supreme court specifically cited Garcia's reference in her letter to the Lemon Law and explained that "[n]o reasonable person could confuse the letter as something other than an attempt to invoke and comply with the law." *Id.* Garcia's demand for a replacement vehicle thus met the requirement of offering to transfer title, so the manufacturer did receive notice that Garcia was invoking the Lemon Law. *Id.* at 371.

In light of the statute's purpose, Ms. Maven's request for a refund should be valid. Allowing her to recover her money for a defective vehicle is exactly the remedy this statute sought to provide. The statutory remedy should be available to her even though she did not explicitly offer to transfer title. Just as Garcia was not required to use "magic words" to communicate an offer to transfer title, Ms. Maven should not be required to use any particular words. Although Maven requested a refund rather than a replacement, both remedies are specifically available under the statute. Therefore this difference in remedy is not significant.

An offer to transfer title could be inferred based on the dictionary definitions of Ms. Maven's words. Ms. Maven requested a "refund," which is defined as "to give back." *Websters Third New International Dictionary, Unabridged,* p. 1910 (2002). Just as it would be nonsensical to interpret Garcia's request for a "replacement" as implying an intention to keep the defective vehicle, it would be nonsensical to interpret Ms. Maven's request for a "refund" as implying an intention to keep her defective vehicle. Items are commonly returned for a refund, even items of less value than a vehicle. It is logical to infer that Ms. Maven intended to transfer title of the vehicle.

CONCLUSION

14. *This writer sets off the concluding paragraph with a separate heading is a format some employers prefer.*

14 Ms. Maven's letter also referred to Wisconsin's Lemon Law, which strengthens her claim that the letter implied an offer to transfer title. Just as Garcia's request for a replacement under the Lemon Law was interpreted as an attempt to comply with the law's requirements, Ms. Maven's request for a refund under the Lemon Law would likely be interpreted as an attempt to comply with the law.

5

Revising for Clarity

ALTHOUGH ACCURACY and thoroughness are the lead dogs in the legal writing race, clarity nips at their heels. If you have ever tried to read a contract, only to give up after a few paragraphs, you understand part of the reason. Legal content that is accurate but unclear is not adequate communication. In fact, it is sometimes not upheld when tested in court. Even experienced legal readers, such as judges, do not enjoy having to work hard to understand legal documents. Judges praise writers who communicate clearly, thus making their job easier. You want to be one of those writers.

Clarity can be enhanced in legal documents through organization at all levels: large-scale, paragraph, and sentence. The overall goal at all levels is to use organization that reinforces the meaning, rather than organization that runs counter to the meaning. Using organization to reinforce meaning is a particularly important tool when writing for educated readers. Because they have had extensive reading experience, educated readers come to understand the natural structures of the language. They employ this knowledge of structure as they read, even though this understanding is usually unconscious. The structure tells them what parts of a sentence, paragraph, or document are most important structurally. This structure helps them focus their attention on those parts. If the important content is placed in those structurally important points, the reader absorbs that content quickly and accurately.

This chapter explains techniques that are particularly useful for increasing the clarity of a legal document. They include techniques that can clarify a document's overall organization, its paragraphs, and its sentences. Although these techniques are presented as tools for revising an early draft, they may be used at any time in the writing process. The techniques may seem to overlap somewhat because several different techniques may help you correct similar problems. All of the techniques, however, approach writing from different angles, allowing you to see your content anew even when you have been working with it for days or weeks.

While these techniques are useful tools for increasing clarity, they are not rules you must follow. Nor are they revising rituals you must follow in a specific order or at specific times. Instead, they are explanations of factors that make legal writing clearer. They are presented to help you understand how writing and reading work and how you can make a few changes that add substantial clarity. Study the techniques, try them on your documents, and then select the techniques that work best for you and add them to your personal writing process.

Clarifying the Large-Scale Organization

In the overall organization of a document or a major section, two components are structurally important: headings and thesis sentences.

■ Headings

Effective headings allow a reader to preview a document's main points before reading and to review those points later when referring to the document. They also help the reader see the overall logical organization of the document. Two factors make headings more effective: substantive content and parallel structure.

■ Substantive Content

While headings that reveal structure are helpful, headings that also communicate content are more effective. For example, the following subheadings come from a memo explaining a five-part test. The headings are accurate and reveal the structure of the Discussion, but they tell the reader nothing about the substance.

Example, Headings with No Substantive Content

    A. First Part of the Test

    B. Second Part of the Test

    C. Third Part of the Test

    D. Fourth Part of the Test

    E. Fifth Part of the Test

In contrast, the following headings, when preceded by the following overview sentence, reveal the structure and the substance.

Example, Summarizing Sentence from Overview Paragraph and Subsequent Headings

---

The five factors the court uses when evaluating a restrictive covenant include (1) whether the restraint is protecting a legitimate interest of the employer, (2) whether the restraint is limited to a reasonable time period, (3) whether the restraint is limited to a reasonable territory, (4) whether the restriction is overly harsh or oppressive to the employee, and (5) whether the restraint is unreasonable to the public.

1. Does the restraint protect the employer's legitimate interests?

2. Is the restraint limited to a reasonable time period?

3. Is the restraint limited to a reasonable territory?

4. Is the covenant overly harsh or oppressive to the employee?

5. Is the restriction reasonable to the general public?

Similarly the following headings, which cover the same tests but follow a different order and use different phrasing, also reveal both structure and substance.

Example, Summarizing Sentence from Overview Paragraph
and Subsequent Headings

When determining whether a restrictive covenant is enforceable, the court evaluates that covenant to make sure it (1) has a reasonable territorial limit, (2) is not harsh or oppressive to the employee, (3) has a reasonable time period, (4) protects the employer's legitimate business interests, and (5) is not contrary to public policy.

A. Reasonable Territorial Limit

B. Not Harsh or Oppressive to the Employee

C. Reasonable Period of Time

D. Protection of the Employer's Business Interests

E. Not Contrary to Public Policy

Sometimes writers argue that revealing too much in the headings will discourage the reader from reading the text, especially if the reader disagrees with the points made. But this is not the situation in legal writing. Legal readers naturally question any conclusion that is presented, whether they agree or not. Presenting the conclusion initially simply encourages the reader to ask the question that the text will answer.

■ Parallel Structure

For both clarity and professional appearance, headings that include logically parallel content should be at parallel levels of organization and should be grammatically parallel. Parallel structure is essentially a form of repetition. By repeating the structure of a previous point, the text communicates to the educated reader that the point's content is logically parallel. Like items in a list, headings should be parallel in substance, structure, and relationship to the overall point. For example, in the previous good examples of headings, those headings communicate the substance of the points in parallel structure; as a result, they are clear and easy to read. In contrast, the following headings communicate substance, but their lack of parallel structure obscures that substance and confuses the reader about the structure.

Example, Non-Parallel Headings

1. Legitimate Interests

Reasonableness of the Time Period

Is the territory reasonable?

A covenant cannot be harsh or oppressive to the employee.

E. Policy concerns and divisibility.

Not only is the format inconsistent, but structure is also inconsistent. Some headings are phrases, while others are complete sentences. One is a declarative sentence while another is a question. They are also not parallel substantively because some headings contain more detail than others.

Such nonparallel structure is obvious here, but is surprisingly easy to create in an actual document when the headings are separated by pages of text. To check your headings, print out the document and read those headings without looking at the intervening text. Also compare your overview paragraph to the headings and make sure they use parallel wording and present the points in the same order. This one step of checking for parallels can help you avoid embarrassing errors and can make the text clearer.

■ Thesis Sentences

Thesis sentences can clarify your organization in four ways:

- by communicating points clearly,

- by relating points to the overall topic,

- by showing the logical progression or the reasoning, and

- by helping the reader scan accurately.

Thesis sentences contain conclusions and help both the reader and the writer identify the paragraph's assertion and check the support in the paragraph that follows. When the reader knows the conclusion up front, he or she can then see if the support logically leads to that point. In contrast, if the thesis sentence comes at the end of the paragraph, the reader is left to speculate about where the content is leading. When he or she discovers the point at the end of the paragraph, the reader then needs to go back over the content to check the support, which is a substantial inefficiency. But when the thesis sentence appears at the paragraph's beginning, the reader is ready to move to the next point by the time he or she finishes reading the paragraph; the reader has already checked the logic and is convinced that the reasoning is sound.

A great thesis sentence also shows the reader how this thesis contributes to the logical progression of the overall document. It clarifies your large-scale organization by telling your reader how each point is relevant to your answer to his or her initial question. In essence, a great thesis sentence, like Janus, faces in two directions, focusing on the point at hand, but also linking that point to the larger discussion.

Two writing techniques help thesis sentences clarify a document: repeating key terms and using introductory phrases as transitions. When these techniques are used well, thesis sentences show the reader how the logic flows through the writing. Good legal writers do not all use exactly the same technique to show the links, but they all do somehow show the reader how one paragraph links to the next.

■ Repetition of Key Terms

Repetition is a convenient technique for legal writing because the need for accuracy already requires you to repeat the same term for the same idea. For example, see how repetition is used in the following thesis sentences from the first three paragraphs of a Discussion. (The repeated word is marked in bold italics when introduced, regular italics when repeated.)

Example, Thesis Sentences That Make Effective Use of Key Terms

1. In Wisconsin, courts enforce covenants not to compete only if they pass a *five-part test*.

2. Under the *first part of the test,* a reasonable *territorial limit* must not extend beyond the geographic area in which the employee has served customers.

3. The *territorial limit* in Petrov's covenant extends beyond the geographic area Dominski served.

As these sentences illustrate, each thesis sentence repeats a term used in a previous thesis sentence, and that term provides a substantive link between the two paragraphs. This repetition moves the logic of the Discussion along, acting like the repeated terms in a syllogism: Socrates is a *man*; all *men* are *mortal*; Socrates is *mortal*. The repetition is a natural outgrowth of using legal terms precisely, and it helps the reader understand the relationship between the paragraphs.

Thesis sentences linked in this way improve clarity in several ways. First, they remind the reader of the content that has gone before. Just by repeating a term, the writer triggers the reader's memory of the previous point. The sentence then links that point to the one in the new paragraph. Second, these thesis sentences communicate the writer's logic to the reader even when the reader is skimming. Even when they are tired or distracted, most readers pay attention at the beginning of a paragraph. If the key content is placed there and is clearly linked to the previous and following thesis sentences, the reader is likely to understand the writer's point, even though the reader may miss some of the nuance in the supporting sentences.

■ Introductory Phrases

Introductory phrases can provide the link you need between paragraphs. Sometimes, especially when a paragraph is introducing a new topic, you can introduce your new point with a phrase that explains how the new point relates to the previous one. For example, consider the following thesis sentences from another Discussion using the same legal standard.

Example, Effective Transition Between Thesis Sentences

1. Courts sometimes determine the reasonableness of a territory by considering the geographic area the employee actually served.

2. Rather than geographic limitations, courts have at other times based the standard for reasonableness on the employee's specific customer routes.

These phrases are also useful to signal that the text is moving from presentation of the law to its application.

By carefully wording headings and thesis sentences, you can greatly increase the clarity of a document. Making the document clearer leads to more successful communication of content to your reader. Additionally, making the document clearer will impress the reader with the writer's ability, and this is a welcome benefit in a career where much of your reputation will rest on your writing.

Applying What You Have Learned

Exercise 5-1
Clarifying Large-Scale Organization

The following excerpt includes the sub-headings and first sentences from a sample memo discussing the reasonableness of a covenant not to compete against a former employer. Read through these sentences and, beginning with Subsection B, identify places where this writer uses the clarity techniques of using parallel structure, repeating key terms, and using introductory phrases as transitions.

Example for Discussion

In Wisconsin, courts enforce covenants not to compete only if they pass a five-part test.

A. Reasonable Territorial Limit

Under the first part of the test, a reasonable territorial limit must not extend beyond the geographic area in which the employee has served customers.

The territorial limit in Oswald's covenant extends beyond the geographic area Finley served.

B. Not Harsh or Oppressive to the Employee

Under the second part of the test, covenants not to compete must be reasonable in their restriction of the employee's activities.

It is unreasonable to prohibit an employee from working in an entire industry.

Oswald's covenant prohibits Finley from working in an entire industry, as did Nalco's covenant.

Under the alternative line of reasoning, a covenant is also unreasonably harsh when it prevents an employee from earning a living, considering the economic conditions and the employee's training for the specific occupation.

Oswald's covenant will not prevent Mr. Finley from earning a living.

When considering all the factors related to unreasonableness to the employee, the court will probably find this covenant meets this part of the test.

C. Reasonable Period of Time

When applying the third part of the test, Wisconsin courts determine whether the period of time covered by the covenant is longer than is reasonable.

Based on this precedent, the time limit in Oswald's noncompete covenant is probably reasonable.

D. Protection of the Employer's Business Interests

Under the fourth part of the test, Wisconsin courts consider whether the employer needs protection from the employee's potential competition.

An employer may establish the need for protection based on the employee's ability to inspire customer loyalty or to generate a high income for the employer.

The loyalty of Finley's clients supports Oswald's argument that a noncompete clause is reasonably needed to protect Oswald's business interests.

E. Not Contrary to Public Policy

The final part of the test involves weighing the facts to determine whether the covenant is contrary to public policy.

A court will not find Oswald's noncompete covenant contrary to public policy.

Clarifying Paragraphs

Paragraphs are the writing components that establish the merit of a memo's reasoning. While the headings and thesis sentences reveal the overall organization and highlight the main points, the paragraphs explain what the main points actually mean. The paragraphs also provide the content that convinces the reader of the validity of your points. When each paragraph lays out the logic clearly, the reader will follow that logic quickly, moving through the document and reaching the same logical conclusion the document presents. Paragraphs, in short, convince the reader.

Clarifying paragraphs, then, means clarifying your reasoning. To do this, two techniques are especially helpful: (1) editing your paragraphs for unity and (2) repeating key terms to underscore the logical flow of the document.

■ Editing for Unity

To show your reasoning clearly in each paragraph, make sure that all the information in the paragraph is relevant to the paragraph's point. Although this seems obvious, it is easy to miss when writing a document. Content can be grouped in more than one way; you will often find that your idea of a paragraph's point shifts as you are writing out the support. Like a hiker with no established trail to follow, you may find your logic curving toward a new point when you meant to be moving in a straight line.

Thesis sentences provide a ready measuring stick for checking paragraph unity. You have already checked your thesis sentences to make sure they present the overall organization clearly. Now you can use them to check the merit of your support. To make sure that the rest of the paragraph supports that point, reread each paragraph and compare its thesis sentence to the rest of the paragraph.

The reader will make similar use of thesis sentences. When the reader sees the thesis at the beginning of a paragraph, he or she knows your conclusion up front. The reader then reads the paragraph to see if your support logically leads to that point. When the thesis sentence appears at the paragraph's beginning and when subsequent sentences convince the reader that your reasoning is logical, the reader is convinced and ready for the next point by the time he or she finishes reading the paragraph.

When you find details that are not relevant to a paragraph's thesis sentence, remove them. If you think the content must be included somewhere in the document, place the removed information in a separate file. You may find that the information you removed is needed for support in another paragraph, and you can move the sentence to that location in the document. Sometimes you will find that the content has already been included elsewhere, and the sentence you omitted was redundant.

If the thesis sentence does not precisely state the point supported by the paragraph, try revising that thesis sentence. The thesis may be broader or narrower than the content in the paragraph. For example, the first sentence of the following paragraph is too narrow because it refers to the outcome in a precedent case. Instead, the first sentence should state the legal rule used in that case that is relevant to the client's situation. As currently worded, the opening sentence is narrower than the point the paragraph's content supports, and this makes it harder for the reader to see what this paragraph contributes to the overall reasoning of the Discussion.

Example, Paragraph with Thesis Sentence that is Too Narrow

In one precedent case, a consumer request was ambiguous because it offered three different options to the manufacturer. *Berends v. Mack Truck, Inc.* 2002 Wi Ct. App. ¶ 13, 643 N.W.2d 158, 162. Offering the manufacturer the choice of further repair is inconsistent with the statutory remedies, and thus a letter that includes that option fails to provide sufficient notice. *Id.* "For purposes of triggering the thirty day time limit established by [the statute], the consumer must either demand that the manufacturer provide a new vehicle or demand that the manufacturer refund the purchase price." *Id.* ¶ 15. Under this reasoning, Mr. Berends' letter to Mack Truck failed to provide sufficient notice to the manufacturer because it included the option to "repair these defects within seven business days" when asking for a refund or a replacement. *Id.* ¶ 2.

Including this option created an ambiguity about whether the statute was being invoked. *Id.* ¶ 13.

That lack of unity is easily remedied by rewording the opening sentence to summarize the legal point that this case illustrates.

Example, Revised Paragraph with a Thesis Sentence that Fits the Content

The statute requires that the consumer's request to a vehicle manufacturer specify unambiguously that the consumer is requesting a refund or a replacement vehicle. *Berends v. Mack Truck, Inc.* 2002 WI Ct. App. ¶ 14, 643 N.W.2d 158, 163. Offering the manufacturer the choice of further repair is inconsistent with the statutory remedies. *Id.* Thus a letter that includes that option fails to provide sufficient notice. *Id.* ¶ 15. "For purposes of triggering the thirty day time limit established by [the statute], the consumer must either demand that the manufacturer provide a new vehicle or demand that the manufacturer refund the purchase price." *Id.* Under this reasoning, Mr. Berends letter to Mack Truck failed to provide sufficient notice to the manufacturer because it included the option to "repair these defects within seven business days" when asking for a refund or a replacement. *Id.* ¶ 2. Including this option created an ambiguity about whether the statute was being invoked. *Id.* ¶ 13.

Sometimes you will need to divide a paragraph because it really covers more than one point. This is likely to be true with paragraphs that are more than a half-page long. For example, the following paragraph blurs two related points, creating a long paragraph with reasoning that is harder to follow.

Example, Paragraph that Blurs Two Points

Ms. Maven's request for a refund should be interpreted to be valid if the court infers an offer to transfer title. Just as Garcia was not required to use "magic words" to communicate an offer to transfer title, Ms. Maven should also not be required to use any particular words. Her vehicle is defective, and allowing her to recover her money is exactly the remedy this statute sought to provide. Ms. Maven requested a "refund," which is defined as "to give back" or "repayment or balancing of accounts." *Websters Third New International Dictionary, Unabridged*, p. 1910 (2002). The statutory remedy should be available to her, even though she did not explicitly say that she was offering to transfer title, to fulfill the statute's purpose is to protect the consumer of a defective vehicle. Just as it would be nonsensical to interpret Garcia's request for a "replacement" as implying an intention to keep the defective vehicle, it would be nonsensical to interpret Ms. Maven's request for a "refund" as implying an intention to keep her defective vehicle. Commonly items are returned for a refund, even items of less value than a vehicle. Although Maven requested a refund rather than a replacement, both of those remedies are specifically available under the statute. Therefore this difference in remedy is not significant in terms of the statute's overall purpose. It would only be logical to infer that Ms. Maven intended to transfer title of the vehicle back to the manufacturer.

In contrast, the logic is much easier to follow in the revision, which divided the content into two paragraphs.

Example, Revised as Two Paragraphs Focused on Different Points

In light of the statute's purpose, Ms. Maven's request for a refund should be valid. Her vehicle is defective, and allowing her to recover her money is exactly the remedy this statute sought to provide. The statutory remedy should be available to her even though she did not explicitly say that she was offering to transfer title. Allowing her recovery would fulfill the statute's purpose, which is to protect the consumer of a defective vehicle. Just as Garcia was not required to use "magic words" to communicate an offer to transfer title, Maven should also not be required to use any particular words. Although Maven requested a refund rather than a replacement, both of those remedies are specifically available under the statute. Therefore this difference in remedy is not significant in terms of the statute's overall purpose.

Under the dictionary definitions of Ms. Maven's words, the court could infer an offer to transfer title. Ms. Maven requested a "refund," which is defined as "to give back." *Webster's Third International Dictionary, Unabridged*, p. 1910 (2002). Just as it would be nonsensical to interpret Garcia's request for a "replacement" as implying an intention to keep the defective vehicle, it would be nonsensical to interpret Ms. Maven's request for a "refund" as implying an intention to keep her defective vehicle. Items are commonly returned for a refund, even items of lesser value. It would only be logical to infer that Maven intended to transfer title of the vehicle back to the manufacturer.

You may have already discovered the paragraphs that need dividing when you reviewed your thesis sentences for the logical flow of the large-scale organization. For example, if you noticed a place where the text skipped a logical step, you may have discovered that the needed step was not absent, but buried within another point. By lifting the information out and giving it its own paragraph, you clarified both points and improved the logical flow.

Sometimes you may find paragraphs in which the support is inadequate. These paragraphs are the ones legal readers label as "conclusory." Although these paragraphs are often noticeably shorter than other paragraphs, length is not the measure of inadequate support. When the support is inadequate, the writer has not tied his or her reasoning to something that the reader considers reliable. For example, a writer might state a legal standard based on an opinion in a precedent case without providing any background about the opinion cited as the source of that legal standard. Without this information, the reader cannot tell if the writer has interpreted the opinion accurately. More commonly, a writer makes a conclusion about the legal significance of some facts without stating those facts.

Example, Paragraph with Inadequate Support

Maven's second letter, like Garcia's letter, probably provided sufficient notice without explicitly offering to transfer title. Like Garcia, Maven specified a specific remedy. Although Maven chose a different remedy than Garcia, the choice of a different remedy probably would not change the Court's reasoning.

In jumping to this conclusion, the writer fails to convince the reader of its validity.

When you find holes in your support, plug them. Although laying out the support when applying the law to the facts can feel like stating the obvious, remember that the reader needs enough information to be able to check your reasoning. The following paragraph presents that needed information.

Example, Paragraph with Adequate Support

Maven's second letter, like Garcia's letter, probably provided sufficient notice without explicitly offering to transfer title. Like Garcia, Maven specified a specific remedy. Just as Garcia's letter specifically requested a replacement, Maven's specifically requested a refund. Although Maven chose a different remedy than Garcia, the choice of a different remedy probably would not change the Court's reasoning. The court would likely use the plain meaning rule, again interpreting the meaning in light of the legislative intent behind the statute. Therefore, the court would determine whether the word "refund" implied an offer to transfer title. "Refund" is defined as "to give back" or "repayment or balancing of accounts." *Websters Third New International Dictionary, Unabridged,* p. 1910 (2002). Since a refund commonly occurs when goods are returned, as implied by "give back" and "balancing of accounts," the court could reason that the offer to transfer title back to the manufacturer is implied in the request.

Often you will need to revise both the thesis sentence and the content to unify a paragraph. Keep adjusting the content until all parts are congruent and the paragraph will be logically strong. Although the idea of unifying each paragraph can seem daunting, it often takes less editing than you expect. Just as slight changes in thesis sentences smoothed the logical flow of the large-scale organization, similar changes in wording are often all you need to smooth the flow of content within a paragraph.

Applying What You Have Learned

Exercise 5-2
Editing for Unity

Read the following paragraph, which has an accurate thesis sentence but is not unified around that thesis. Strike out all irrelevant information so the paragraph is more unified.

Maven's second letter probably would be found to imply an offer to transfer title, thus meeting the other notice requirement. Although it did not explicitly offer to transfer title, the reasoning used in *Garcia* supports implying that offer. In contrast, Maven's first letter did not invoke the lemon law because she did not specify the remedy she wanted. The first letter included an option that was not specified in the statute because she also asked the manufacturer to inform her of repair steps they suggested. Garcia's offer was implied because he cited the Lemon Law and asked for a replacement. Similarly, Maven's second letter cited the Lemon Law and asked for a refund. Although Maven requested a refund rather than a replacement, that difference can be argued to be immaterial because both replacement and refund are remedies specified under that statute. Although the manufacturer in *Garcia* argued that the offer to transfer title was unclear unless explicitly stated, the court rejected that reasoning, explaining that "when a consumer demands a replacement vehicle under the Wisconsin Lemon Law, the consumer impliedly offers to transfer title to the old vehicle." *Garcia v. Mazda Motor of America, Inc.*, 2004 WI ¶ 19, 682 N.W.2d 365, 371. Just as the *Garcia* court found that it would have been nonsensical to conclude that a consumer would demand a replacement without offering to transfer title to the original vehicle, it would be nonsensical to conclude that Maven would request a refund without offering to transfer title to her vehicle. Although the first letter was ambiguous because it suggested that repair might be possible, the second letter did not include that option.

■ Repeating Key Terms

Just as you used the repetition of key terms to link thesis sentences, you can use repetition of words to link sentences within a paragraph. These repeated words form a verbal chain of logic that links each sentence to the one before and the one following. Generally, each sentence provides further development of an idea that was part of the previous sentence. You can show the reader which idea you are developing next by using the word that represents that idea, usually early in the sentence. Thus by rephrasing your sentences, you are often able to clarify the logic without needing to reorganize the paragraph.

In the following example paragraph, repeated words form a logical chain that moves the reader through the explanation of the law. The repeated words are in bold italics when they are introduced, then in italics when they are repeated in the subsequent sentence.

Example, Paragraph Using Repeated Terms to Clarify the Chain of Logic

To invoke a remedy under the Lemon Law, the consumer's ***notice*** to the manufacturer must specify the remedy the consumer wants. Wis. Stat. § 218.017 (2)(b) (2005-06). If the *notice* ***offers*** options other than the two statutory remedies, it is ***defective***. *Berends v. Mack Truck.*, 2002 WI Ct. App. 69 ¶ 13, 643 N.W.2d 158, 162 (Wis. App. 2002). "*Offering* the manufacturer another opportunity to ***repair*** the vehicle is inconsistent with a demand under [the statute]." *Id.* ¶ 2. When Berends requested relief under the Lemon Law, he offered **three options**, including *repairing* the truck's defects as well as either a refund or a replacement. *Id.* ¶ 2. When reviewing Berends' *request*, the appellate court reasoned that"[b]y providing Mack Truck a *third option*, Berends failed to follow the unambiguous language of [the statute], rendering his *notice defective.*" *Id.* at 163.

The thesis sentence does not need to include all the words you will repeat in the paragraph. In fact, when too many terms are introduced at once, the paragraph can be harder to follow. In the previous sample paragraph, terms appeared gradually as the logic progressed. In the following example, the terms appeared too quickly, and the reader has to untangle the knot of ideas to understand the paragraph.

Example, Paragraph Using Too Many Terms at Once

To invoke a remedy under the ***Lemon Law***, the consumer's ***notice*** to the manufacturer must specifically ***request*** only **one option**, not including ***repair***. Wis. Stat. § 218.017 (2)(b) (2005-06). *Notice offering options* other than these two statutory remedies is defective. *Berends v. Mack Truck.*, 2002 WI Ct. App. 69 ¶ 13, 643 N.W.2d 158,162 (Wis. App. 2002). "*Offering* the manufacturer another opportunity to *repair* the vehicle is inconsistent with a demand under [the statute]." *Id.* ¶ 14. Berends' *request to* the manufacturer of his nonconforming Mack truck offered three *options*, including *repairing* the truck's defects, a refund,or a replacement under the *Lemon Law. Id.* ¶ 2. The appellate court reasoned that"[b]y providing Mack Truck a third *option*, Berends failed to follow the unambiguous language of [the statute], rendering his *notice* defective." *Id.* ¶ 14.

In summary, reread the document and compare each thesis sentence to the rest of the paragraph. Revise until the thesis and support are unified. Sometimes you will need to revise the thesis sentence, sometimes the paragraph's content, and sometimes both parts. Keep revising until you see congruency, and the paragraph will be logically strong.

Applying What You Have Learned

Exercise 5-3
Adding Clarity by Repeating Terms

Select any three consecutive paragraphs from one of the sample memos at the end of Chapter 4. Read those paragraphs and underline the repeated key terms you find in the paragraphs. Also compare the thesis sentences with each other, also looking for parallel terms. Then discuss what you find, determining where and how the repetition of terms is useful. Also note any places where the repetition seems distracting rather than clarifying. Finally, discuss the general uses and limitations you found related to this technique.

Clarifying Sentences

While large-scale elements reveal the content's organization and paragraphs reveal the logical support, sentences transmit the actual content to the reader's mind. Sentences divide the content into manageable pieces. Just as you cut your food into bites so you can chew and swallow it, sentences cut the content into bites that the reader can absorb easily and file into memory. When the content is familiar and easier to understand, the reader can handle larger bites; this reading is like eating Rice Krispy Treats. But when the content is less familiar and tougher to understand, the reader wants smaller bites; this is more like eating tough meat. Legal content is tough meat, so you need to use shorter, simpler sentences.

■ Controlling Sentence Length

Keeping the sentences shorter and simpler is easier to do when you identify the parts of the basic English sentence. By controlling this sentence structure, you keep the sentences readable even as you vary that structure to meet the needs of the content. When you master that sentence structure, you can adapt it to fit the logic of the content. You will not have to worry about your writing becoming boring; the logic of the content will require sufficient changes in the sentence structure.

Although you can keep the sentences short and simple, you will not be using the most elementary structure. The simplest English sentence includes only a subject and verb, and sometimes objects of the verb.

Example, Simple Sentence

subject	*verb*	*object*
The dog	**bit**	**the man.**

In legal writing, however, ideas are usually not simple enough for this short a sentence. Usually legal writers need to add more information for accuracy and to communicate your points. As you learned in Chapter 4, however, you want to keep your subject and verb together for clarity. You also want to state your main point in the subject and verb. That means you will add any other needed information at the beginning of the sentence, at the end, or in both places. Thus the basic sentence structure in legal writing is the following.

Example, Basic Structure for Clear Sentence

introductory phrase	*subject*	*verb*	*object*	*additional phrase*
As the man was walking by, /	the dog /	attacked /	him, /	biting him hard enough to break the skin.

If sentences are difficult to read, the writer usually has overloaded the sentence with explanatory phrases. Sometimes the sentence includes more than one phrase before or after the verb. Often the sentence has too much information between the subject and verb. For example, the following sentence has both of these problems.

Example, Sentence with Too Much Added Information

Maven's first letter did not provide sufficient notice to Zelta because it offered a remedy not available under the Lemon Law when it included the phrase, "Unless you can repair this car right away," along with her request for a refund, which was similar to Berends' reference to the option of repairing the defects.

The content becomes clearer, however, when (1) the sentence is divided into three main points, (2) each sentence keeps the subject and verb together, and (3) each sentence is revised to include no more than one phrase before and one after the subject and verb.

Maven's first letter did not provide sufficient notice to Zelta. Along with her request for a refund, the letter included the phrase, "Unless you can repair this car right away." Like Berends' reference to repairing the defects, Maven's language thus offered a remedy not included in the Lemon Law.

As with all writing techniques described in this text, you do not have to follow this structure rigidly in all sentences. It provides a useful starting point, however, when you are trying to get a complex idea into a sentence. It also provides a useful tool for fixing sentences that have gotten cumbersome.

— *FIGURE 5-1* —
THE BASIC COMPONENTS OF A CLEAR SENTENCE

Components and Examples of Clear Sentences

introductory information	+ subject	+ verb	+ object and added information
Along with her request for a refund,	the letter	included	the phrase "Unless you can repair this car right away."
Like Berends' reference to repairing the defects,	Maven's language	offered	a remedy not included in the Lemon Law.

134

███████████████████████████████

Components and Examples of an Overloaded Sentence

introductory information	+ subject	+ more info	+ verb	+ object and added info	+ more info added
Because it offered a remedy not available under the Lemon Law,	Maven's first letter,	by including the phrase "Unless you can repair this car right away," along with her request for a refund,	did not provide	sufficient notice to Zelta,	similar to Berends' reference to the option of repairing the defects..

To identify sentences that may need revision, try printing up your draft and drawing a dark slash mark after each period in the text. When you have completed this mark-up, it is easy to find potential problem sentences. Just look for places where there are more than three lines of text with no slash marks. Read those longer sentences out loud. If you stumble when reading them, or if you run out of breath before you reach the end of the sentence, then that sentence is a candidate for revision.

Applying What You Have Learned

Exercise 5-4
Revising to Increase Clarity

Using the techniques you have just learned, revise the following two one-sentence paragraphs to increase clarity. To do this, try using the following techniques:

- dividing the long sentences into shorter ones,

- keeping the subject, verb, and object of the verb together, and

- having only one phrase before or after the subject-verb-object part of the sentence.

The statutory test that Georgia uses to determine whether a contract is valid includes four prongs requiring "[1] parties able to contract, [2] a consideration moving to the contract, [3] the assent of the parties to the terms of the contract, and [4] a subject matter upon which the contract can operate." Ga. Code Ann. §13-3-1 (2004). This memo, however, concerns the component of assent because the remaining three prongs are satisfied by the facts.

The parties' assent to the terms, a basic requirement of contract law, is required, as has been codified in statutes, to have a binding contract and such codification exists in the Official Code of Georgia, which reads, "consent of the parties being essential to contract, until each has assented to all the terms, there is no binding contract; until assented to, each party may withdraw his bid or proposition." *Id.*

■ Clarifying the Interrelationship of Ideas

In English, the sequence of words in a sentence affects its meaning. This fact is illustrated in the following series of five sentences, which all use identical words but communicate five different meanings.

Example, Changes in Meaning Caused by Changes in Word Order

The dog bit only the man's leg.

The dog only bit the man's leg.

The dog bit the only man's leg.

The dog bit the man's only leg.

The man bit the dog's only leg.

If the words are delivered in a different order, the reader will process them differently. For this reason, check the location of modifying phrases to avoid creating any ambiguity.

Even when accuracy is not affected, the sequence of words and phrases may affect a sentence's clarity. You have seen this effect in thesis sentences, where introductory phrases showed the logical link between one paragraph and the next. You have also seen this effect within paragraphs, when you used verbal chains to link sentences. Usually the repeated term occurred early in the sentence, while the new term appeared later in the sentence. Using sequence to increase clarity within sentences is yet another application of this concept.

To enhance a sentence's readability, you want to use each part of the sentence so that the sentence's sequence of words reinforces the logic of the content. Thus you can generally use the introductory phrase to set up the context that makes the main point meaningful. Use the subject and verb to communicate the main point of the sentence. Use the phrase after the subject and verb to communicate detail needed to explain the main point or to introduce the concept that will be the main point in the subsequent sentence.

For example, use the introductory phrase, which comes first in the sentence, to provide the link to the previous sentence. Doing this prepares the reader to attach the new knowledge to the previous sentence, just as you want the reader to do. For example, you may use an introductory phrase to move the reader from the law to its application.

Example, Introductory Phrase Showing Application

Under the dictionary definitions of Ms. Maven's words, the court could infer an offer to transfer title.

You may use an introductory phrase to signal a contrasting point of law.

Example, Introductory Phrase Showing Contrast

Unlike Mr. Berends, Ms. Maven did not include the option of replacing the vehicle in her letter.

You may use it to introduce a condition that might flow from an application of the previous legal concept.

Example, Introductory Phrase Showing Condition

If the court follows this precedent and interprets the statute broadly, it will likely find that Maven's letter implied an offer to transfer title.

When the opening phrase sets up the context of the sentence's main point, the reader is much more likely to understand and remember that main point.

Word each introductory phrase accurately, because this wording can make a tremendous difference in the overall clarity of the sentence. When reading your sentence, the reader receives two kinds of information: words that express your ideas and structural signals that explain how those ideas relate to each other. The words that express your ideas include your legal terms and facts; they will usually be nouns, active verbs, and some adjectives and adverbs. But the other words that signal structure are also important because they tell the reader how to link your ideas. These structural signals include prepositions, conjunctions, and subordinating conjunctions

Use the phrase after the subject and verb to add extra detail, explanation, or other information needed to finish the point. This is the most readable position for this information. Just as you can carry many grocery items more easily in a grocery bag, your reader can remember details more easily after the main point provides the logical framework that holds those details. The subject, verb, and object of the sentence provide that framework. For example, the following sentence is rather long and includes a lot of detail, but it is tolerably clear because the subject, verb, and object begin the sentence and clarify the framework for those details.

Example, Main Point Beginning Sentence

subject	+ verb	+ object phrase	+ details

The statute / requires / a replacement vehicle or refund / within thirty days after the consumer has met all the requirements under the statute.

— *FIGURE 5-2* —

THE BASIC COMPONENTS OF A CLEAR SENTENCE

introductory information	+ main point (subject, verb, object)	+ added information

Effective Uses of Those Components

Introduce a contrasting point	State the point	Add information as needed
Although she did not explicitly offer to transfer title	*that offer is implied*	*by her request for a refund and her reference to the Lemon Law.*

Refer to a relevant situation	State what happens when this occurs	Add in information as needed
When interpreting a consumer protection statute,	*the court construes the meaning broadly*	*in light of the social problem the statute was written to address.*

Refer to previous reasoning	Application	Add information as needed
In light of the statute's purpose,	*Maven's request would provide adequate notice*	*because it both refers to the Lemon Law and asks for a remedy provided under the statute.*

Applying What You Have Learned

Exercise 5-5
Clarifying Sentence Structure

Revise the sentences in the following paragraphs so that introductory information is placed before the subject and added information comes after the object. Also remove unneeded information, and keep the subject and verb together and focused on the main point.

Through signatures of the parties, assent to contract is commonly achieved, but the law recognizes at least two other methods of showing assent. First, in *Cochran v. Eason*, 180 S.E.2d 702, 703 (Ga. 1971), when a party initialed all the various terms used in the contract the party or the party's representative signed, the court said that action may satisfy the assent requirement. Even without the signature of all of the parties, the Georgia Supreme Court held in *Cochran* that an agreement was enforceable when family members had agreed to divide an estate. *Id.* at 704. Each page of the agreement was initialed by both of the parties' duly authorized attorneys, and secondly, both non-signing parties' attorneys "were given repeated opportunity to submit their clients' positions to the contrary" if they did not assent. *Id.* at 703-04. The court inferred that the parties assented to the agreement by looking at two factors. *Id.*

Georgia courts have also said that performance under the contract by the parties, aside from initialing a contract, can be sufficient to demonstrate assent to the contract's terms. In *State v. U.S. Oil Co.,* 389 S.E.2d 498, 499 (Ga. Ct. App. 1989), the Georgia Court of Appeals held that a contract allowing the State to purchase gasoline from any provider was enforceable even though U.S. Oil never agreed to that provision in its original contract. The court reasoned that once U.S. Oil began supplying its gasoline to the State, its performance under the contract tacitly showed assent to the terms of the contract, which made the contract legally binding. *Id.*

Using Structural Words

Although you have clarified the logical connection between many points by repeating key terms in headings, thesis sentences, and other sentences, you will also use structural words in legal writing. These structural words can include prepositions, conjunctions, pronouns, and linking verbs.

Structural words work as efficient instructions to the reader, and they are powerful tools for increasing clarity. Each structural word tells the reader how to relate the current ideas to those preceding and how to file the content in the reader's memory. For example, when a sentence starts with the word "if," the reader knows that the following phrase is a possible situation but not necessarily a true one.

> *If* the request includes options other than these two statutory remedies, *then* it does not provide sufficient notice.

The reader also knows that a comma will come at the end of the "if" phrase, and after that comma the sentence will state a consequence, something that will happen if the situation in the "if" phrase occurs. That is a lot of information, all compressed into one, two-letter word: "if." Many similar structural signals in English are equally precise and efficient. Experienced, educated readers, such as lawyers, become particularly efficient at processing these structural signals, and they depend on those signals to help them absorb information quickly and accurately.

Because structural words communicate so much information about how ideas are logically related, they must be precise. As you learned in Chapter 1, legal readers are literal, and they expect you to use the same word for the same idea throughout a document. Legal readers also follow structural words literally. For example, when a sentence starts with "additionally," the legal reader expects the information that follows "additionally" to be another point logically parallel to the previous one. The reader also expects the information following "additionally" to support the same proposition that the previous sentence supported. Legal readers use structural words like drivers in a convoy use turn signals; if you write "additionally," but then state a point that contradicts the previous sentence, you have done the equivalent of turning on your left turn signal on a busy interstate, but then switching to the right lane instead. The driver trying to follow you in the convoy will be, at best, surprised and annoyed. More likely, the driver will no longer be following you.

Overuse of one particular structural word can indicate a lack of precision. When using structural words as transitions between paragraphs or sentences, you may find that you use only one or two words most of the time, perhaps repeating one word three or four times on a page. For example, if you use "however" frequently, you may be combining points that could be better presented in separate paragraphs. Other times, overuse of one structural word may mean that you are using the word out of habit rather than out of conscious choice. If so, some other word will probably be more precise. For example, "similarly" may be more precise for a comparison than "additionally." To help you choose the most accurate structural word quickly, consult the following list of transitions grouped by their logical functions.

— FIGURE 5-3 —
STRUCTURAL WORDS

Logical Function	*Structural Word(s)*
Signaling similarity	similarly, analogously, as, accordingly
Signaling contrast	not. . . but; but; conversely; however; in contrast; nevertheless; on the contrary; while; yet
Introducing conditions	although, even if, if, only if, provided that, unless, when, whenever, whereas, while
Introducing results	if . . . then; when. . . then; accordingly; as a result; consequently; hence; so; so that; therefore; thus

Introducing reasons for a result	because, if, since, for
Introducing examples or explanations	as if, as though, for example, specifically, namely
Signaling a list	first, second, third, etc.; both . . . and; either . . . or; neither. . . nor; additionally; also; and; furthermore; last; nor; or

Logical Function	*Structural Word(s)*
Showing time relationships	after, afterward, as, as long as, before, before this, during, earlier, later, meanwhile, now, once, since, simultaneously, then, until, when, whenever, while
Showing relationship of place	where, wherever
Summarizing	finally, in conclusion, in summary

Applying What You Have Learned

Exercise 5-6
Clarifying Paragraph Structure

The following sentences, which contain no structural words, are arranged in random order. Rearrange them to make a logical paragraph. Then add structural words to make that order clearer to the reader.

- Emma's clients are all located in Dane County.

- Quinn's covenant is overly broad.

- The territorial limitation of Quinn's covenant is unreasonable.

- The restriction to "anywhere east of the Mississippi" is unreasonable.

- Quinn's covenant exceeds the territory Emma has actually served.

- The Behnke covenant's geographical territory exceeded that actually served by the employee.

- Quinn's covenant specifies a geographic territory "anywhere east of the Mississippi."

- Emma has never sold insurance outside the area.

— *FIGURE 5-4* —

Checklist of Techniques for Enhancing Clarity

1. Clarifying Large-Scale Organization
Read headings.
- Do they contain substantive content?
- Are they written in parallel structure?

Read thesis sentences.
- Does each sentence use a key term from a previous thesis sentence?
- If not, does it have an introductory phrase that provides a link to the previous thesis sentence?

2. Clarifying paragraphs
Read each paragraph for unity.
- Does all the content support the paragraph's thesis?
- Are there any holes in the support?

Read each paragraph for verbal chains.
- Does each sentence repeat a key term or somehow show the logical link to the previous sentence?

3. Clarifying sentences
Are the subject and verb clear?
- Is the main point in the subject and verb?
- Are the subject and verb close to each other?

If there is an introductory phrase, is it clear?
- Is there only one phrase before the subject?
- Does it set up the context in which the main point is meaningful?
- Is a comma inserted to separate that phrase from the subject?

If there is an additional phrase at the end of the sentence, is it clear?
- Does it provide information to make the main point clear or accurate?
- Does it introduce a concept that will be discussed in the following sentence?

Are the structural words effective?
- Are they accurate?
- Are they varied to avoid overuse?

6

Receiving and Presenting Information Orally

ALTHOUGH THIS TEXT FOCUSES on legal writing, listening and speaking are integrally related to that writing. This brief chapter provides tips to help you effectively complete those aural and oral tasks.

Listening

This skill, usually taken for granted, is more important than most beginning law students appreciate. Often your teacher or your employer will give instructions orally. Because lawyers expect you following their instructions to the letter, you must learn to listen to these instructions with special care. Note deadlines, suggested sources for information, budget limitations, format requirements, and other such details. Ask questions as needed about jurisdiction, best sources to use to find relevant law, and approaches the speaker has in mind. For example, you might ask the following questions.

Examples, Useful Questions for Employer

- Do you want that memo to include a summation of the facts? An issue statement?

- Would you recommend starting with any particular key research terms?

- Are there any special limits on use of computer research for this project?

- If I find other possible legal theories to pursue, do you want me to explore those or check with you first?

Although you want to ask substantive questions, avoid general questions or comments that sound like whining or complaining. These questions might resemble the following.

Examples, Ineffective Questions and Comments

- Are you sure I can do this?

- I'm not sure I can get it done by that time.

- I've never done anything like this before.

- How long do you think this will take?

- This is a little overwhelming.

These general questions do not require information in the answer, but rather reassurance. You will generally have very little time with your supervising attorney or teacher, so you want to use that time to get information you need, rather than soothe your emotional uncertainty.

Special listening skills are required when getting oral feedback about your work. Although all of us want to hear praise for our hard work, often legal supervisors or teachers do not take the time to salve our egos. Instead, feedback will often detail only criticisms of your work. When hearing criticism, remember that your supervisor is really trying to help. It is in the supervisor's interest that you do well, and he or she is eager to help you do the best you can. If you focus on taking the criticism in this way, you can sidestep the disappointed, wounded feeling that is a common response to criticism.

Taking notes can also help you avoid reacting to the criticism right away. When our work is criticized, most of us want to explain to the speaker why we did what we did. But resist the urge. Instead, focus on understanding what the speaker is saying. Ask for clarification when you need it, but avoid making excuses or talking about why you did what you did. Interrupting the criticism to defend your actions will only sound defensive.

After listening, thank the person for the feedback, whether you agree with it or not. Wait until later, when you have time to reread your notes and reflect, to determine whether you think the criticism is valid. If you manage to do this, to listen and simply accept the criticism, you will do a lot to impress your teacher or supervising attorney. Although everyone expects it, few people know how to accept criticism gracefully. If you are one of those few, you will impress the criticizer as mature and fair, and that impression will likely be stronger than any impression made by your previous errors. You can, by listening and accepting criticism, turn the situation to your advantage.

In summary, expect your efforts to be criticized. Be pleasantly surprised by any compliments. Remember always that your supervising attorney or teacher is eager for you to learn and improve quickly, and that desire, rather than any mean-spiritedness, is the source of the criticism.

Speaking

When preparing for your presentation, write out a one-sentence statement of your main point, with two or three sentences that summarize the overall support of your point. It is a good idea to write this out, at least the first sentence. Speakers usually take a little time to get to their main point, even in professional speeches. Your supervising attorney's time is valuable, however, and you need to be ready to get to your point quickly. Just as you begin paragraphs with the main point and then support it, begin your presentation with the main point. It is then easier for the listener to follow your presentation of the supporting detail, stopping you when he or she has all the supporting information he or she desires.

If there are any important caveats to your answer or information, state those specifically. Avoid general statements of doubt, however, such as the following.

Examples, Ineffective Phrases for Caveats

- I'm not 100% sure about this answer, though.
- Of course, policy considerations might make this incorrect.

The previous sentences communicate uncertainty but do not explain the reason behind that uncertainty. Instead, state the limitations to your answer more factually and specifically, as do the following sentences.

Examples, Effective Phrases for Caveats

- One precedent case, however, uses a different standard.
- But the opposition may argue that this approach violates the spirit of due process, if not the letter.

In these sentences, the listener understands that it is the law that is unsettled, not the researcher answering the question.

Also avoid lapsing into a diary of your research process.

Example, Ineffective Information

- First I checked the references under the statutes annotated, but none of those pertained to our issue. Then I. . .

Instead focus on the answer you found.

━━

Example, Effective Information

- This restrictive covenant is invalid under Wisconsin law because it covers an area broader than that actually served. Under Wisconsin Statute. . .

Use legal authority to back up your points, rather than as thesis of your presentation.

— *Figure 6-1* —
CHECKLIST FOR RECEIVING AND PRESENTING INFORMATION ORALLY

When getting an assignment

1. Listen. You really do not want to ask your supervisor, "What was that again?"

2. Listen for between the lines hints about what is important—timeliness, accuracy—by hearing what the supervisor's reminders are.

3. Take notes. Do not trust your memory.

4. Even when you feel overwhelmed or scared, do not complain or whine.

5. Ask questions as needed:

    - jurisdiction?

    - approaches the boss has in mind?

    - sample of preferred format for document? (different bosses and firms have their own preferences)

    - time or budget limitations?

When presenting your work

1. Be on time.

2. Do not whine or complain. If you need to state some caveat, do so factually.

3. Organize your presentation around your answer, rather than around a chronology of your search.

When getting feedback

1. Expect the writing to be criticized. Be pleasantly surprised if it is not.

2. Listen and take notes. Focus on getting information.

3. Avoid making excuses. You are not expected to avoid making errors, but you are expected to learn from them. Ask questions as needed for clarification.

4. Pay attention to any advice carefully; do not question it. You can think about it later and decide whether you agree. You job now is to listen.

5. Thank the person for the feedback. A good attitude toward criticism can greatly impress a boss.

7

Persuading in a Legal Context

What is Persuasive Legal Writing?

PERSUASION IN GENERAL is a matter of guiding individuals to accept a particular position or take a particular action. The individual may accept or reject any persuasive information, whether the issue is what newspaper to buy, what politician to elect, or whether to accept a legal settlement. In all forms of persuasion, the individual decision maker is preeminent.

To persuade legal readers, the writer needs to provide logical reasons, not just emotional appeals. While people often make less important decisions based on impulses and emotions, they do not want to make most important decisions on that basis. Persuasive legal writing always involves important decisions, so it always needs to base its persuasion on substantive reasons. The appeal to the reader's emotions is important, but it is not as likely to dominate over substance.

Who Reads Persuasive Legal Writing?

The reader will often be a judge. Attorneys write to persuade trial judges to grant their motions or deny their opponent's motions. On appeal, they may write to a panel of judges asking them to reverse or remand a trial judge's decision. To do this, they write briefs to the court. They write as petitioners to an appellate court, arguing that the trial court made an error that is substantial enough to justify changing the decision. Or they write respondent's briefs, arguing that the trial court did not make any error and that its decision should be upheld. Attorneys write to persuade the state's highest court to review the appellate court's decision. If the court agrees to review an appellate decision, then they would write another brief to that court to persuade it to reverse or modify the appellate decision. In other situations, they write an *Amicus* brief, which is a brief written by someone not representing either party, but writing as a "friend of the court."

Sometimes the reader is another attorney representing a client. For example, an attorney might write a letter explaining why a party should accept the settlement offer. Attorneys write collection letters to persuade people to pay bills. They write letters to subcontractors explaining why they must fulfill contractual obligations on time. Although they address their letters to individuals, the letter will usually be read by the individual's attorney.

When shifting from objective and persuasive writing, the changes are important yet subtle. The reader differs somewhat but retains the same goals.

The purpose becomes more specific, but remains focused on helping the reader make a decision.

— FIGURE 7-1 —
WRITING SITUATION FOR OBJECTIVE LEGAL DOCUMENTS

WRITER:
**Attorney or
Law Clerk**

Writing
Decisions
BEFORE

READER:
**Senior Attorney,
Client, Others**

PURPOSE:
**Providing reliable analysis and
answer to a legal question**

WRITER:
**Attorney or
Law Clerk**

READER:
**Judge, Other Attorney,
or Non-Lawyer**

Writing
Decisions
AFTER

PERSUASIVE PURPOSE:
**Providing reliable analysis
and favorable answer to a
legal question**

How Do I Persuade My Reader?

In persuasive legal writing, you are writing to a legal reader who is much like the reader of a research memo. This legal reader also values thoroughness, clarity, and conciseness. You began developing your understanding of these legal readers in Chapter 1, where you learned that the legal reader values clarity and conciseness over novelty or eloquence. These basic values have not changed just because the document being read is persuasive rather than objective. The writing techniques that you have already learned remain important.

Like the reader of a memo, the legal reader is persuaded by documents that are accurate, relevant, and credible. The reader will use the document to help him or her make an important decision. The legal reader needs to make that decision based on relevant facts and governing law, not personal feelings. This reader therefore values accuracy, thorough reasoning, relevant logic, and clear writing. The reader needs to make the decision within a limited time frame, so the reader also values conciseness and clarity.

Legal readers are persuaded by arguments that will withstand the scrutiny of others. When deciding a case, a judge knows that an appellate court may review the decision. When a supreme court justice is preparing an opinion on an appealed case, the justice knows his or her opinion will be scrutinized by practicing attorneys and scholars. When persuading someone to accept a settlement, an attorney knows that his actions could be scrutinized if his professional conduct is reviewed. The reader wants to make a decision that will stand up to this scrutiny.

Persuasive legal writing still needs to accurately explain the law, the facts, and the reasoning linking those facts to the law. This content is similar to that of an objective document on the same topic. This same content is required whether the document is persuasive or objective because legal readers follow the same process to make a decision. Each legal reader wants to believe that he or she is applying the law fairly and consistently. To persuade this reader, you must still show how the law supports your decision.

Unlike the reader of a memo, this reader needs to be motivated enough to act in your favor. This reader does not approach your request from an uninformed, neutral position. He or she has information about the other side's arguments and of the other options available. A judge will have a brief from your opponent, and an attorney reading a settlement letter, who has his or her client's welfare in mind, will read your persuasive letter with healthy skepticism.

Adding information to create this additional motivation, rather than writing for a different purpose, is the adjustment you will need to make for persuasive legal writing. For example, you need to present the arguments in favor of the action you want, refute the arguments against that action, and explain the situation so that your reader wants to help your client or take the action you advocate. And you must do all this while keeping your writing clear and confident.

This motivation is not created solely by logic, although logic dominates your persuasive document. You are trying to persuade the decision maker to see your point of view on the issues. Although the law may show the reader that an outcome is logical, sympathetic facts make the reader want to apply the law in that way. Judges are skilled at interpreting the law in various ways, and they will use their skill to interpret it in a client's favor if the client appears deserving. Similarly, your clients have values and goals that affect their decisions. And other attorneys and the clients they represent want to make decisions that advance their own interests. Although legal readers work within the law, they are also human beings who have a sense of justice, have personal goals, and have natural sympathies for fellow humans. Always try to show the reader that the outcome you advocate will feel right as well as be logical.

The goal of persuasion is to base the argument on both the logical application of the law and the human sense of justice. Present the argument so that the reader sees its validity and also wants your client to win.

What Does Persuasive Legal Writing Look Like?

Adjusting to persuasive legal writing is not primarily a matter of learning a new format. Persuasive legal writing will generally be in the form of a letter or a brief to the court. A persuasive letter uses the same format as any other business letter. A brief includes a heading similar to a complaint and other sections similar to a legal research memo.

The important adjustment for persuasive legal writing is that the content is arranged and emphasized to make the outcome favoring your client seem more logical than any other option. For example, in the Discussion of a legal research memo, the content was structured around all the possible legal standards a court might use, whether they favored the client or not. In an Argument, however, the content is structured around the one or two legal approaches that lead to the result your client desires. Although the document may address alternative legal standards, the organization and focus remains on the legal standards and the line of reasoning that you are advocating. Similarly, a persuasive letter focuses on the reasoning you advocate, rather than all possible approaches.

A persuasive legal document has an organization that is tightly focused and thesis sentences that state the preferred position. Generally, unfavorable arguments are relegated to the body of the paragraphs, where they are dismissed along the way rather than being presented in a thesis sentence.

Persuasive legal writing therefore takes the same organizational techniques used in objective writing and reapplies them to a narrower purpose. While all objective documents may describe a broad legal landscape and highlight a few points of interest, a persuasive document leads the reader down a precise path through that landscape, leading to the desired location and keeping the eye fixed on that location. As other paths become visible, the persuasive text explains why those paths are not worth following, keeping to the chosen path.

— FIGURE 7-2 —
COMPARING OBJECTIVE AND PERSUASIVE WRITING

WRITING ASPECT	OBJECTIVE WRITING	PERSUASIVE WRITING
Large-scale Organization	• Both arrange points in a logical order • Both explain law and then apply it to the facts	
	• Starts with point most obvious to your reader	• Starts with your side's strongest point
	• Explains other side's point and then explains your response	• Explains why other side loses
	• Explains court's possible concerns and answers	• Explains why concerns raised by other side are not a problem
Small-scale Organization	• Both start paragraphs with thesis sentences	
	• May start a paragraph with other side's point or take a whole paragraph to explain it	• Places references to other side's points mid-paragraph
	• Explains other side's points before explaining answer	• Refers to other side's points but does not explain them

WRITING ASPECT	OBJECTIVE WRITING	PERSUASIVE WRITING
Sentence Structure	• Both put main points in subject and verb • Both provide a logical connection to previous sentence	
	• States precedent's position affirmatively	• States your point affirmatively
	• Focuses subject and verb on most important point	• Focuses subject and verb on point most favorable to you
	• Uses dependent clauses to state minor points	• Uses dependent clauses to minimize unfavorable points
Word Choice	• Both use precise, accurate terms	
	• States unfavorable points specifically	• States unfavorable points in more abstract language
	• Uses transitions to smooth flow	• Uses transitions to aid emphasis

8

Drafting Briefs for Trial Courts

ONE PERSUASIVE DOCUMENT you will produce is a brief to a trial court. Neither a legal research memo nor a case brief, a brief to a trial court is a document that an attorney writes to persuade courts to rule in a client's favor.

Throughout the course of one litigated case, an attorney might write multiple briefs to a trial court, each focused on a different decision the court must make. For example, if a defendant filed a Motion to Dismiss a client's claim, the defendant's attorney might submit a brief in support of the motion, and the plaintiff's attorney would submit a brief opposing the motion. If the plaintiff's attorney was successful and the judge denied the Motion to Dismiss, then both parties would proceed through discovery. In discovery, the plaintiff might request a document that the defendant refused to release. The plaintiff's attorney might then file a Motion to Compel Discovery and a brief in support of that motion. During the trial, the defendant's attorney might object to the admission of some evidence and ask the court to suppress it. In support of that Motion in Limine, the judge might request briefs from both sides before deciding the motion. So it goes throughout the litigation process until the matter is resolved. Although attorneys argue many motions orally, other motions require more detailed support and written briefs.

Purpose of Briefs to Trial Courts

A brief to a trial court helps the court see the merit of the client's position. It explains how a decision in the client's favor is both correct under the law and just in the context of common sense and common social values. It presents the law and facts the court can use to decide the issues in the client's favor.

A brief to a trial court generally argues the one most plausible interpretation that favors the client. While the brief may discuss alternative interpretations of the law or the facts, they are presented in the context of explanations of why they are inferior to the chosen interpretation. Although the brief needs to explain why the opposition's argument should fail, defeating that argument is not all that is needed to win. An attorney must find a way to defeat opposing arguments without losing focus on the client's argument.

Structure of Briefs to Trial Courts

The structure of a brief to a trial court is similar to that of a legal research memo, but not identical. Rather than providing a dramatic change of form, the brief redirects similar components to a persuasive purpose. The brief begins with a Caption, like a complaint. The brief includes Issues, which follow the general form of Questions Presented. There are, however, no Brief Answers, because the court ultimately decides the answer. The brief next includes a Statement of Facts; an Argument, which is a persuasive version of a memo's Discussion; and a Conclusion. Thus all the sections of a brief to a trial court will be somewhat familiar.

The components included in a brief vary depending on the rules of the court, the complexity and length of the brief, and the customs of local practice. For example, many jurisdictions do not require Issue Statements, relying instead on the Point Headings within the Argument to provide an overview of these issues. Many courts do not require an inclusion of an Applicable Statutes section, while others want the relevant statutory language attached in an appendix. In some jurisdictions, the Conclusion includes only formulaic language stating the action requested by the party. In others, the Conclusion provides a tight, persuasive summary of the Argument's points. When writing a brief to a trial court that is new to you, always check the court's rules and customs related to briefs.

When writing a brief to a trial court, the main change you will make, compared to writing a legal research memo, is in the way you focus your content. This shift in focus applies throughout the document.

— FIGURE 8-1 —

PARTS OF A BRIEF TO A TRIAL COURT

Part & Purpose	Components	Structure
Caption • Identifies the case and parties • Identifies role of this document in the litigation	• Parties names and roles • Filing identifier • Name of document • Name of court	• Follows specific court rules

Part & Purpose	Components	Structure
Introduction (sometimes omitted) • Provides a context to make the issues under-standable	• Summary of general situation and legal question • Procedural summary leading to question at hand	• Is only one paragraph in length, unless the brief is quite long
Issues Presented (sometimes omitted) • States the question upon which the case turns • Presents that question so the it favors the client's position	• Relevant law favoring client • Core question • Relevant facts, present-ed to suggest the desired outcome	• Presents each issue as a separate, numbered question • Is structured like Questions Presented • Phrases content to help reader see the client's position • Includes no Brief Answer
Applicable Statutes (sometimes omitted) • Quotes the relevant statutory authority	• Statutory language • Citation • Notes all editing with scrupulous accuracy	• Conforms to the court's citation rules and customs • Uses ellipses to mark any omissions • Uses brackets to mark any changes
Statement of Facts or of the Case • Tells the story behind the Issues in a way that favors the client	• Legally significant facts • Needed background facts • Relevant sympathetic facts	• May be organized by chronology, topic, or location

Part & Purpose	Components	Structure
Argument • Explains what law the court should use to decide the issue • Explains how that law supports a decision in the client's favor	• Mandatory authority on point, whether favorable or not • Explanation of how the favorable authority is the most relevant and just • Explanation of how the law, applied to the facts, leads to favorable decision	• Presents the law and then the application of law to the facts • Organizes around the favorable law • When arguing multiple points, provides an overview paragraph • In each section, explains relevant law and why it is best law for the court to use in its decision • Includes Point Headings that affirmatively state each major point • Begins each paragraph with an affirmative statement of the paragraph's point
Point Headings • Makes the Argument's structure more apparent • Summarizes the major points	• Relevant legal terms • Affirmative statement of client's position	• Organizes so content is logically parallel • Uses parallel structure
Conclusion (sometimes omitted) • Reminds court of overall purpose of the brief	• Statement of the action the client is requesting • May summarize the reasons presented in the Argument	• Is one paragraph long

■ Caption

The format and content of the Caption are governed by the rules and customs of the court receiving the document.

— FIGURE 8-2 —
SAMPLE CAPTION

STATE OF WISCONSIN   CIRCUIT COURT   DANE COUNTY
_____

PETROV SULLIVAN, LLC,
Plaintiff

          v.   Case No. 09999

DAPHNE DOMINSKI,
Defendant
_____

DEFENDANT'S BRIEF IN SUPPORT OF
MOTION FOR SUMMARY JUDGMENT

■ Issues Presented

Persuasive Issues are structured like Questions Presented but have a markedly different effect on the reader. While an objective Question Presented shows the reader how the legal issue is debatable, a persuasive Issue shows the reader how that issue is not debatable. An Issue is worded, as much as possible, to suggest that the only logical outcome is the one the client wants. This suggestion appears through slight changes in wording, without becoming misleading and inaccurate. Nevertheless, persuasion is possible.

The facts in the Issue do not need to tell the whole story; that is the task of the Statement of Facts. Instead, the facts portion of an Issue creates a snapshot, a quick, favorable vignette. The two following Issues illustrate how this is done through the wording of the law and the choice of facts. For example, an attorney arguing that an employee was not eligible for worker's compensation might write the following.

Example, Persuasive Issue, One Side

Under Wisconsin Statutes Section 102.03(1)(f)(2005-06), which excludes compensation to employees "engaged in a deviation for a private or personal purpose," was a produce buyer deviating for a private purpose when he stopped for a drink in a local bar before traveling from the public library to the produce warehouse?

The attorney for the other side, arguing for eligibility, might write the following.

Example, Persuasive Issue, Other Side

Under Wisconsin Statutes Section 102.03(1)(c)(2005-06), which extends coverage to workers injured while going to and from their employment while "performing a service for the employer," was a produce buyer performing a service when he was traveling from the library, where he had researched current crop and weather conditions, to the produce warehouse to retrieve some files needed for a meeting?

These two Issues tell the court that different portions of the statute determine the outcome in this case, that different legal criteria are relevant, and that different facts are important. Both Issues are arguably correct; by reading the two Issues, the court can see the crux of the argument. A clerk for the judge might then create the following objective Issue.

Example, Neutral, Objective Issue

Under Wisconsin Statutes Section 102.03(1), was an employee "performing a service for the employer at the time of the injury" when the employee completed work-related research at a public library, stopped to have a beer, took a public bus back to work, and was hit by a speeding car while walking from the bus to his place of employment?

Although an effective Issue alone cannot guarantee a victory, a poor Issue can increase the chances of a loss. When both sides have crafted effective Issues, the court will be able to see the legal decision that must be made and the possible alternatives. But when one side fails to clarify its view of the issue, the other side's version stands unchallenged, and creates an important first impression that the law favors that side.

■ Statement of Facts

Some litigators and judges believe that the Statement of Facts is the most important part of a brief. They argue that the court is sufficiently skilled in the law to find a way to rule in favor of the side that the court believes should win. And, they argue, the Statement of Facts is the portion of the brief that makes a court want a particular party to win. Although many other attorneys and judges would not go this far, all would say that the Statement of Facts is important.

A persuasive Statement of Facts, like the one in a legal research memo, includes all the facts to be used later in the document. As in a memo, you need to have completed some of your research on the relevant law before you can begin to identify the facts you need to include. You will want the Statement of Facts to include facts that meet any of the following criteria.

To make the Statement of Facts persuasive, you may include some facts for strategic reasons, rather than choosing only the facts that are legally relevant. You may include some facts because you think they will persuade the court to want to find in favor of your client. For example, in a tort case you might include facts about a plaintiff's financial hardships when discussing the effects of the defendant's actions, even though the proximate cause of those hardships may be debatable. You may also decide to emphasize some facts by stating them in more detail, again because the facts will be persuasive with your reader.

Applying What You Have Learned

Exercise 8-1
Selecting Relevant Facts

Review the following facts and then decide which ones you would emphasize to persuade each of the following readers that lawyers perform a crucial role in a free society. Compare these choices with the choices you would need to make to convince a judge.

Possible Readers to Persuade

    A. A tenured professor in the field in which you majored as an undergraduate

    B. A class of kindergartners

    C. A person serving a ten-year term for possession of cocaine

    D. A building contractor who has been sued by unhappy customers

Possible Facts

1. Lawyers explain a client's case to the judge.

2. Many of our great leaders, such as Thomas Jefferson, have been lawyers.

3. It takes a lawyer to protect you from another lawyer.

4. Lawyers know how to research the law and find the best way to get what you need.

5. Many lawyers provide services to people who cannot afford to hire them.

6. A lawyer can predict what will happen if a new law is passed, so they can help us create better laws.

7. If someone is doing something that hurts you, you can go to a lawyer and ask the lawyer to help. The lawyer can use the law to help you.

8. A good lawyer can persuade the jury to find in your favor.

9. A good lawyer can help keep you out of court in the first place.

10. We need judges to decide legal issues, and they need to become lawyers first to learn how the law works.

11. If you can't beat them, join them.

12. Many of our senators and legislators through the centuries have been lawyers.

13 By learning to deal with an adversarial system, lawyers become the gladiators of a civilization that no longer settles matters by fighting.

14. You need a lawyer to explain contracts to you.

15. A lawyer knows how to work the system.

16. Lawyers are a necessary evil in a society governed by law.

17. A lawyer may be able to help a convicted person get paroled sooner.

18. Most lawyers want to help people more than to win battles.

19. Any system requires technical specialists, and lawyers are the technical specialists in our legal system.

20. Legal questions, unlike elections, need to be decided by someone who focuses on justice rather than popularity.

When organizing the Statement of Facts, you can use the same approaches you used with a legal research memo's facts, with a few strategic modifications. You may group the facts by topic, by chronology, or by location. Your choice, however, will be based on your decision about which grouping presents your client in the most sympathetic light. For example, if you represented the defendant in a convenience store robbery, you might organize based on chronology so that you could show how the defendant was drawn into the situation by other accomplices. If you were the prosecutor, however, you might organize by topic so that you could begin the facts with a description of the clerk's fear and of the harm done to the convenience store. That approach would create sympathy for the clerk and store owner, not the hapless felon.

Often you will choose your organization based on your desire to open the statement with a paragraph that creates sympathy for your client. Just as the opening scene of a movie creates a strong first impression about the nature of the story, the opening paragraph of a persuasive Statement of Facts can create a strong first impression of your client. Organize the facts to make the most use of this strategic paragraph.

— FIGURE 8-3 —
CHECKLIST FOR PERSUASIVE STATEMENT OF FACTS

1. Include facts that are

    • relevant to the elements of a statute or regulation;

    • relevant to precedent cases;

    • relevant to policies and goals of those statutes, regulations, and precedent cases; and

    • emotionally favorable with respect to the legal criteria.

2. Organize the facts in the way that allows you to create a favorable impression of your client's position in the first paragraph. That organization may be

    • by topic,

    • by chronology, or

    • by location.

3. Use the opening paragraph of the Statement of Facts to create a favorable first impression.

■ Argument

When writing the Argument, the first persuasive concern will be choosing the content. You will select the precedent to include and identify the arguments that can overcome any unfavorable precedent or law. Then you can organize that content to present it persuasively.

■ *Choosing the Argument's Content*

When you are selecting content, be clear about what you are asking the court to do. The law included in a Brief in Support of a Motion for Summary Judgment would differ substantially from the law in a Brief in Support of a Motion to Dismiss. Stay focused on the relevant legal standard. This standard is sometimes called the standard of review, although other attorneys reserve this term for appellate briefs only. The judge must identify the legal standard that would stand up under appellate scrutiny because no judge likes having his or her opinions reversed.

Also look first to the mandatory authority, if any exists on your issue. The content must include the mandatory authority applicable to that legal standard and the authority that addresses the issues. Even if that authority is not as favorable as authority from another jurisdiction, you cannot avoid mandatory authority. Instead focus on finding some interpretation of that authority that either supports your client's position or limits that authority so that it will not apply to your client's situation. This may seem impossible at times, but that is rarely true.

To understand how the mandatory authority supports your position, identify the aspects of that law that support the desired outcome. These aspects might include the literal language of the law, the courts' past application of that law, or the legislative goals or policies behind the creation of that law. When you identify that aspect of the law, study the legal authority for precedent, reasoning, relevant facts, and quotes that support your position. Select information from these supporting authorities and use it to explain how those authorities adequately address your client's situation.

If the mandatory authority does not seem to support your position, look again carefully for aspects of the authority that may support your client's position. This may become apparent if you look for ways your case differs from the precedent and can therefore be distinguished. For example, some of the reasoning used in the precedent cases might not apply to your client's situation, and therefore the reasoning should lead to a different result. Or the legislative goals or policies behind the law may not be met if the law is applied against your position. You may find factual differences that can make the law inapplicable to your client's situation. Use this reasoning, policy, or factual difference to explain how the mandatory authority does not bar the result you want, and may even support it.

If mandatory authority does not adequately address your position, use persuasive authority, or case law from other jurisdictions that is relevant because it deals with similar statutes or with similar factual situations. When selecting persuasive authority, look first to other jurisdictions that your court will respect. This might include jurisdictions that your court has referenced in previous cases. You might consider other state jurisdictions that fall within your federal circuit, which often includes nearby states with similar cultural backgrounds. If the Argument focuses on interpreting new statutory language, look for other jurisdictions that have similar statutes with similar wording. Finally, look for legal opinions discussing similar, relevant facts.

Before presenting persuasive authority in the Argument, you need to convince the court that it should consider persuasive authority. To do this, explain why and how the mandatory authority cannot resolve the issue. Sometimes this may be relatively simple, as when you are litigating a new statute that has never been interpreted by a court in your jurisdiction. If, however, there is some precedent that arguably does address your situation, then develop your reasoning thoroughly on this point. Getting the court to accept persuasive authority may be the determining factor in winning your case.

— *FIGURE 8-4* —
CHECKLIST FOR CHOOSING ARGUMENT'S CONTENT

1. Choose the law appropriate to the trial court's task at hand.

- Determine exactly what you are requesting and the legal criteria for that request.

- Determine the mandatory authority that the court must use to resolve the issue.

- If mandatory authority appears to favor your position, identify the aspects of that law that support your desired outcome, which might be any of the following:

– the literal language of the law,

– the courts' past application of that law, or

– the legislative goals or policies behind the creation of that law.

- Select supporting legal authorities and reasoning that emphasize these favorable aspects.

- If mandatory authority appears to be against your position, look again carefully for aspects of the legal authority that may support you, which might be either of the following:

    – legislative goals or policies that will not be met if the law is applied against your position or

    – distinguishing facts that can be interpreted to make the law inapplicable to your client's situation.

- Select information from legal authorities that emphasizes the distinction.

- If mandatory authority does not support your position, use persuasive authority.

- Identify reasoning that explains why the mandatory authority does not resolve the issue.

- Identify persuasive authority that can be used to resolve the issue. For example, that persuasive authority may do any of the following:

    – apply a statute with similar language;

    – address similar facts; or

    –– come from a nearby, respected jurisdiction.

2. **Choose the facts that correspond to the legal criteria, which may include any of the following:**

    - facts relevant to the elements of a statute or regulation,

    - facts relevant to significant facts in precedent cases,

    - facts relevant to policies or goals of statutes or precedent,

    - facts that are emotionally favorable with respect to the legal criteria, or

    - facts that demonstrate how a common sense of justice favors an outcome in your client's favor.

■ *Organizing the Argument*

The organization of the Argument follows the same pattern as a Discussion, again with strategic differences. Like a Discussion, the Argument presents the relevant legal standard and then applies it to the facts. The presentation of the legal standard, however, begins with a strategically chosen point about the applicable law. Often cases are won and lost in the battle over how the law should be interpreted and applied. Therefore begin your persuasive focus by explaining the legal standard from the most favorable point of view possible. As you present that law, shape it to emphasize favorable points. Focus your thesis sentences on the aspects of the law that support your position and move any limitations or weaknesses into the body of the paragraph.

To see how this persuasive focus shifts the organization and the wording of sentences, consider the following three versions of the same information. The following, objective paragraph explains two divergent approaches that a court might use to address the same legal question. The two subsequent persuasive paragraphs present the law as it might be presented in the argument by the two opposing sides.

Example, Objective Opening Paragraph from a Discussion

When determining whether a witness may testify, courts in the Seventh Circuit generally allow witnesses to testify, but have also established the court's right to decide competency as a matter of law. As a result, the law is not completely settled on this question. In most cases, the courts have considered the question as part of the witness's overall credibility and have therefore allowed a witness to testify and the jury to evaluate the merit of that testimony. Some precedent, however, distinguishes the question of competency from credibility. In making this distinction, this precedent holds that competency is a matter of law, while credibility is a matter of fact. Because competency is a matter of law, it therefore is within the court's discretion, and a judge may decide not to allow a witness to testify.[1]

The following excerpt from the beginning of an Argument on this law focuses on the court's discretion. This party wants the court to exercise that discretion and declare an unfavorable witness incompetent to testify. The party is asking the court to do something that is allowed, but is rarely done. To support this view, the Argument refers to authority stating that the court has the discretion to make the decision the party needs.

---

1. Citations are omitted from these samples for brevity.

Example, Persuasive Version, One Side

A witness's competency is a question of law for the judge to decide, while a witness's credibility is a question of fact for the jury. This circuit has granted broad discretion to trial judges, based on the judge's opportunity to observe the witness's physical manner of articulation and the continuity of testimony. "The facts necessary for the evaluation of the witness's competency are questions that are peculiarly within the knowledge of the trial judge."[1]

This next excerpt focuses on the court's common precedent, which favors allowing the witness to testify and treating the issue as one of credibility. Because this party wants the witness to testify, this Argument focuses on legal authorities that support its view of the way the issue should be handled.

Example, Persuasive, the Other Side

Rule 601 of the Federal Rules of Evidence presumes witnesses are competent. It was adopted as part of the new rules because the old standards of mental capacity had proven elusive. According to these notes, one effect of Rule 601 is to abolish mental capacity as a basis for rendering a person incompetent. Subsequent court decisions support the rule. . . .

Each of the preceding sample Argument excerpts began with a statement of the law and then supported that statement with relevant authority from the jurisdiction. What differs is not the writing style but the selection of authorities to include and emphasize. Later in these Arguments, each of the writers deals with the opposition's law; however, each writer does so in explaining how the law is distinguishable or not determinative of the issue. For example, the first party deals with the fact that the court rarely uses this discretion to exclude a witness in the following sentence.

Example, Persuasive Thesis Sentence, One Side

Although a witness's incompetency is most often recognized by a judge in the course of that witness's testimony at trial, no law precludes a judge from determining incompetency earlier when the requisite facts present themselves.[2]

---

2. Citations are omitted from these samples for brevity.

The second party handles the existence of the court's discretion by pointing to the rarity of its use as a pre-emptive decision.

Example, Persuasive Thesis Sentence, Other Side

Judges do not often use their discretion to impeach a witness's competence at the outset, but assume competency and allow the jury to assess the credibility of the witness's testimony.

After organizing the law you want the court to use, insert needed counterarguments in the places where the reader would logically raise the opposition's argument. For example, if the opposition would question your application of the facts to a particular part of your five-part test, then explain why the opposition is incorrect within the explanation of the correct application of the facts. If, however, the opposition would question your choice of law, counter that argument as you present the law. In this way you can address the opposition without letting their arguments dictate your organization or dominate your reader's thinking.

— *FIGURE 8-5* —
CHECKLIST FOR ORGANIZING THE ARGUMENT

1. Begin with the law that you want the court to use.

2. Make sure your thesis sentences state your position rather than the opposition's.

3. Insert counters to the opposition's arguments within the body of paragraphs on your points, in places where the reader might raise the opposition's point.

■ **Conclusion**

The Conclusion's form depends on the customs of your jurisdiction and your law firm. Some writers consider the Conclusion as a mere formality. Others use it as an opportunity to make one final, strong statement of their position, so the reader is left with a clear image of the overall argument. In either situation, the Conclusion is always short, usually just one paragraph.

Applying What You Have Learned

Exercise 8-2
Selecting Relevant Legal Language

Read the following fact situation, assuming you represent Angelina Martinelli.

Angelina Martinelli moved from a small town to a farm. When she moved, she left her 2003 Volkswagen with her adult daughter, Sophia Martinelli. Angelina gave Sophia permission to display the car to be sold, but not to actually sell it. Sophia took the car to Jeremiah Giesen's used car lot in the town and authorized him to display the car for sale. Geisen subsequently put a dealer's plate on the Volkswagen and drove the car to Alexander Brouillet's used car dealership in a nearby town. Giesen sold the car to Brouillet for $9,000 in cash, keeping the money for himself. Geisen did not deliver title for the vehicle to Brouillet. Angelina Martinelli learned of this and now wants to commence an action against Brouillet to recover her car.

To make this claim work, you must argue that Brouillet was not a "buyer in the ordinary course of business." If he does not fall under that definition, he will have to return the car. But if he is a "buyer in the ordinary course of business," then he can legally keep the car and Ms. Martinelli will instead have to sue Giesen for the car's value.[3]

---

3. Even though you may think the client should pursue other legal arguments, reconcile yourself to working within the limits stated here. These limits have been chosen to keep this project simple. The statutory language, while based on real statutes, has been edited to make the chain of reasoning less complex.

Now read the statutory language quoted below and identify the phrases that support your argument on Ms. Martinelli's behalf. Beside each identified phrase, list the facts that you can use to support your application of the statute on Ms. Martinelli's behalf. As you do this, it may help to ask yourself the following questions.

- Given your facts, which part of the relevant statutory definitions does Brouillet fail to meet?

- How can you link that failure to other statutes to show that Brouillet is not a "buyer in the ordinary course of business"?

• *Section 999.101(9)*

"Buyer in ordinary course of business" means a person that buys goods in good faith, without knowledge that the sale violates the rights of another person in the goods, and in the ordinary course from a person in the business of selling goods of that kind. A person buys goods in the ordinary course if the sale follows the usual or customary practices in the kind of business in which the seller is engaged. A buyer in ordinary course of business may buy for cash, by exchange of other property, or on secured or unsecured credit. Only a buyer that takes possession of the goods or has a right to recover the goods from the seller under ch. 999 may be a buyer in ordinary course of business.

• *Section 999.104(1)*

"Between merchants" means any transaction with respect to which both parties are chargeable with the knowledge or skill of merchants.

• *Section 999.104(2)*

"Merchant" means a person who deals in goods of the kind or otherwise by his or her occupation holds himself or herself out as having knowledge or skill peculiar to the practices or goods involved in the transaction or to whom such knowledge or skill may be attributed by his or her employment of an agent or broker or other intermediary who by his or her occupation holds himself or herself out as having such knowledge or skill.

• **Section 999.104 (12)**

"Good faith" in the case of a merchant means honesty in fact and the observance of reasonable commercial standards of fair dealing in the trade.

• **Section 999.101(20)**

A buyer of goods acquires all title which the purchaser's transferor had or had power to transfer. A person who does not have a valid title has power to transfer a good title to a good faith purchaser for value. When goods have been delivered under a transaction of purchase the purchaser has such power even though the delivery was procured through fraud.

• **Statute 999.190**

Possession of a vehicle is completed by the delivery of the vehicle, the existing certificate of title, an application for a certificate of title containing the name and address of the buyer, and the required fee.

Now read the following Wisconsin legal opinion, which deals with similar facts and similar statutes and see how it uses the statutes and facts to support a decision in favor of the car's original owner.

406 Wis. 165 NORTH WESTERN REPORTER, 2d SERIES

42 Wis.2d 16

Marcella MATTEK, Respondent,

v.

**Sam MALOFSKY d/b/a Sam Malofsky
Motor Company, Appellant.**

Supreme Court of Wisconsin.

March 7, 1969.

Action to replevy automobile. The County Court for Outagamie County, Raymond P. Dohr, J., rendered judgment, and defendant appealed. The Supreme Court, Hallows, C. J., held that where owner left automobile in son's possession and authorized him to put it out for display purposes, son took automobile to licensed used car dealer and authorized him to place it on his lot for display purposes, and dealer sold automobile to a second used car dealer and delivered no certificate of title and first dealer kept the money for himself, delivery of automobile to second dealer constituted "entrustment", but second dealer as merchant was not "buyer in ordinary course of business" because he was chargeable with knowledge of automobile registration law that on transfer of automobile he must deliver certificate of title to transferee, and owner could recover automobile from second dealer.

Affirmed.

1. Sales ⟐234(7)

The provisions of Uniform Commercial Code-Sales that any entrusting of possession of goods to merchant who deals in goods of that kind gives him power to transfer all rights of entruster to buyer in ordinary course of business and defining "entrusting" are applicable to sales between merchants where merchants buy from one another in ordinary course of business. W.S.A. 401.201(9, 19), 402.103 (1) (b), 402.104(3), 402.403(2, 3).

2. Sales ⟐234(7)

The purpose of provisions of Uniform Commercial Code-Sales that any entrusting

of possession of goods to merchant who deals in goods of that kind gives him power to transfer all rights of entruster to buyer in ordinary course of business and defining "entrusting" is to protect a person from a third-party interest in goods purchased from general inventory of merchant regardless of that merchant's actual authority to sell those goods. W.S.A. 402.-403(2, 3).

3. Sales ⟐234(7)

A merchant may be a buyer in ordinary course of business from another merchant under provision of Uniform Commercial Code-Sales that any entrusting of possession of goods to merchant who deals in goods of that kind gives him power to transfer all rights of entruster to buyer in ordinary course of business if he meets four elements: (1) Be honest in fact, (2) be without knowledge of any defects of title in goods, (3) pay value, and (4) observe reasonable commercial standards; in observance of reasonable commercial standards merchant is chargeable with knowledge or skill of a merchant. W.S.A. 402.-403(2, 3).

4. Automobiles ⟐20

Where owner left automobile in son's possession and authorized him to put it out for display purposes, son took automobile to licensed used car dealer and authorized him to place it on his lot for display purposes, and dealer sold automobile to a second used car dealer and delivered no certificate of title and first dealer kept the money for himself, delivery of automobile to second dealer constituted "entrustment", but second dealer as merchant was not "buyer in ordinary course of business" because he was chargeable with knowledge of automobile registration law provision that on transfer of automobile he must deliver certificate of title to transferee, and owner could recover automobile from sec-

MATTEK v. MALOFSKY　　　　Wis. **407**

Cite as 165 N.W.2d 406

ond dealer. W.S.A. 342.19(2), 402.403 (2, 3).

See publication Words and Phrases for other judicial constructions and definitions.

5. Customs and Usages ⬤=8

Evidence of custom or usage of automobile dealers contrary to automobile registration law cannot be used to defeat rights of third party whatever value of such evidence may be in adjusting disputes between dealers. W.S.A. 342.19(2).

6. Statutes ⬤=223.2(20)

The automobile registration law must be construed with Uniform Commercial Code-Sales and it is proper to refer to registration law to determine when a used car dealer is supposed to know or what knowledge he is chargeable with when he claims to be a buyer in ordinary course of business. W.S.A. 342.19(2) 402.403(2).

———————————

The plaintiff Marcella Mattek commenced this action to replevy a 1964 Plymouth automobile from the defendant Sam Malofsky, a used-car dealer in Appleton. Mrs. Mattek was the owner of the automobile and lived in Menasha with her 23-year-old-son Gene Mattek. She moved to Forestville and left the automobile in Gene's possession and knew that Gene's intention was to sell the car. She did not authorize him to sell it but did authorize him to put it out for display purposes. Gene took the automobile to Doug Frakes, a licensed used-car dealer in Menasha, and authorized him to place the car on his lot for display purposes. Sometime later Frakes drove the automobile with his dealer's plate on it to Malofsky's lot in Appleton and sold it to him for $1,750. No certificate of title was delivered. Frakes kept the $1,750 for himself and Mrs. Mattek commenced this action to recover her car.

Fulton, Menn & Nehs, Appleton, for appellant, Peter S. Nelson, Appleton, of counsel.

Fred A. Reiter, De Pere, for respondent.

HALLOWS, Chief Justice.

Two issues are presented on this appeal: (1) Whether the provisions of sec. 402.403, Stats.[1] are applicable to sales between merchants; and (2) whether an automobile dealer who buys a used car from another automobile dealer, who has lawful possession of the car, without obtaining or inquiring about the certificate of title to the used car is a "buyer in the ordinary course of business" within the meaning of sec. 402.403.

1. "402.403 Power to transfer; good faith purchase of goods; 'entrusting'. (1) A purchaser of goods acquires all title which his transferor had or had power to transfer except that a purchaser of a limited interest acquires rights only to the extent of the interest purchased. A person with voidable title has power to transfer a good title to a good faith purchaser for value. When goods have been delivered under a transaction of purchase the purchaser has such power even though:

(a) The transferor was deceived as to the identity of the purchaser; or

(b) The delivery was in exchange for a check which is later dishonored; or

(c) It was agreed that the transaction was to be a 'cash sale'; or

(d) The delivery was procured through fraud punishable as larcenous under the criminal law.

(2) Any entrusting of possession of goods to a merchant who deals in goods of that kind gives him power to transfer all rights of the entruster to a buyer in ordinary course of business.

(3) 'Entrusting' includes any delivery and any acquiescence in retention of possession regardless of any condition expressed between the parties to the delivery or acquiescence and regardless of whether the procurement of the entrusting or the possessor's disposition of the goods have been such as to be larcenous under the criminal law.

(4) The rights of other purchasers of goods and of lien creditors are governed by chs. 406, 407 and 409."

[1, 2] We think the provisions of sec. 402.403 are applicable to sales between merchants. We come to this conclusion because the purpose of sec. 402.403(2) and (3) is to protect a person from a third-party interest in goods purchased from the general inventory of a merchant regardless of that merchant's actual authority to sell those goods. This section does not expressly or by implication restrict such protection of a sale by a merchant to a member of the consumer public. If the policy of negotiability of goods held in the inventory of a merchant is to be promoted, it would seem to apply between merchants where merchants buy from one another in the ordinary course of business. The protection is afforded to "a buyer in the ordinary course of business," and by other provisions of the Uniform Commercial Code the term "buyer" includes a merchant.

[3] In sec. 401.201(9), Stats., a buyer in the ordinary course of business is defined as "a person who in good faith and without knowledge that the sale to him is in violation of the ownership rights or security interest of a third party in the goods buys in ordinary course from a person in the business of selling goods of that kind but does not include a pawn broker." Good faith is defined in sec. 401.201(19), Stats., to mean "honesty in fact in the conduct or transaction concerned." This definition applies to a member of the consumer public only, because in sec. 402.103(1) (b) " 'good faith' in the case of a merchant" is is defined to mean "honesty in fact and the observance of reasonable commercial standards of fair dealing in the trade." In addition, sec. 402.104(3), Stats., relating to the general standard applicable to transactions between merchants charges each merchant with the "knowledge or skill of merchants."

Consequently, a merchant may be a buyer in the ordinary course of business under sec. 402.403 from another merchant if he meets four elements: (1) Be honest in fact, (2) be without knowledge of any defects

of title in the goods, (3) pay value, and (4) observe reasonable commercial standards. In the observance of reasonable commercial standards, however, a merchant is chargeable with the knowledge or skill of a merchant.

[4, 5] We think Malofsky was not the buyer in the ordinary course of business within the meaning of sec. 402.403, Stats. Although the delivery of the automobile to Frakes, a used-car dealer, constituted an entrustment, Frakes could by subsequent sale pass title to a buyer in the ordinary course of business. However, Malofsky as a merchant was not a buyer in the ordinary course of business because he was chargeable with the knowledge that the registration law, sec. 342.19(2), Stats. of 1963, which provides that while a dealer need not apply for a certificate of title for a vehicle in stock or acquired for stock purposes, he shall upon the transfer of such vehicle give the transferee evidence of title, and in the case of a vehicle which has a certificate of title, the certificate of title shall be reassigned and delivered to the transferee. Malofsky should have known the used automobile had a certificate of title outstanding and that Frakes was required to give him such certificate of title. Under the standards set forth in sec. 402.104(3), Stats., applicable to transactions between merchants, Malofsky is chargeable with this knowledge and his failure to procure a certificate of title or some evidence of title was unreasonable as a matter of law. Evidence of custom or usage of automobile dealers contrary to the statute cannot be used to defeat the rights of a third party whatever the value of such evidence may be in adjusting disputes between dealers.

The case of Commercial Credit Corp. v. Schneider (1953), 265 Wis. 264, 61 N.W. 2d 499, relied upon by Malofsky, is not in point. That case held it was unreasonable for a person to rely upon the certificate of title of an automobile for the disclosure of a lien interest; the facts here

CONGRESS BAR AND REST., INC. v. TRANSAMERICA INS. CO.   Wis. **409**
Cite as 165 N.W.2d 409

involve the failure to produce any certificate of title. Cases which involve the doctrine that automobiles are personal property and pass by the usual rules of intention of the parties and not by delivery of certificate of title are also not pertinent. In those cases the certificate of title is considered generally to be a significant factor but is not controlling. McWhorter v. Employers Mut. Casualty Co. (1965), 28 Wis.2d 275, 279, 137 N.W.2d 49; Udovc v. Ross (1954), 267 Wis. 182, 64 N.W.2d 747, 66 N.W.2d 200; Annot. (1951), *Motor vehicle certificate of title or similar document as, in hands of one other than legal owner, indicia of ownership justifying reliance by subsequent purchaser or mortgagee without actual notice of other interests,* 18 A.L.R.2d 813.

This is the first case interpreting the impact of sec. 402.403, Stats: However, in Hudiburg Chevrolet, Inc. v. Ponce (1962), 17 Wis.2d 281, 116 N.W.2d 252, decided before the adoption of the Uniform Commercial Code in Wisconsin, this court adopted the voidable title theory of sec. 402.403. But it should be noted that while a seller under this section has power to pass a better title than he possesses, nevertheless, the buyer must meet certain requirements to be entitled to the protection of that section.

[6] A case from a lower court, almost on all fours with the present case, is Atlas Auto Rental Corp. v. Weisberg (1967), 54 Misc.2d 168, 281 N.Y.S.2d 400, where the court held the provisions of the U.C.C. 2–403 applied to transactions between merchants but a dealer who purchased a used car without any bill of sale or owner's registration took the risk that his transferor was not the owner. We think sec. 342.19(2), Stats. of 1963, of the Motor Vehicle Code must be construed with the Uniform Commercial Code and it is proper to refer to the Motor Vehicle Code to determine what a used-automobile dealer is supposed to know or what knowledge he is chargeable with when he claims to be a buyer in the ordinary course of business.

Judgment affirmed.

— *FIGURE 8-6* —

SAMPLE BRIEF TO A TRIAL COURT WITH COMMENTARY— DOMINSKI

Note: this trial brief follows the Bluebook citation format, using italics

EXPLANATION

1. *Each court has its own rules for the format and content of the caption for all legal documents in a case. Captions allow the court to track the procedure in a case and provide a clear, organized record.*

2. *The first Issue emphasizes the client's point of view by focusing on the wording in the law that supports that position. In contrast to this wording, the subsequent facts make the covenant look too broad. That is exactly the point the writer needs to make to win.*

3. *In this Issue, the quote from the covenant contrasts with the employee's actual work, emphasizing the point essential to the writer's argument.*

1 STATE OF WI CIRCUIT COURT DANE COUNTY

PETROV SULLIVAN, LLC,
   Plaintiff

   v.   Case No. 09999

DAPHNE DOMINSKI,
   Defendant

DEFENDANT'S BRIEF IN SUPPORT OF MOTION FOR SUMMARY JUDGMENT

ISSUES

2   I. Under Wisconsin Statutes Section 103.465 (2005-06), which specifies that a covenant not to compete is void if its territorial restriction is broader than "reasonably necessary for the protection of the employer," is an insurance agency's covenant overbroad when it restricts an employee from working anywhere in Dane County even though the employee's customers reside only in the City of Madison?

3   II. Under Wisconsin precedent that has voided covenants not to compete when they are overly harsh to the employee, is an insurance agency's covenant not to compete overly harsh when it restricts an employee from "engage[ing] in the marketing of insurance, the underwriting of insurance, or any other activity relating in any way whatsoever to the insurance industry," even though the employee had only sold property and casualty insurance?

182

4. *This writer chose to open the facts with a focus on the opposition, making Petrov look like the active instigator in this case. The writer continues this approach in the Argument, where "Petrov" is often the subject of a sentence, the one taking action. To make a persuasive theme like this work, the writer needs to implement it consistently. If the writer does this, the document will be unified. If not, the story can seem unfocused.*

5. *This paragraph includes several non-essential facts: (1) Ms. Dominski is a native of Madison and (2) she began this job right after college. These facts may build some sympathy for Ms. Dominski. The fact that she was just out of college when she signed the contract might help offset the fact that she did agree to this restriction. But the writer did not overplay this point by adding adjective phrases, such as "Ms. Dominski, a young woman fresh from college and inexperienced in the details of contract law." That overdone phrase probably would have made the reader groan or laugh rather than be sympathetic.*

6. *This paragraph begins with a description of Dominski's specialization. This is an important point in the second subsection of the Argument, so it needs to be emphasized here. When emphasizing facts, choose facts that are legally significant as well as sympathetic. Facts that are sympathetic but not so important (as the two non-essential facts in the previous paragraph) can be included but logically should not be over emphasized.*

7. *This paragraph also begins with a key point, emphasized clearly in the opening phrase, "All of Ms. Dominski's customers." The reader will not miss a fact if it appears in the first five words of a paragraph.*

4 ## STATEMENT OF FACTS

Petrov Sullivan LLC (Petrov) filed a complaint asking against Ms. Dominski asking the court to enforce a covenant not to compete in her employment contract. (Compl.) In response, Ms. Dominski filed a motion for summary judgment in her favor, asserting that the covenant is void because it is overly broad and harsh as a matter of law. (Def.'s Mot. Summ. J.)

5 Petrov is a Wisconsin insurance agency and brokerage firm that serves professional, commercial, and private clients throughout the Midwest. (Stip. Facts ¶ 1.) Petrov hired Ms. Dominski, a native of Madison, to work as an insurance agent at Petrov's Madison office soon after she graduated from college in 1990. (Stip. Facts ¶ 2.) In her employment contract, Petrov included the following covenant not to compete.

> If the undersigned agent terminates employment with Petrov Sullivan LLC, the agent agrees not to engage in the marketing of insurance, the underwriting of insurance, or any other activity relating in any way whatsoever to the insurance industry, anywhere in Dane County, Wisconsin, for two years after the date of termination.

(Stip. Facts ¶ 5.)

6 During her eleven years working for Petrov, Dominski specialized in property and casualty insurance. (Stip. Facts ¶ 3.) Petrov's marketing strategy involves having employees develop expertise in specific areas of insurance law. (Stip. Facts ¶ 1.) Petrov also encourages employees to develop good working relationships with their customers, with whom they are often the sole contact. (Stip. Facts ¶ 1.)

7 All of Ms. Dominski's customers reside in Madison. (Stip. Facts ¶ 5.) Many are people she met through her volunteer work in Girl Scouts, United Business Women, Friends of Public Broadcasting, and the Red Cross. (Stip.

Facts ¶ 6.) Others are acquaintances from her church, slow pitch softball league, curling club, neighborhood association, and civics club. (Stip. Facts ¶ 6.) Dominski maintained her involvement in all these organizations on her own time. (Stip. Facts ¶ 6.)

8. The writer omits Ms. Dominski's motivations in this paragraph, which would not be helpful to the case. Instead, the writer focuses on Petrov's actions.

8 Ms. Dominski resigned from Petrov effective January 2, 2004. (Stip. Facts ¶ 4.) Learning that Ms. Dominski was considering staying in the insurance business, Petrov filed its complaint seeking to prevent Ms. Dominski from working in the insurance field anywhere in Dane County.

9. Depending on the court rules, Applicable Statutes may be included as a section in the brief, may be attached as an appendix, or may not be included.

9 <u>APPLICABLE STATUTES</u>

Wis. Stat. § 103.465 (2005-06) Restrictive covenants in employment contracts.

10. The statute is edited to omit some unneeded language. Editing can be done to make the relevant language easier to see, as long as it does not change the meaning.

10 A covenant by an assistant, servant or agent not to compete with his or her employer or principal . . . after the termination of that employment or agency, within a specified territory and during a specified time is lawful and enforceable only if the restrictions imposed are reasonably necessary for the protection of the employer or principal. Any covenant, described in this subsection, imposing an unreasonable restraint is illegal, void and unenforceable even as to any part of the covenant or performance that would be a reasonable restraint.

<u>ARGUMENT</u>

11. Point Headings highlight the main points in the Argument so the reader can review that Argument quickly, either before or after reading the whole brief.

11 I. SUMMARY JUDGMENT IS JUSTIFIED BECAUSE THE UNDISPUTED FACTS SUPPORT THE JUDGMENT AS A MATTER OF LAW.

12. This Argument begins with a focus on the legal standard the court will use in granting a summary judgment. Even experienced attorneys sometimes neglect this step, but they usually regret it. The first thing the judge will do is determine the proper legal standard to use to decide the case. Occasionally, when the judge repeatedly uses the same standard, this section may be omitted. Persuasive writers need to understand the judge's situation and provide that judge with the information he or she needs to use the law in the way the writer wants.

12 A summary judgment shall be granted when there is no genuine issue as to any material fact and when the moving party is entitled to judgment as a matter of law. Wis. Stat. § 802.08(2) (2005-06). A summary judgment is appropriate when no material facts are at issue and when the application of law is clear. *Tomlin v. State Farm Mut. Auto. Liab. Ins. Co.*, 95 Wis. 2d 215, 218-19, 290 N.W.2d 285, 287 (1980).

13. *If you looked up the opinion cited in this paragraph, you would find that the references are accurate but that the writer has often phrased the references to point toward the desired outcome. For example, "A summary judgment is not appropriate when material facts are at issue or when the application of law is unclear" has now become "A summary judgment is appropriate when . . . ." The writer is careful not to mis-state the law. But, within that limitation, writers can often edit to make a point clear.*

14. *Here the writer keeps the reader focused on "summary judgment" in the thesis sentences of the opening paragraph. This focus unifies this section. An important point comes at the end of this last paragraph. To give it some emphasis, the writer has used a short sentence.*

15. *This point heading flows smoothly from the first one. Always check the point Headings to make sure they fit together logically and grammatically.*
The opening sentence picks up the term "enforceable" from the heading to smooth the transition. The opening paragraph also focuses on the legal standard for this point, again giving the judge what he or she needs to decide the case.

13 When deciding a motion for summary judgment, the court follows a standard methodology. *Grams v. Boss*, 97 Wis. 2d 332, 338-39, 294 N.W.2d 473, 476-77 (1980). The court initially examines the pleadings to determine whether a claim has been stated and whether a material issue of fact is presented. *Id.* If the plaintiff has stated a claim for which relief may be granted, the court then determines whether the moving party has made a *prima facie* case for summary judgment. *Id.* To make a *prima facie* case, a moving defendant must show a defense that would defeat the plaintiff. *Id.* When the defendant has made a *prima facie* case and no material facts are disputed, the court next determines whether those facts support any reasonable alternative inference sufficient to entitle the opposing party to a trial. *Id.*

14 Summary judgment should be granted when the moving party meets its burden of demonstrating a right to a judgment with such clarity as to leave no room for controversy. *Id.; Coleman v. Outboard Marine Corp.*, 92 Wis. 2d 565, 571, 285 N.W.2d 631, 634 (1979). Ms. Dominski meets this standard.

15 II. AS A MATTER OF LAW, PETROV'S COVENANT NOT TO COMPETE IS UNENFORCEABLE.

In Wisconsin, a covenant not to compete is enforceable only when it conforms to the statutory requirements: "Any covenant . . . imposing an unreasonable restraint is illegal, void and unenforceable . . . . " Wis. Stat. § 103.465. When applying this statute, courts apply a five-part test. *Lakeside Oil Co. v. Slutsky*, 8 Wis. 2d 157, 161-68, 98 N.W. 2d 415, 418-22 (Wis. 1959). Under this test, the covenant must

(1) provide a reasonable territorial limit,

(2) not be harsh or oppressive to the employee,

(3) provide a reasonable time restriction,

(4) protect the business interests of the employer, and

(5) not be contrary to public policy.

16. *This final sentence of the paragraph would be just as accurate without the "even if" phrase. However, retaining it helps emphasize this key point.*

17. *The writer starts the paragraph with the client's point. This technique adds clarity and strength to the Argument. Avoid beginning with a presentation of the other side's argument or background facts. That approach leaves the reader wondering where you are headed and can create the impression that the Argument is weak or unfocused.*

18. *Sub-headings help the reader see the organization quickly and, when worded as affirmative statements of the writer's position, help emphasize the argument.*

19. *The first sentence of each paragraph under sub-heading A states a point that, if true, leads the judge to find for the client. This clear focus for thesis sentences is a major aspect of effective persuasive writing. Try to start a paragraph with a statement that not only summarizes the paragraph but also presents that summary so the reader can see how the point supports the overall legal argument.*

20. *The opening sentence of this paragraph has the subject and verb rather far apart. Although a writer would avoid this sentence structure in a memo, where clarity and ease of understanding are paramount, the writer may occasionally use this structure for emphasis in a brief. This document is more formal and the situation is more important. Thus a slightly more formal, oratory style is workable. But do not overdo it. This reader is still a busy lawyer.*

21. *If you compare this paragraph to the one presenting the precedent, you will see many parallel phrases and structures. This is effective and useful, because the repetition of structure helps the reader see the comparison. To achieve this parallelism, writers may need to revise the paragraph explaining the precedent, rather than just revising the application paragraph. While writing the application, an attorney will often clarify his or her understanding of the important points of the precedent. Such revision of the precedent is fine as long as it does not create any inaccuracy.*

Id. at 163-67. **16** If a covenant fails any part of this test, a court will not enforce any part of the covenant, even if part of the covenant would have been valid. *See* Wis. Stat. § 103.465.

17 Petrov's covenant fails two of these requirements: its territorial limit is unreasonably broad and its restrictions on the employee's activities are so broad as to be harsh and oppressive to the employee. Since it fails these parts of the test, the covenant is unenforceable as a matter of law under Wisconsin Statutes Section 103.465.

18 *A. The Covenant's Territorial Limit is Unreasonable.*

19 The territorial limit of a covenant not to compete is unreasonable when it extends beyond the geographic area in which the employee has served customers. *Wis. Ice & Coal Co. v. Lueth,* 213 Wis. 42, 43, 250 N.W. 819, 820 (Wis. 1933). The Wisconsin Supreme Court ruled that Wisconsin Ice and Coal's covenant not to compete was overly broad when its restricted territory included not only the area covered by the employee, but also the areas covered by forty-five similar workers. *Id.* Covenants not to compete are allowed only to provide the employers with protection that they reasonably need. *Id.* Employers do not need protection from an employee's influence with customers the employee has not met, and therefore such a broad restriction was unneeded. *Id.*

20 The measure of an appropriate territorial restriction in Wisconsin is the territory actually served, not the territory of potential customers. *Id.* Allowing an employer to enforce such a broad restriction would break down all proper limitation on covenants not to compete. *Id.* at 45. Based on this reasoning, the court voided Wisconsin Ice and Coal's covenant. *Id.*

21 Petrov's territorial limit is similarly unreasonable because it extends beyond the geographic area Ms. Dominski actually served. The covenant restricts Dominski from working in the insurance business "anywhere in Dane County," but her customers all reside within

Madison. (Stip. Facts ¶ 5.) To serve all of Dane County, Petrov employs fifteen insurance agents. (Stip. Facts ¶ 1.) As was true with Wisconsin Ice and Coal's covenant, Petrov's restricted territory includes not only the area covered by the employee, but also the areas covered by many other similar workers. Thus Petrov's covenant, as that of Wisconsin Ice and Coal, should be void.

22 Petrov's overbroad restriction, if enforced, would break down the proper limitation on covenants not to compete as surely as Wisconsin Ice and Coal's restriction would have. Petrov does not need protection from Ms. Dominski's competition for customers she has not served. Petrov's territorial restriction is not based on the actual area the employee served. It is therefore overly broad and unenforceable.

B. The Covenant's Broad Restrictions Are Harsh and Oppressive to the Employee

23 Under the second part of the test, covenants not to compete will not be enforced if they are unreasonable in their restriction of the employee's activities. *Nalco Chem. Co. v. Hydro Techs., Inc.*, 984 F.2d 801, 805 (7th Cir. 1993). Under this rule, Nalco's covenant was unreasonable because its restrictions were broader than needed to protect the employer's interest. *Id.*

24 It is unreasonable to prohibit an employee from working in an entire industry. *Id.* In *Nalco*, a water treatment company had two employees sign an employment agreement that included a covenant not to compete. Under that covenant, employees leaving Nalco could not "for the period of two (2) years immediately after its termination, engage or assist in the same or any similar line of business." *Id* at 804 n.2. This restriction was ruled overbroad because Nalco was a large company, including twelve major work divisions and dealing in several aspects of handling water. *Id.* at 802. The court reasoned that this covenant encompassed virtually all aspects of the water treatment industry and went beyond those areas in which the employees actually worked. *Id.* at 805.

---

22. *This thesis sentence uses an intrusive phrase effectively to emphasize a point. The phrase "if enforced" intrudes between the subject ("restriction") and the verb ("would break down"). This makes the reader stop and pay extra attention to the intrusion. Here, that is appropriate because the writer wants to emphasize that this is not something the reader should do, and "if" makes that point clearer.*

23. *This opening sentence is similar to the sentence in a memo on this content. Yet this is more persuasive because it is phrased from the perspective of not enforcing the covenant, the perspective retained throughout this Argument*

24. *This paragraph could have been part of the previous one, but beginning a new paragraph here draws attention to this paragraph's opening sentence. If the two had remained in one paragraph, the paragraph would have been too long.*

The paragraph includes quite a bit of detail about Nalco, but what is interesting is what it does not include. It does not talk about why the employees left, what they planned to do after leaving, or what their training had been. By leaving out all facts that are unneeded to make this particular point, the writer keeps the Argument concise and focused. And since the writer is emphasizing the point that the company did not need this much protection, keeping the focus off the employees is appropriate. In fact, it is essential to make this Argument work for this client.

25. *This writer has made this Argument sound much stronger than it did in the original memo. In that memo, the writer had presented two lines of reasoning and said the outcome depended on which line of reasoning the court followed. In this brief, however, the writer focuses solely on the line of reasoning that supports the client's position, presenting that thoroughly and persuasively. In a memo, the writer must consider all the plausible arguments, even though they may be contradictory or confusing. But in a brief, the writer presents the law that supports the Argument, and presents it in a way that makes it look straightforward and clear.*

26. *The writer has added a little punch to a main point in this sentence by stating a key concept in the verb "violate," replacing the noun form "are in violation." In the second sentence, the long introductory phrase refers to opinions and a law review article. These references, suggest that this issue has been discussed at length. This longer build up also makes the final quoted sentence appear short, rather like a punch line.*

27. *The phrasing of this paragraph's opening sentence ("Such a clear violation . . .") is rather unusual and dramatic. Some writers might think this is overdone; others would like it. The degree of drama a writer interjects into an Argument is part of his or her personal style. But be careful about overdoing it. If the reader notices the sentence and thinks it is overdone, the technique loses its effectiveness.*

25 This restriction was broader than necessary to protect Nalco's legitimate interests. *Id.* The court explained that employers must draft noncompete covenants carefully to avoid this overbreadth because employees' job specialization is increasing. *Id.* In light of the covenant's broad restriction, court found Nalco's covenant invalid because it was overly harsh to the employees. *Id.*

Petrov's covenant prohibits Dominski from working in an entire industry. Like Nalco's, Petrov's covenant goes beyond the areas in which Dominski actually worked. Nalco's covenant restricted former employees from working in "the same or any similar line of business." *Id.* Similarly, Petrov's covenant restricts Dominski from working in "any other activity relating in any way whatsoever to the insurance industry." (Stip. Facts ¶ 5.) Dominski had only worked in Petrov's property and casualty insurance divisions, with no involvement in marketing or underwriting. (Stip. Facts ¶ 3.) Yet Petrov's covenant restricts her from working in these areas. (Stip. Facts ¶ 5.) Therefore, just as Nalco's restriction was broader than needed to protect Nalco's legitimate interests, Petrov's covenant is broader than needed.

26 Overly broad restrictions on the employee's activities violate the public policy against barriers to competition. *Id.* at 805-06, (citing *Lakeside Oil*, 8 Wis. 2d at 166-67). Citing Wisconsin precedent and a law review article, the Nalco court summarized the clarity of this policy concisely: "The disapproval afforded broad restraints of business activity is secret." *Id.* at 805.

27 Such a clear violation of this policy cannot be enforced. Petrov's broadly worded restriction flies in the face of this policy. The covenant goes beyond the protection Petrov may have justly claimed. The covenant attempts not just to protect Petrov's legitimate interests, but also to discourage any competition from skilled employees who once worked for Petrov. This covenant is broader than necessary and thus overly harsh to the employee.

28. *This Conclusion summarizes the argument but is not particularly dramatic. Perhaps because the previous paragraph was rather dramatic, the writer needed to pull back a little in this one. In general, dramatic pieces of persuasion should be surrounded with more ordinary, factual writing. This allows the reader to digest the emphasized point and prevents the writer from losing credibility by overdoing the writing.*

29. *The attorney's signature here is more than a formality; it means the attorney is stating the information in the document is accurate to the best of the attorney's knowledge. Stop and think before you sign your name to make sure this is true.*

30. *The court sometimes requires a certificate like this to show that the opposition has received the required copy.*

28 ## CONCLUSION

Under Wisconsin statutory law, when a covenant fails any part of the test, a court voids the whole covenant. Petrov's covenant not to compete applies to a territory that is overbroad, thus failing the reasonable territory part of the test. The covenant's restrictions are also harsh and oppressive to the employee because it covers areas of activity in which the employee never worked. In sum, the covenant fails two parts of the test and thus is unenforceable as a matter of law under Wisconsin Statutes section 103.465.

29 Respectfully Submitted

DATED: January 2, 2006

_____
Attorney for the Defendant

30 ## CERTIFICATE OF SERVICE

I, Victoria Flood, attorney for the Defendant, hereby certify that I have served the Plaintiff with a complete, accurate copy of this Brief in Support of A Motion for Summary Judgment by placing the copy in the United States Mail, sufficient postage affixed and addressed as follows:

Petrov Sullivan LLC
c/o Atty. Jared Jerdee
2001 Williamson St.
Madison, WI 53703

DATED: January 2, 2008

_____
Attorney for the Defendant

— *FIGURE 8-7* —
SAMPLE BRIEF TO A TRIAL COURT WITH COMMENTARY— ELLERKAMP

Note: This trial brief follows Bluebook citation format, using underscoring.

EXPLANATION

1. *Courts usually have requirements for the headings of all documents submitted to them. Typically the heading for all documents is similar. So the writer can use the same template for all the documents in a case, just changing the title of the document as needed.*

2. *Some courts require Introductions that provide an overview of the case. If an introduction is optional, the writer has to decide whether to include one. To make the decision, consider whether an Introduction will help the reader. The important goal here is to let the reader see, within the first few sentences of the document, the merit of the client's position.*

In this Introduction, the writer focuses on the law. This is appropriate here because the law, more than the facts themselves, provide the client's strongest support.

---

1 <u>STATE OF WI CIRCUIT COURT DANE COUNTY</u>

Quinn Randall LLC,
    Plaintiff,

        v.   Case No. 09998

Emma Ellerkamp,
Defendant.

DEFENDANT'S MEMORANDUM OF POINTS AND AUTHORITIES IN SUPPORT OF MOTION FOR SUMMARY JUDGMENT IN DEFENDANT'S FAVOR

2 <u>INTRODUCTION</u>

The plaintiff, Quinn Randall LLC (Quinn), is suing its former employee, Ms. Ellerkamp, for breach of contract based on a non-compete covenant included in Ms. Ellerkamp's employment contract. That covenant, however, does not conform to Wisconsin law because it restricts the employee's actions in a territory larger than the area actually served by the employee. Under Wisconsin Statutes Section 103.465 (2005-06), if a noncompete covenant includes restrictions that are not reasonably necessary for the employer's protection, the whole covenant is void. Thus the plaintiff has based its suit on an invalid noncompete covenant and, since there are no disputed material facts, the plaintiff's suit fails as a matter of law.

3. *This Issue includes the statute's citation. Adding that information emphasizes the law, which is the focus of the coming argument.*

4. *While the Introduction explains the legal situation, the Statement of Facts presents the human situation. Here we learn about how the client's position is fair and just. For example, this version focuses on Quinn's actions after Ellerkamp resigned and suggests Quinn's motivations. It omits any explanation about Ms. Ellerkamp's motivation for leaving or her expectation that former clients may remain loyal to her.*

The line between writing persuasive facts and misleading ones is not bright, but it is important. Beginning legal writers sometimes go too far in an effort to persuade the reader. To avoid doing this, ask yourself whether the other side could say that your fact statement is inaccurate. If so, you have gone too far. If, however, the other side would dislike your version but could not call it inaccurate, then you are still on the safe side of the line.

Choosing and organizing the facts well is generally more important for persuasion than any wording of those facts. For example, this Statement of Facts is persuasive, even though the wording has not changed that much compared to the original memo. What has happened is that this version omits unneeded or unhelpful details and focuses on the helpful ones.

This writer uses short sentences rather frequently, so they do not create any particular emphasis in the facts. Overall, however, the short sentences give the facts a clipped, no nonsense tone that is appropriate for this Argument because the argument relies on the logic of the law rather than on particular sympathy for this client.

5. *These facts seem to stop more than end. Often it is better to finish strongly, but this writer is probably wise not to try to create a dramatic ending when none exists. For a stronger finishing point, the writer could have returned to the idea of how Quinn was trying to restrict Ellerkamp.*

3 ISSUE STATEMENT

Under precedent interpreting Wisconsin Statues Section 103.465 to require non-compete covenants to meet a five-part test, does a covenant fail the reasonable territory part of the test when the covenant restricts an employee from marketing insurance "anywhere east of the Mississippi River," even though the employee worked only in Dane County, Wisconsin?

4 <u>STATEMENT OF FACTS</u>

Defendant Emma Ellerkamp resigned from her insurance sales position at Quinn. (Compl. ¶ 6.) To preclude her from working in the insurance field, Quinn filed a complaint against Ms. Ellerkamp to enforce a non-compete covenant in the employment contract she had signed twelve years earlier. (Compl. ¶ 4.) Ms. Ellerkamp filed a motion for a summary judgment declaring the non-compete covenant invalid because it violates Wisconsin Statues Section 103.465 . (Def.'s Mot. Summ. J.)

After she graduated from UW-Madison in 1990, Ms. Ellerkamp worked for Quinn as one of sixteen insurance agents in its Madison, Wisconsin, office. (Compl. ¶ 2, ¶ 4; Stip. Facts ¶ 2.) Quinn is sells many kinds of insurance to varied clients, including businesses, professional organizations, and individuals. (Compl. ¶ 2; Stip. Facts ¶ 1.)

When beginning her work, Ms. Ellerkamp signed an agreement containing the following non-compete covenant. "The undersigned agent agrees that in the event the agent terminates employment with Quinn Randall LLC: For two years after the date of termination, the agent will not engage in the marketing of insurance in Madison, Wisconsin, or anywhere east of the Mississippi River." (Compl. ¶ 9.) Quinn has never had any offices outside Wisconsin. (Stip. Facts ¶ 6.)

5 While working for Quinn, Ms. Ellerkamp sold property and casualty insurance. (Stip. Facts ¶ 3.) She built her clientele in Madison and surrounding communities through her participation, during non-work hours, in various professional and civic associations and in her work with charities. (Stip. Facts ¶ ¶ 4, 7.)

ARGUMENT

6. *The Argument begins with a quick overview before launching into the first point. This overview is not needed to get from the Argument heading to the first point about the summary judgment standard. Rather, it is needed to let the reader know what the second point is and how points A and B fit together to form a unified argument.*

[6] Ms. Ellerkamp meets the standard for a summary judgment. First, Quinn's non-compete covenant, upon which Quinn relies, is invalid as a matter of law. Second, neither party disputes any material facts. Therefore, summary judgment in Ms. Ellerkamp's favor is legally justified.

A. Standard for Summary Judgment

7. *The writer attacks the problem head on by stating that the standard for a summary judgment is high. Rather than avoiding that possible weakness, the writer tackles it, explaining the standard clearly but wording it in terms of when summary judgment is granted, rather than when it is not.*

Here the writer quickly sets aside a non-controversial point, that there is no genuine issue of material fact. Then the writer returns to the issue that is critical in this case.

This portion of the Argument includes information that was not in the research memo, and therefore had to be researched separately. When writing any persuasive document for the court, a wise attorney makes sure he or she knows and addresses the procedural or other standards the court will use to decide the issue. Failing to do this can lose an otherwise winnable case. The wording of these sentences may seem surprisingly objective. Effective persuasive writing often does sound much like objective writing. In fact, a good persuasive document can read like an objective document explaining a clear-cut point of law. The persuasion occurs in the organization and choice of law.

[7] A court grants a motion for summary judgment when the moving party demonstrates a right to a judgment with such clarity that it leaves no room for controversy. Grams v. Boss, 97 Wis. 2d. 332, 338, 294 N.W.2d 473, 477 (1980). The moving party bears the burden of establishing "that no genuine issue exists as to any material fact and that the moving party is entitled to a judgment as a matter of law." Lambrecht v. Estate of Kaczmarczyk, 2001 WI 25, ¶ 24, 241 Wis. 2d 804, 623 N.W.2d 751. In this case, no genuine issue of material fact exists: both parties have stipulated to the facts. The only remaining question is whether the defendant is entitled to a judgment as a matter of law.

8. *The writer here takes the time to explain the logic of the argument carefully. That is important because if the court is not convinced on any one step in the logic, the client will lose the case. When explaining your reasoning, try to avoid undue repetition. But, above all, include enough explanation to persuade your reader.*

[8] When deciding a motion for summary judgment, the court follows a standard methodology. Grams, 97 Wis. 2d at 338, 294 N.W.2d at 477. The trial court first determines whether the plaintiff has stated a claim for relief. Lambrecht, 2001 WI 25, ¶ 21. The court then considers the moving party's proof to determine whether that party has made a *prima facie* case for summary judgment. Id. All inferences to be drawn from the underlying facts must be viewed in the light most favorable to the party opposing the summary judgment. Id. ¶ 23.

Ms. Ellerkamp is entitled to summary judgment. The covenant violates Wisconsin Statutes section 103.465 so clearly that no room remains for legal controversy. Because the statute specifies that any non-compete covenant failing the test cannot be enforced even partially, Ms. Ellerkamp has made a prima facie case that Quinn has no legal basis for its claim. Thus Ms. Ellerkamp is entitled to summary judgment as a matter of law.

B. Quinn's Non-Compete Covenant is Unenforceable Based on Undisputed Facts.

9 In Wisconsin, a non-compete covenant is unenforceable when it imposes restrictions that are not reasonably necessary for the employer's protection. Wis. Stat. § 103.465. To determine whether the covenant meets this standard, the courts apply a five-part test. Lakeside Oil Co. v. Slutsky, 8 Wis. 2d 157, 161-68, 98 N.W. 2d 415, 418-22 (1959). The five questions asked under this test are **10** (1) does the covenant protect legitimate employer interests? (2) is the restraint reasonable as to duration? (3) is the restraint reasonable as to territory? (4) is the covenant not overly harsh to the employee? and (5) is the restriction reasonable with respect to public interest? Id. at 163-67, 98 N.W. 2d at 419-22. **11** When applying these factors, the court also considers public policy goals that generally disfavor non-compete covenants. Streiff v. Am. Family Mut. Ins. Co., 118 Wis. 2d 602, 614, 348 N.W.2d 505, 512 (1984).

12 When a covenant fails even one part of this test, the whole covenant is void.

> Any covenant, described in this subsection, imposing an unreasonable restraint is illegal, void and unenforceable even as to any part of the covenant or performance that would be a reasonable restraint.

Wis. Stat. § 103.465. Thus, the legislature has specifically eliminated the courts' discretion to modify covenants.

13 Voiding the whole covenant is necessary to prevent employers from drafting unfair clauses to deter employees from attempting to compete even though the employers

9. Now, after explaining the legal steps needed in the decision, the writer gets to the law regarding non-compete covenants. It is similar to the wording from the research memo, except that it is worded to focus on the outcome the writer wants: "a covenant not to compete is unenforceable when . . . ."

10. Arguably the writer would not need to include all five parts of the test, since only one is going to be discussed below. But this brief is already concise, and the overall approach is one of thorough and careful reasoning. In light of those factors, including all the elements makes sense and enhances credibility.

11. Here and later in the Argument, the writer emphasizes the policy behind the law. Rather than organizing the law from a historical approach, the writer moves the background history from the memo into the discussion of the policy.

12. This point needs to be conveyed to win this case, and the writer does this by stating it in a thesis sentence and then supporting it thoroughly. The governing law needs to be emphasized because courts in the past did try to revise the law and because the dissenting opinion suggested that revising the original covenant made sense. To counter that opinion, the writer needs to drive home the point that the legislature spoke clearly on the matter. The writer does not, however, dwell on the other side's argument before answering it.

13. Many beginning legal writers make the mistake of setting up the opposition's argument before contradicting it. That may be a useful ploy in debate, but not in writing. When a writer takes the time to set up the opposition's argument, he or she is ceding the reader's attention to the opposition. Here the writer keeps the focus on the client's position. Part of that position is the policy behind the law, which happens to counter the opposition's argument.

knew the clause would be unenforceable. Streiff, 118 Wis. 2d at 608, 348 N.W.2d at 509. The legislature enacted this statutory language specifically to prevent courts from revising non-compete covenants: "[I]t is clear that our legislature has . . . opted not to give effect even to so much of the covenant as would be a reasonable restraint." Id. at 614-15, 348 N.W.2d at 512.

14. *Here the writer quickly outlines the connections between the narrow argument just made (that the territory is too broad) and the ultimate point (that summary judgment is justified here). This helps the reader avoid getting lost in the details of the rather technical argument.*

14 Under Wisconsin Statutes Section 103.465, Quinn's covenant is unenforceable and should be stricken as a whole. The covenant violates the third part of the test because the covenant restricted activities in a territory that is unreasonably broad. Therefore, because Quinn is left without a legal basis for its claim, Ms. Ellerkamp is entitled to summary judgment as a matter of law.

15. *At this point, the writer is using law from the research memo. If you compared the corresponding paragraph from the research memo, you would see how some details are omitted and how slight changes in the wording make the point more affirmative.*

15 Non-compete covenants are unreasonable as to territory when they cover an area larger than actually served by the employee. Union Cent. Life Ins. Co. v. Balistrieri, 19 Wis. 2d 265, 270, 120 N.W.2d 126, 129 (1963); Behnke v. Hertz Corp., 70 Wis. 2d 818, 823-24, 235 N.W.2d 690, 693-94 (1975). Under facts similar to this case, the court found a non-compete covenant covered an unreasonable territory when it restricted an insurance salesperson from working in any state where his employer was licensed to operate, even though he had sold insurance only in Milwaukee County. Union Cent. Life, 19 Wis. 2d at 270, 120 N.W.2d at 129. The court reasoned that the employer did not need protection from the employee's influence over customers with whom he had never worked. Id. at 270-71, 120 N.W.2d at 129. Because the covenant imposed unnecessary territorial limitations on the employee, it was stricken completely. Id., 120 N.W. 2d at 129.

16. *Here the writer reminds the reader of the legal standard, again fending off an argument the opposition will make without stopping to make that argument for the opposition.*

16 Courts determine the reasonableness of a non-compete covenant based on its actual wording, not on what could have been written. Streiff, 118 Wis. 2d at 614-15, 348 N.W.2d at 512. If the state were to enforce the reasonable parts of a non-compete covenant that violates some parts of the test, then employers could draft ominous covenants because most employees would fear breaking contractual obligations and would not contest the covenant. Id. 348 N.W. 2d at 512. The employers would have much to gain and nothing to lose by drafting such covenants. To avoid this outcome, the legislature chose a different approach.

> The legislature has in sec. 103.465 instructed the court as to the equities between the parties. Under sec. 103.465 if an indivisible covenant imposes an unreasonable restraint, the covenant is illegal, void, and unenforceable even as to so much of the covenant as would be a reasonable restraint.

Id. 348 N.W.2d at 512.

17. *Here and elsewhere in the brief, the writer uses an intrusive phrase to emphasize a particular point. In this thesis sentence, the writer emphasizes "anywhere east of the Mississippi" by inserting it between the subject and verb. That structure draws attention to the phrase so the contrast with "Dane County" is more dramatic. Although often this writer relies on careful logic to make the argument, here the writer uses a key fact to make the point. But the writer follows up this fact with a careful, reasoned explanation of the point. This writer wants to make sure the reader follows the logic of the Argument.*

17 Quinn's restriction, covering "anywhere east of the Mississippi," is unreasonable because it is much larger than Dane County, the area Ms. Ellerkamp actually served. Just as Behnke's covenant applied to a geographical territory that exceeded the area actually served by the employee, Quinn's covenant applies to a territory that exceeds the area Ms. Ellerkamp actually served. Furthermore, Quinn's covenant exceeds the territory served by the entire company; Quinn has offices only in the Midwest but none in the Eastern United States. The covenant's territory so clearly exceeds what is reasonable that it leaves no room for controversy.

18. *In this final paragraph, the writer reminds the reader that the law focuses on the clause as it is written. That is done in the thesis sentence by a reference to the facts, or to what might have been the facts, rather than a more abstract reference to the law. Perhaps the writer believes the reader understands the law by this point, so these thesis sentences will imply the legal point clearly enough to work.*

18 Although Quinn could have created reasonable territorial limits, in fact it did not. Quinn chose to ignore the statutory restrictions when drafting this covenant, just as the legislature feared employers would do. Quinn created an ominous covenant to deter employees from changing employers. Because Quinn's covenant is unenforceable as a matter of law, declaring it invalid comports with the purpose behind the statute as well as with the letter of the statute.

CONCLUSION

19. *In general, the strength of this brief is its clear focus. For example, this brief does not discuss whether the clause is severable, although the writer discussed that issue at length in the research memo. Similarly, the writer omits any argument about the covenant being overly harsh to the employee. The writer decided to be bold, focus on one argument, and make that argument thoroughly. This takes courage, but can be effective when the one argument is strong.*

19   Quinn's covenant not to compete has an unreasonable territorial restriction that is unenforceable as a matter of law. Ms. Ellerkamp is entitled to summary judgment because no material facts are in dispute and no reasonable view of the evidence supports Quinn's complaint.

20. *The attorney's signature here is more than a formality; signing it means the attorney is saying the document is accurate to the best of the attorney's knowledge. So stop and think before you sign your name.*

20   Respectfully Submitted,

_____
Attorney for the Defendant

DATED: January 12, 2008

21. *The certificate of service is a form added at the end of the brief to provide assurance that the opposing party has been properly notified of this Motion, which is needed to fulfill legal due process.*

21   **CERTIFICATE OF SERVICE**

I, John Solache, as the Defendant's attorney, certify that I served the plaintiff with a complete, accurate copy of this Brief in Support of a Motion for Summary Judgment by mailing a copy via the United States Mail, with sufficient postage, addressed as follows:

Quinn Randall LLC
c/o Atty. Keisha Mathis
Suite 712, Pyare Square
5500 West University
Madison, WI 53709

DATED: January 12, 2008

_____
Attorney for the Defendant

9

Revising for Persuasion

REVISING TO ENHANCE persuasion is first a matter of revising for clarity because much of a brief's persuasiveness comes from its content and organization. A document is most likely to persuade a reader by choosing the right motivation and presenting it clearly.

When revising for persuasion, you will edit strategically to make key, favorable points stand out. You will also edit to de-emphasize unfavorable points without becoming misleading. Just as you organized your Argument to emphasize the law that favored your desired outcome, you must now revise to emphasize the relevant content supporting that outcome.

This strategic revision occurs in the Statement of Facts, Issues, and Argument. In the Statement of Facts, you will emphasize the facts that help the judge see your client's position favorably. In the Issues, you will emphasize the way the key facts favor the legal outcome you advocate. In the Argument, you will revise the thesis sentences to present the reasoning behind your client's position, pulling the reader's focus to that position on the law and its application. When all the parts work together to present the persuasive position, the brief will be unified, consistent, and effective.

Revising the Statement of Facts

Revising the Statement of Fact involves

- deciding what facts to emphasize and de-emphasize,

- selecting and using writing techniques to create that emphasis or de-emphasis, and

- revising the rest of the facts so they fit smoothly around the emphasized and de-emphasized facts.

To decide what facts to emphasize, review the facts and select two or three that exemplify the view you want your reader to have of the overall situation. For example, if you were representing a defendant who had shot another man who had threatened him, you might select the facts that show why the defendant would have reason to fear the man he shot. Such facts might be that the defendant weighed 60 pounds less than the shooting victim, that the victim had previously beaten the defendant, or that the defendant was alone in an isolated area when the victim approached him. You would probably not want to select facts that are irrelevant to that issue, such as the defendant having a history of being teased about his appearance or the victim being vain about his physique.

Then decide what facts, if any, you need to de-emphasize. For example, in the previous situation you might de-emphasize the fact that your client was carrying a gun or that he knew he would be walking in a dangerous area. You are likely to de-emphasize the facts that the opposition will emphasize.

After selecting the facts you want to emphasize or de-emphasize, select the emphasis techniques you will use. To decide what technique might be best, review the following table of techniques and samples. As you review that table, you will probably find that you understand some techniques but find others confusing. That is not a problem; you do not have to master all the techniques. Instead, select one from a personal short list of techniques that you understand and feel comfortable using. In each of the sample briefs at the end of Chapter 8, for example, the writer relied on a few favorite techniques to create emphasis. These choices created different writing styles in the two briefs.

When you review the list of techniques below, identify the techniques that you are most likely to use, marking them so you can refer to the list quickly when you are revising the facts. Then try out those techniques on facts from your brief to see how the techniques work for you.

— *Figure 9-1* —
REVISION TECHNIQUES THAT EMPHASIZE FACTS

1. Place the fact in a short sentence.

2. Place the fact at the beginning of a sentence or paragraph.

3. Describe the fact more specifically, using concrete words rather than abstract ones.

4. Use an active verb to communicate the fact.

REVISION TECHNIQUES THAT DE-EMPHASIZE FACTS

1. Place the fact in a sentence with other facts that make the unfavorable fact seem less unfavorable.

2. Place the fact toward the middle of a paragraph.

3. Explain the fact in less detail, using more abstract words.

4. Use passive voice to downplay an action.

After revising the facts, you will almost always need to revise the remaining facts to fit around that emphatic point. As you do so, revise with clarity in mind. Resist the urge to add more emphasis to other facts just because you now know how to do it. Adding too much dramatic emphasis is no more effective than having a teacher constantly shouting to a class of fifth graders. All emphasis is lost because the audience learns to tune out the drama and the content.

Always be sure that your facts remain accurate. If your persuasive techniques cross over the line and become misleading, you run the risk of destroying your credibility with the court, not only on this case, but also on all future cases.

— FIGURE 9-2 —
EXAMPLES OF EMPHASIS TECHNIQUES FOR STATEMENTS OF FACT

TECHNIQUE	EFFECTIVE VERSION	INEFFECTIVE VERSION
Place the fact in a short sentence	Quinn has no offices outside Wisconsin.	Quinn, however, currently does not have any existing offices in any area outside the state of Wisconsin.
Place the fact at the beginning of a sentence or paragraph	All of Ms. Dominski's customers reside in Madison.	According to Ms. Dominski's customer list, her customers all reside in Madison.
Describe the fact more specifically, using concrete words, rather than abstract ones	Many of Dominski's customers are people she met through her volunteer work in Girl Scouts, United Business Women, Friends of Public Broadcasting, and the Red Cross.	Many of Dominski's customers are people she met through community organizations.
Use an active verb to communicate the fact	Ms. Ellerkamp built her clientele through contacts she made while participating in various community organizations.	Ms. Ellerkamp's clientele included her acquaintances from various community activities.

EXAMPLES OF DE-EMPHASIS TECHNIQUES FOR STATEMENTS OF FACT

TECHNIQUE	EFFECTIVE VERSION	INEFFECTIVE VERSION
Place the fact in a sentence with other ameliorating facts	Just after graduation from college, Ms. Dominski began working for Petrov, where she signed an employment contract that included a covenant not to compete.	In January, Ms. Dominski resigned from Petrov because she planned to open her own insurance business in Madison. She anticipated that many of her current clientele would bring their business to her new firm.
Explain the fact in less detail, using more abstract words	In January, Ms. Dominski resigned from Petrov. Subsequently, Petrov filed this complaint against Ms. Dominski seeking to enforce the covenant not to compete.	In January, Ms. Dominski turned in her resignation, hoping to open her own insurance business focusing on business clients. Subsequently, Petrov filed this complaint against Ms. Dominski seeking to enforce the covenant not to compete.
Use passive voice	Ms. Dominski attended training sessions offered by Petrov.	Petrov provided training for Ms. Dominski.

Applying What You Have Learned

Exercise 9-1
Evaluating a Statement of Facts

Consider the following overdone excerpt based on the Dominski sample Brief included in Chapter 8. Notice how the bias in this version makes you question the accuracy and overall merit of Daphne Dominski's case. Mark the points in the account where you see the bias and identify what the writer did wrong.

When Ms. Dominski began working for the huge insurance conglomerate called Petrov, she was a new college graduate still "wet behind the ears." Without realizing the problems that a covenant not to compete could create for her, Daphne naively signed Petrov's sleazy contract and enthusiastically threw herself into her new job. Not only did she work diligently during her office hours, but she also made use of her connections as a Madison native and as an active volunteer in many organizations. She gained scores of new clients for Petrov through her volunteer work, **never** giving this benefit a second thought, but only glad to build up the business of her new employer.

She continued this effort for ***twelve years!*** She also studied diligently to develop a specialty in property and casualty insurance, doing her best to forward the chosen marketing strategy of her boss. Using her own personal free time, Daphne unselfishly worked in multiple charities. She has been the **Brownie leader** for a group of eleven impressionable second graders. She helped recruit speakers for the United Business Women's luncheons for three years. She has collected donations for the WHA silent auction, then worked the phones during the auction and even swept up the studio after the auction was done! She has also volunteered for the Red Cross, helping organize and pack emergency supplies for flood victims, helping build a dike of sandbags to hold back the raging Mississippi that threatened the historic town of Prairie du Chien. But that's not all. She has even donated—over 3 gallons—of her own blood!! Wow!! And Daphne's good works don't stop there. *No way.* She is a regular attendee of the First Congregational Church, where she often serves as a greeter or usher. She is a dues-paying member of her neighborhood association, still living in the same neighborhood where she once played as a toddler. For her employer, Petrov, she has done more than they could have possibly hoped for to develop good working relationships with individual customers.

When Ms. Dominski *finally* resigned from her job working under these oppressive conditions, Petrov did not arrange a going away party for her. No, not this boss! Instead, Petrov "slapped her in the face" with a Complaint seeking to prevent her from working in the insurance field any more. Petrov *cruelly* insists on restricting her from working in insurance in the **whole** Midwest.

Rather than persuading the judge, the Statement of Facts in the previous application exercise is likely to be annoying. The writer has wasted the court's time with irrelevant details, such as "still living in the same neighborhood where she once played as a toddler." The writer has inserted his or her personal opinion by using adverbs such as "diligently," "unselfishly," and "cruelly" and adjectives such as "lowly," "oppressive," and "sleazy." The emotional tone is increased by informal language such as contractions ("That's not all.") and interjections ("Wow" and "No way"). The writer has also used informal descriptions of actions that add emotionalism, such as "slapped her in the face with a Complaint," and "enthusiastically threw herself into her new job." Finally, graphics are sprinkled throughout the facts to add emphasis, including italics, boldface, different type size and font. These graphics, however, create the impression of an advertising brochure rather than a reliable, factual account. When this level of emotion appears in the telling of the story, the reader has to wonder how accurately the facts are being reported.

To avoid this problem, check your facts for accuracy and revise as needed. Avoid using boldface, underlining, italics, or other graphic devices to add emphasis. Instead, use more substantive techniques, such as stating facts more specifically or using short sentences. Never use quotation marks around a casual phrase. If the phrase is so casual that it needs quotation marks, remove it and substitute a different phrase. Although the revised version might seem less persuasive, that is probably not the case.

— *Figure 9-3* —

CHECKLIST FOR REVISING THE STATEMENT OF FACTS

1. After completing your Argument, identify two or three facts that are legally significant and favorable to your client.

2. Place those facts in positions of emphasis, such as the following.

   • State it in a short sentence.
   • Place it in the first sentence of a paragraph.
   • Explain the fact in more specific detail.
   • State the action in active voice.

3. Identify any unfavorable facts and move them out of positions of emphasis by one of the following methods.

   • State it in a longer sentence with other facts that make the fact less unfavorable.
   • Place it toward the middle of a paragraph.
   • Explain the fact more generally and in less detail.
   • State the action in passive voice.

4. Check the statement to make sure you have not overdone the emphasis.

5. Check the statement for overall readability.

Applying What You Have Learned

Exercise 9-2
Writing a Persuasive Statement of Facts

Read the following objective Statement of Facts regarding a negligence case. Then, representing either Elkelund or Grissom, write a persuasive version of the facts.

Elle Elkelund is suing her upstairs neighbor, Gerald Grissom for negligence. She wants to recover damages for her ruined wedding cake, ruined wedding reception, and general emotional distress.

On Sunday, June 22, Mr. Grissom legally purchased fireworks in Indiana on his way back to his apartment in Madison, WI. He subsequently stored these fireworks in a plain brown bag placed in a plastic trash bin located near the balcony door of his efficiency apartment. The fireworks included some fireworks that are legal in Wisconsin, but also some bottle rockets and other fireworks that are illegal in this state, although legal in Indiana.

On the following Friday evening, June 27, Mr. Grissom had eight friends over to watch some fights on television and share some beer and pizza. Mr. Grissom and most of his friends also smoked cigarettes as they watched the fight. The gathering went well, and around 9:00 Mr. Grissom realized he was running low on beer. He left to purchase more beer at a nearby convenience store while his friends remained in the apartment, waiting for the next fight to begin.

As they waited, one of the friends accidentally stepped into a plate of pizza that was sitting on the floor. This led the friends to decide to clear up the mess so they could walk around the room without further disasters. As they cleaned up, they put all the trash into a trash bin under the kitchen sink. One of the friends emptied ash trays into this bin. Another friend emptied items from the small trash can near the glass door, thus inadvertently throwing away the fireworks. Yet another friend loaded and started the dishwasher, which was next to the sink.

When Mr. Grissom returned with the beer, he noticed that the smoky room smelled a little odd, but he did not investigate. He noticed also that his friends had picked up trash off the floor and generally cleaned up the room, but he did not look carefully to see what had been done. He did not notice that the ash trays had been emptied or that the fireworks were missing from the small trash can. He simply kidded his friends a little, thanked them, and returned to the couch, opening another can of beer. As they watched television, the trash under the sink began to smolder, but no one noticed. The battery in the smoke detector was dead, and Mr. Grissom had not bothered to replace it. In about thirty minutes, the fireworks exploded. Mr. Grissom, having consumed at least five beers, could not readily locate the fire extinguisher in the kitchen. Eventually they did extinguish the fire, but they did not realize that the fire had heavily damaged the hose leading from the dishwasher to the drain. As the dishwasher continued to run, water seeped through the walls and ceiling down to Ms. Elkelund's kitchen in the apartment below, dripping onto the counter.

Ms. Elkelund was not in the apartment at the time because she was at the rehearsal for her wedding, which was occurring at 11:00 a.m. the next day. Ms. Elkelund's wedding was to be a small but elegant affair, with a state supreme court justice officiating and with the governor and other prominent citizens in attendance. Ms. Elkelund was marrying the son of Ukraine's Ambassador to the United States, and the wedding colors were the colors of that national flag, light blue and yellow. In keeping with the Ukrainian theme, Ms. Elkelund had arranged to have a special Ukrainian cake created, and she had picked it up in Chicago on Friday. The cake was sitting on her kitchen counter, next to the special wedding mints, and paper napkins embossed with the couple's names and the wedding date. These items had cost Ms. Elkelund $1,100.

When Ms. Elkelund returned home at 11:00 p.m., she discovered that the dripping water ruined her wedding cake, the mints, and the napkins. Since it was too late to make any other arrangements, she was forced to purchase several sheet cakes from a local grocery store at a cost of $145. These cakes were decorated in red, white, and blue for the Fourth of July. She also purchased plain white napkins and ordinary mints for an additional cost of $9. Ms. Elkelund was distraught and cried through the night. She feels that her whole wedding was ruined, and that the damages greatly exceeded the cost of the items lost and purchased as replacements. In her wedding pictures, the stress shows. Her eyes are reddened and her smile looks forced.

Revising the Issue

After you have completed the Argument and Statement of Facts, review your Issues to make sure they include the same key words you used elsewhere in the brief to the trial court. The Issue should state the relevant law, the relevant facts, and tie them together with a question that, when answered, will determine the outcome of the case. If the Brief does not include an Issue, then the Point Headings should fulfill the purpose of an Issue, and they should be revised with similar goals in mind.

The Issue is only one sentence, so the scope of your revision is much smaller than the revision of the Statement of Facts. Nevertheless, you may be able to change some wording of the law, facts, and question to emphasize the merit of your client's position.

■ Law Portion

The Issue's law portion should include the relevant, favorable legal terms you emphasized in the legal synthesis in your Argument. You may be able to quote relevant, favorable phrases from the statute to emphasize how the law favors the client's position. For example, if the Issue was the following, a small revision could add some persuasiveness to the defendant's issue.

Example, Original Issue

Under Wisconsin Statutes Section 895.52(2)(2005-06), covering landowner's liability for injuries incurred by recreational users of the land, is Outagamie County entitled to immunity when a spectator was injured while watching members of the high school football team play touch football on the County's property in a regularly scheduled gym time?

Example, Issue with Law Revised

Under Wisconsin Statutes Section 895.52(2)(2005-06), which grants immunity to landowners whose property is used for recreational activities other than organized team sports, is Outagamie County entitled to immunity when a spectator was injured while watching members of the high school football team play touch football on the County's property in an open gym session?

■ Fact Portion

You may be able to revise the facts portion of the Issue by rewording those facts somewhat to emphasize favorable facts and minimize unfavorable ones. For example, see how the following revision adds some persuasiveness to the original issue.

Example, Issue with Facts Also Revised

Under Wisconsin Statutes Section 895.52(2)(2005-06), which grants immunity to landowners whose property is used for recreational activities other than organized team sports, is Outagamie County entitled to immunity when a spectator was injured while watching high school students play touch football on the County's property during open recreation?

■ Question

When revising the core question, compare the Issues with the Point Headings; often the same key terms will appear in both. Although using the same terms in all these places may seem repetitious, it provides a useful clarity and reminder for the reader. The core question should relate logically to both the law and the facts portions, pulling those two parts of the Issue together. When you accomplish this, the Issue should express the unifying and central points needed to win your case.

As you revise portions of the Issue for persuasiveness, expect only subtle improvements. You are working within the constraints of one sentence and within the boundaries of accuracy.

— *FIGURE 9-4* —
CHECKLIST FOR REVISING ISSUES

1. Revise the law or the question in your Issue to state the key legal criteria.

2. Revise the facts portion of the Issue to emphasize key favorable facts using one of these techniques.

   • State the favorable facts more concretely or specifically
   • Arrange the facts so that the favorable ones come at the beginning or end of the list.

3. Reread the Issue as a whole and revise as needed to keep it accurate and clear, even if that means reducing your emphasis.

Applying What You Have Learned

Exercise 9-3: Writing Persuasive Issues

Using the same law used in Ms. Maven's situation, which is described in the sample memos at the end of Chapter 1 and in Chapter 4, read the following objective facts and determine how you would apply that law to these new facts. Assuming you are Mr. Fautz's attorney, write a persuasive Issue for his brief arguing that Xeron's motion should be denied. Then, assuming you are the attorney for Xeron, write an Issue arguing that the motion should be granted.

Xeron Motors has filed a motion for summary judgment against Mr. James Fautz dismissing Fautz's action under Wisconsin's Lemon Law. Mr. Fautz is suing Xeron because it failed to replace his Xeron sports car, which is still under warranty.

Fautz bought a 2008 Xeron sports car on September 15, 2007. Within a few days of buying the car, he discovered that the car began vibrating badly at speeds over 60 m.p.h. and drifting to the left, so that he had to exert substantial effort to keep the car within its lane. He returned it to the dealer, who said the alignment was off. After three days, he picked up the car, but he found that the car still had the same problems. He returned it to the dealer, who kept it for fifteen days, making various repairs. When he picked it up the second time, he took the car onto the highway to test it and found that it had the same problems. He returned it immediately to the dealer, who kept it for another eighteen days making additional repairs. Nevertheless, when Fautz picked up his car on October 25, the problems remained.

Fautz wrote a letter to Xeron Motors on November 1 asking for a replacement vehicle. After summarizing the problem and the efforts of the dealer, the letter stated, "This sports car is a lemon. I want a replacement vehicle within 30 days or I'll sue."

On December 15, Fautz filed a complaint against Xeron Motors *pro se*, citing the Lemon Law statute. Xeron filed a motion for summary judgment, arguing that Fautz had not provided adequate notice to invoke the Lemon Law. On Fautz's behalf, we will argue that his letter did provide adequate notice because it specified that he wanted a replacement vehicle and because he referred to the car as a "lemon." His letter thus logically implied that he was invoking the statute and that he was offering to return title of the defective car to Xeron.

Revising the Argument

To make the Argument more persuasive, you can apply the same structural techniques and same process you used when revising the Statement of Facts. When drafting the Argument, chose the legal arguments you wanted to emphasize or de-emphasize. Now you can

(1) revise your thesis sentences,

(2) move unfavorable points out of positions of emphasis,

(3) use other writing techniques to create that emphasis or de-emphasis on remaining key points, and

(4) revise the rest of the Argument so it fits smoothly around these revised sentences.

■ Revising Thesis Sentences

Clear thesis sentences can communicate the organization of the Argument, just as they did in your Discussion. In an Argument, the thesis sentences state the strong points of your argument. To check your thesis sentence, read them sequentially, without the supporting text, to make sure they flow together smoothly and logically.

As you do this, also check to make sure the thesis sentences state your position affirmatively. For example, when presenting the legal standard you want the court to use, begin each paragraph with a statement about the law that favors your client's position. Avoid starting a paragraph with the opposition's position, as the following paragraph does. In this paragraph, the writer's position does not appear until the italicized sentence late in the paragraph, and then it is stated negatively rather than affirmatively.

Example, Ineffective Placement of Thesis Sentence

To complain about the illegality of a search, the defendant must have an expectation of privacy in the place searched. *United States v. Miller*, 425 U.S. 435, 436 (1976); *United States v. Robinson*, 414 U.S. 218, 219, (1973). Although the defendant's office, desk, and files were within a public building, *this is not sufficient to invalidate his expectation of privacy.* The uncontroverted testimony in this case indicates that the Defendant did expect his office, desk, and files to be private. Furthermore, he exercised exclusive use and control over these areas and things present in those areas, and so his expectation of privacy was reasonable. (R. 207-09).

To begin the paragraph affirmatively, the writer can reword the thesis sentence.

Example, Effective Placement of Thesis Sentence

A warrantless search is illegal when it is conducted in an area where the defendant has an expectation of privacy. United States v. Miller, 425 U.S. 435, 436, (1976); *United States v. Robinson*, 414 U.S. 218, 219, (1973). The State implies that because the defendant's office, desk, and files were within a public building, he knowingly exposed them to the public. This is simply not the fact in this case. The uncontroverted testimony in this case indicates that the defendant did expect his office, desk, and files to be private and that he exercised exclusive use and control over these areas and things present in those areas. (R. 207-09).

■ Moving Unfavorable Points out of Positions of Emphasis

Although you must not overlook the opposition's arguments, avoid giving those arguments undue emphasis. To make sure you have done this, find statements in the Argument about the opposition's contentions and make sure that they appear within the body of paragraphs, rather than in thesis sentences. Also make sure that the contentions are not given more explanation than the counterarguments to those contentions. Just as you placed unfavorable facts in a context that made them seem less unfavorable, you want to place unfavorable arguments in a context that minimizes their impact. Sometimes you can do this by relegating the opposition's argument to a dependent clause.

Example, Effective Handling of Opposing Point

The defendant had a valid expectation of privacy with respect to the contents of his desk at work. *Although the State implied that the defendant knowingly exposed files in his desk to the public,* the defendant's uncontroverted testimony contradicts that implication. When asked about his expectation, the defendant . . . .

Sometimes you may need to spend a whole sentence explaining the opposition's position.

Example, Effective Handling of Opposing Point

A warrantless search is illegal when it is conducted in an area where the defendant has an expectation of privacy. *United States v. Miller*, 425 U.S. 435, 436, (1976); *United States v. Robinson*, 414 U.S. 218, 219, (1973). *The State implies that because the defendant's office, desk, and files were within a public building, he knowingly exposed them to the public.* But the uncontroverted testimony in this case indicates that the defendant did expect his office, desk, and files to be private and that he exercised exclusive use and control over these areas and things present in those areas. (R. 207-09).

Avoid, however, giving the opposition a whole paragraph or more of your Argument's space, as happens when the following sentence structures are used for a defendant's argument.

Examples, Ineffective Handling of Opposing Point

The plaintiff contends that . . . .

This argument, however, is in error because . . . .

Avoid setting out the opposition's position before your own. Instead, begin with your client's position.

Often much of this revision already occurred when you revised the thesis sentences. For example, as you revise the thesis sentence to remove unfavorable information, you will also relegate the opposition's position to a reference within the middle of the paragraph.

■ Emphasizing Key Points

You can also add emphasis to your Argument by revising individual sentence structures and wording, using techniques similar to those used in the Statement of Facts. Those techniques include

• placing the point in the beginning or end of a sentence,

• placing the point in a short sentence, and

• describing a fact in more concrete or specific wording.

These techniques can be used to make certain themes, legal points, or facts stand out in the Argument. Just as you did in the Statement of Facts, use these techniques on a few main points and avoid overdoing your emphasis.

■ *Placing the Point in the Beginning or End of a Sentence*

Placing key language at the beginning of a sentence gets that information into the reader's mind early, before other detail clutters the picture.

Example, Effective Sentence

Petrov's territorial limit is unreasonable because it extends beyond the geographic area Ms. Dominski actually served.

This structure also can be effective in a thesis sentence, where it gains additional emphasis.

Placing the information at a sentence's end creates a punch line. This can be effective at the end of a line of reasoning. It is most effective when the subject and verb come at the end of a sentence, after an introductory phrase, and when that ending phrase is relatively short.

Examples, Effective Sentence

Just as Nalco's restriction was broader than needed to protect Nalco's legitimate interests, *Petrov's covenant is broader than needed.*

This structure is not as dramatic as a short sentence, but for that reason it can be used more often without straining credibility.

■ *Placing the Point in a Short Sentence*

For a stronger emphasis, place information in a short sentence. This can add emphasis to a legal conclusion or a point of law.

Examples, Effective Short Sentences

Ms. Dominski meets this standard.

Petrov's covenant fails two parts of the test.

Citing Wisconsin cases and a law review article, the court summarized this policy: *"The disapproval . . . is not secret."*

Using a short sentence in an Argument often requires some preparation. Few points can be stated simply, so using a short sentence often is a matter of dividing a longer sentence into two. For example, the following sentence adds emphasis at the end in a short phrase.

Example, Effective Sentence

Although Quinn could have created reasonable territorial limits, it did not.

If the writer wanted to emphasize the point even more, he or she might divide the sentence.

Example, Effective Short Sentence

Quinn could have created reasonable territorial limits for its covenant not to compete. *But it did not.*

■ Describing a Fact in More Concrete or Specific Wording

This technique usually happens naturally as you include specific facts about relevant points of law.

Example, Effective Sentences

Under that covenant, employees leaving Nalco could not *"for the period of two (2) years immediately after its termination, engage or assist in the same or any similar line of business . . . ."* *Id.* This restriction was ruled overbroad because Nalco was a large company including *twelve major work divisions and dealing in several aspects of handling water.*

If you have supported your statements about the law and explained your reasoning adequately, you may have already used this technique. But check for places where your vigilance may have lapsed.

As you interweave your use of these techniques into your writing, you refine the initial draft and increase its persuasiveness. A series of small changes creates a significant overall improvement.

Applying What You Have Learned

Exercise 9-4
Revising for Persuasion

The following paragraphs bury their persuasive points rather than organizing around them. Review the background information below to become familiar with the overall argument. Then decide how you would revise the Argument paragraphs. (These paragraphs follow the background information.) In those paragraphs, underline the persuasive points that should be emphasized. Prepare to explain your choices to the class.

After you have decided which points to emphasize, revise the Argument using the techniques illustrated previously.

[overview of relevant facts]

Mr. Baker was injured while sitting on a bench placed at the edge of a football field in an Outagamie County park. Mr. Baker is now suing the County, arguing that it is liable for his injuries. When the injury occurred, Mr. Baker was watching high school students playing flag football at an open gym, which Outagamie County allowed to be held in the park each August. All the players in this game were members of the local high school football team, and their coach was also present. The players were not, however, suited up in their uniforms or practice gear, and they were not required to attend. The open gym was also open to any high school students, although only the football team members had come to play.

[procedural posture of the brief]

Based on undisputed facts, Outagamie County has made a prima facie case that this case should be dismissed because Outagamie County has recreational immunity as a matter of law under the Recreational Use Statute, Wisconsin Statutes Section 895.52(2)(a)(1)(2005-06).

[overview of argument]

Wisconsin's recreational use statute grants immunity to landowners for injuries occurring on their land as a result of recreational activities. Wis. Stat. § 895.52(2)(a)(1)(2005-06). A recreational activity is defined as "any outdoor activity undertaken for the purpose of exercise, recreation or pleasure, including practice or instruction in any such activity." Wis. Stat. § 895.52(1)(g). Also, participating as a spectator at a recreational activity is a recreational activity. *Meyer v. Sch. Dist. Of Colby*, 226 Wis. 2d 704, 710, 595 N.W.2d 339, 342 (1999).

The open gym at which Baker was injured falls within the definition of recreational activity. Wis. Stat. § 895, 52(1)(g). The undisputed facts show that the gym involved an outdoor game (Baker Dep. 2:51) undertaken for the purposes of bonding and practicing the player's skills. (Baker Dep. 1:30-33.) As a spectator at the open gym, Mr. Baker was thus participating in a recreational activity at the time of his injury. Thus, Outagamie County is entitled to recreational immunity as a matter of law. *Id.*

[relevant point heading]

II. OUTAGAMIE COUNTY IS IMMUNE FROM LIABILITY UNDER WISCONSIN STATUTE SECTION 895.52(2)(a)(1) BECAUSE THE OPEN GYM WAS A RECREATIONAL ACTIVITY AND DID NOT FALL UNDER THE ORGANIZED TEAM SPORT ACTIVITY EXCEPTION.

Example, Argument Paragraphs for Revision

Wisconsin's recreational immunity statute does, as the Plaintiff argues, provide an exception to recreational immunity when the activity is an "[o]rganized team sport activity sponsored by owner of the property on which the activity takes place." *Id.* Three requirements must be met to invoke this exception: (1) that the landowner owned the land, (2) that the activity was an organized team sport activity and (3) that the landowner sponsored the activity. Wis. Stat. § 895.52(1)(g)(2005-06). Other than this exception, however, the statute grants immunity to landowners from others injured on their land during a recreational activity. *Id.* § 895.52(2)(a)(1). The purpose behind the statute is to encourage landowners to allow others to use their land for recreation without fear of tort liability. 1983 Wis. Act. 418, §1.

The Plaintiff argues that all three requirements of the exception were met by undisputed facts. The Plaintiff also incorrectly argues that Outagamie County sponsored this event solely by allowing it to take place on their property and by providing a bench for participants to sit on. As shown below, however, the second and third requirements necessary to invoke this exception cannot be met by the undisputed facts of this case. The second requirement is not met because the open gym was a recreational activity, lacking the organization and qualities inherent in organized team sports. (Holt Dep. 3:129-30.) The third requirement is not met because Outagamie County did not sponsor the open gym. Finally, the legislative intent behind the statute and public policy both support granting immunity to the County. 1983 Wis. Acts 418, § 1.

A. The Undisputed Facts Show, as a Matter of Law, that the Open Gym at Issue was Not an Organized Team Sport Activity Because It Lacked the Organization and Competitive Qualities Inherent in Organized Team Sports.

When determining whether an activity is recreational, courts look at "all aspects of the activity," including the activity's nature and purpose. *Meyer*, 226 Wis. 2d at 712, 595 N.W.2d at 343 (quoting *Linville v. City of Janesville*, 174 Wis. 2d 571, 579-80, 497 N.W.2d 465, 469 (Ct. App. 1993)). Wisconsin precedent distinguishes between recreational activities, such as company picnic softball games, and organized team sports activities, such as regular season school and league games. *Kostroski v. County of Marathon*, 158 Wis. 2d 201, 203, 462 N.W.2d 542, 543 (Ct. App. 1990); *Meyer*, 226 Wis. 2d at 710, 595 N.W.2d at 342; *Hupf v. City of Appleton*, 165 Wis. 2d 215, 218, 477 N.W.2d 69, 70 (Ct. App. 1991). The undisputed facts demonstrate that the open gym at which Mr. Baker was injured was a recreational activity. (Baker Dep. 2:73; Sullivan Dep. 1:31-34; Holt Dep. 3:134-36.)

Courts have applied the exception to cases where a spectator was injured while watching a junior varsity football game and where a player was injured after his league softball game. *Meyer*, 226 Wis. 2d at 710, 595 N.W.2d at 342; *Hupf*, 165 Wis. 2d at 218, 477 N.W.2d at 70. At such events, however, attendance is mandatory and players are provided with team uniforms, protective padding, coaches, referees, and scorekeepers. Also, admission fees, concessions, and an abundance of spectators are all commonplace at league and high school games. Application of the organized team sport activity exception has therefore been limited to cases where the activity at issue involved regular season school or league play between competitive teams. *Meyer*, 226 Wis. 2d at 710; *Hupf*, 165 Wis. 2d at 218, 477 N.W.2d at 70.

In *Kostroski*, a spectator was injured at her company picnic softball game. *Kostroski*, 158 Wis. 2d at 203, 462 N.W.2d at 543. In deciding this case, the court reasoned that the atmosphere at such events is generally relaxed and noncompetitive. *Id.* Participants are usually not provided with team uniforms, coaches, umpires, or scorekeepers. *Id.* Furthermore, one would not expect to pay admission at a company picnic softball game. *Id.* The court, therefore, did not apply the organized team sport activity exception. *Id.* The court explained that courts do not apply the organized team sport activity exception to cases involving randomly attended games undertaken for pleasure. *Id.*

— *Figure 9-5* —

CHECKLIST FOR REVISING THE ARGUMENT

1. Revise thesis sentences to state your position affirmatively.

2. Move unfavorable information out of positions of emphasis.

3. Emphasize other key points.

   • Place the point in the beginning or end of a sentence.

   • Place the point in a short sentence.

   • Describe the fact in more concrete or specific wording.

Unifying the Brief

When your revisions are complete, review all the components within the brief to clarify your organization, underscore your main points, and unify the whole document. Compare the Argument and Statement of Facts to be sure both sections present congruent facts. This unifying detail creates a clearer image of the situation in your reader's mind.

To do this, print out the draft and compare the Argument and Statement of Facts side by side. For example, highlight all the facts that appear in the Argument and then read the Statement of Facts to make sure each of those facts is included there. Although the Statement of Facts includes facts that are not specifically used in the Argument, it should not include superfluous information.

Delete any facts that are not needed for clarity, sympathy, or legal relevance. The court will appreciate this efficiency, and the remaining facts will gain emphasis.

Similarly, make sure the Issues and Point Headings are congruent with the Argument. Compare your Issues to your Point Headings and to the Argument's thesis sentences. The words used to describe the law and the facts in your Issues should echo the words used in the Argument. This repetition of key words will help the reader remember those key concepts. Finally, check the overview paragraph and the Conclusion to make sure they are similarly congruent. When all the parts of the brief to a trial court are unified, the reader will better understand and remember the content.

— *FIGURE 9-6* —
CHECKLIST FOR UNIFYING THE BRIEF

1. Compare your Argument and Statement of Facts to be sure both sections present congruent facts.

   • Make sure that the Statement of Facts includes every fact used in the Argument.

   • Delete any facts in the Statement of Facts that are not needed for clarity, sympathy, or legal relevance.

2. Make sure your Issues and Point Headings are congruent with your Argument.

   • Use key legal terms and other words that are used in the Argument.

3. Make sure your overview paragraph and Conclusion are similarly congruent.

10

Preparing Oral Arguments

ALTHOUGH MUCH OF your effectiveness as an attorney depends on writing clearly and accurately, sometimes you must depend on oral skill as well. Usually the skill needed is not the ability to present a great speech, but the ability to participate in and steer a focused conversation.

An oral argument is most often a focused conversation, rather than a speech, because usually the court will interrupt the attorney's presentation to ask a question or make a comment. Rather than being flustered or viewing the court's questions as interruptions, a skilled attorney must view the court's comments as cues from the court that can help the attorney know what the court needs to help it decide in the client's favor.

Understanding the Purpose

If a court requests or grants an oral argument, it is because the judge has questions to ask, colleagues to persuade, or other issues that the written briefs and the judge's own research could not adequately resolve. For example, the attorney may have presented a line of reasoning that appears plausible but has not been used by the court before. The court may want to question the attorney more thoroughly on the argument to test it before basing the decision on that new argument. Or, in the multi-judge panel of a supreme or appellate court, the court may want to hear oral arguments to resolve a difference of opinion between several judges. Thus one judge may ask pointed questions not because he or she questions the reasoning, but because he or she wants to have those points clarified for the other judges.

To be effective in an oral argument, you need to anticipate these questions and recognize them when they occur. To do this, review the case carefully and consider all the questions that might arise, such as the questions listed below.

— *FIGURE 10-1* —
QUESTIONS TO CONSIDER WHEN PREPARING ORAL ARGUMENTS

• What issues will be important to the court?

  – What might be confusing or ambiguous in light of the opposition's arguments?

  – What points might be more controversial because they rely on innovative reasoning?

• What are our strongest arguments?

• What are our weakest?

• What are the opposition's strongest arguments?

• What are their weakest?

Structuring the Components

Although each court determines the structure for its oral arguments, some general patterns exist. Each party's attorney has a limited time to speak, and the court uses some mechanism to show the speakers how much time they have remaining. Some courts use a series of colored lights that indicate how much time is left. Other courts have a timekeeper who briefly interrupts to tell the speaker how much time remains. The parties speak in a predetermined order. For example, at the appellate level, the appellant goes first, the respondent next, with a brief set-aside for the appellant's rebuttal. At the trial court level, the party seeking relief, which is generally the movant, speaks first. The respondent speaks next, although the overall structure of this oral argument is substantially less formal. Sometimes, but not always, the movant has time for a brief rebuttal.

— *FIGURE 10-2* —
ORAL ARGUMENT STRUCTURE

• Case is announced

• Petitioner speaks

• Respondent speaks

• Petitioner rebuts, if time is reserved for this

Court asks questions at any time

When the attorneys speak, they speak to the court, not the opposition. For example, an attorney might begin his or her oral argument by stating the following.

Example, Opening Sentence

May it please the court, I am [name] and I represent [client's name].

When the attorney is the petitioner, he or she may decide to reserve a few minutes for rebuttal.

Example, Reservation for Rebuttal

I would like to reserve two minutes for rebuttal.

The attorney then summarizes the procedural history and his or her key points.

Example, Summary of Facts

Mr. Lundstrom has moved the court to dismiss Mr. Reese's complaint because it fails to state a claim for which relief may be granted. Mr. Reese alleges that he was fired because of age discrimination, but he has alleged no facts supporting his belief. Furthermore, age is not a protected class under the statute on which Mr. Reese relies.

The attorney next asks the court whether it wants a summary of the facts and supplies one if asked. This summary, however, must be only a few sentences long.

Example, Summary of Facts

Mr. Reese worked for approximately two years as a mechanic in Mr. Lundstrom's garage. During the past three months, Mr. Reese had made several costly errors, and Mr. Lundstrom had pointed out these lapses to Mr. Reese. Finally, after Mr. Reese failed to replace a cotter pin, which led to a customer losing a wheel while driving, Mr. Lundstrom fired Mr. Reese. Mr. Reese, who is fifty-seven years old, now claims that the firing was a result of his age, rather than his errors at work.

As you prepare your summaries of the procedure, law, and facts, be prepared to present it more thoroughly if needed. You cannot always assume that the judge, who is busy with many cases, has the particulars of your case readily in mind. The judge may not have had enough time to read your brief as carefully as would be desirable. You may, therefore, need to summarize the argument in your presentation.

After completing this introductory information, you will begin presenting your main points. You must refine the presentation until these main points can be stated in just a few sentences and a few minutes. Although you may have more time to go into detail, that time is not guaranteed. To prepare for this, write out the opening sentences so you can present that information smoothly and concisely. Also practice. Practice enough to be smooth and fluent in your presentation. Note the time it takes you, so you can budget your allotted time adequately.

You probably do not need to write out the body of the argument because you are not likely to present it in one uninterrupted speech. Instead, list the main points, key facts, and key legal authorities in some form that makes them readily accessible. You may note the information on separate cards, so you can move back and forth as needed to answer questions. Or you may prefer to use a legal pad, where all the information can be available on one page. Use the method that is most comfortable for you.

After you have prepared your notes, practice using them. Practice in front of a mirror, standing as you will in the courtroom. Practice in front of friends or colleagues and have them ask questions that occur to them. Rehearse just as you would to prepare for a sporting event, a recital, or a performance of any kind.

Handling Questions

Sooner or later during your oral argument, the court will interrupt to ask a question. The question could be general or specific. For example, the court might quiz Mr. Lundstrom's attorney about the disputability of the facts Reese cited as supporting his age discrimination claim. The court might also inquire about the legal standard on a motion holding and point out that the motion goes no further than the four corners of the complaint. To a great extent, this is when the work of the oral argument really begins. The oral argument begins addressing issues that the briefs alone could not. If you have anticipated these questions, you will be able to show how your position should, nevertheless, prevail.

You must accept the interruption with grace. The attorney must stop talking immediately when the court begins to speak, even if he or she was interrupted mid-sentence. The attorney must also begin listening immediately, listening for clues about the court's concern. Avoid resenting the interruption and avoid feeling defensive, because it will make it hard for you to focus on listening. Remember that the judge may be trying to help you make your case more persuasive. Alternatively, the judge may honestly not understand your argument and may be asking questions to reach that understanding. It is extremely rare for a judge to want to embarrass an attorney. Always assume good will on the part of the court. You will probably be right, and you will be more likely to see what information the court needs.

To help yourself switch into a listening mode, you can classify the kind of question the court is asking. For example, the court may be asking for clarification or more explanation on a particular point. It may want more information about the facts, precedent opinions, or their reasoning. Alternatively, the court may want a clearer sense of the overall, big picture of the law. Or the court may be exploring a question that you can identify as a red herring, or a question that is not in reality a concern in this case.

— *FIGURE 10-3* —
QUESTIONS TO HELP YOU LISTEN TO THE COURT

- Does the court want me to clarify something I just said?

- Is the court asking me to explain one particular point in more detail?

- Does the court want me to give it more information about
    – the facts of this case,
    – the facts of a precedent case, or
    – the reasoning in a precedent case?

- Is the court asking for me to explain the big picture?

Address the court's question directly and then return to your main point, tying the two together logically if you can. One way to do this is to use the question's language as you begin your answer. If you do not understand the court's question, you may ask the court for clarification.

Examples, Rephrasing Language from the Question

One precedent opinion that used this reasoning was . . . .

Although "age" is indeed an immutable trait, it is not included in the list of traits that are considered protected classes, as are gender, race, ethnicity, . . .

After answering a question, return to your presentation, continuing until the court again interrupts you with a question.

As you see that you have only one minute remaining, begin summarizing your main points. You may want write out this summary because it will be only two or three sentences long. If you finish before your time ends, simply sit down. You show confidence by showing that you know when you have made your case.

Organizing the Oral Argument

To organize the body of your oral argument, you may begin with a shorter version of your written argument, but you probably do not want to settle for that alone. Instead, select one or two key points to drive home. While a written brief is an ideal place to set out ideas that may need to be reviewed or studied in detail, an oral argument is the ideal place to emphasize central images and ideas.

When you select the key points to emphasize in your oral argument, you can rule out certain kinds of points. Rule out weaker alternative arguments that you added just for extra support or fall back points. Also omit sympathetic facts that are not central or relevant to your critical points. Omit technical procedural points that are not debatable. Also omit other minor or settled elements or points of law. As you remove points that are necessary but not central to your case, you will find it easier to see what is important.

From the remaining information, consider what is most likely to make a judge want to find in favor of your client. Are there key facts that make a decision in your client's favor a matter of good social policy? If so, work those into your reasoning. Are there legal issues involved that reach beyond this case? Include reasoning related to those points if you think the judge will be concerned about them.

The hardest step in organizing your argument may be making the final choices of those few points that you will emphasize. Resist the urge to throw in all your good arguments. In speaking, emphasizing many points means you are emphasizing nothing. You need to settle on one or two points that are most important.

When you have determined what your main points are, marshal all the information you have so that you can retrieve it easily when you need it to answer questions. Whether you use file cards or file folders or legal pads, you want to have the information ready to grab when you need it. Use highlighting, tabs, post-it attachments, and other visual tools to help you see the information quickly. Consider writing information in short phrases rather than complete sentences. This structure makes it easier for you to find the information quickly.

Know your support well. You need not memorize your information in a certain order. But you do need to know the law, the precedent, the facts, and the procedural history of your case. Have all this information organized so you can retrieve and summarize whatever you need.

— *FIGURE 10-4* —
PARTS OF AN OPENING STATEMENT IN AN ORAL ARGUMENT

PORTION	STRUCTURE	EXAMPLE
Identify speaker	One sentence	May it please the court, I am Michelle Faraday and I represent Mr. Lundstrom.
Procedural History	One sentence	Mr. Lundstrom has moved the court to dismiss Mr. Reese's complaint because it fails to state a claim for which relief may be granted.
Overview of your main points	One to three sentences listing your two main points	Mr. Reese's complaint alleges that he was fired because of discrimination based on his age, but he has alleged no facts supporting his belief. Furthermore, age is not a protected class under the statute on which Mr. Reese relies.

Portion	Structure	Example
Query regarding facts	Question to court about information it wants	Would you like for me to summarize the facts of the case?
Summary of facts, if court wants it	Two to four sentences summarizing the facts	Mr. Reese worked for approximately two years as a mechanic in Mr. Lundstrom's garage. During the past three months, Mr. Reese had made several costly errors in his work, and Mr. Lundstrom had pointed out these lapses to Mr. Reese. Finally, after Mr. Reese's failure to replace a cotter pin led to a customer losing a wheel while driving, Mr. Lundstrom fired Mr. Reese. Mr. Reese, who is 57 years old, now claims that the firing was a result of his age, rather than of the errors Mr. Reese made in his work.

Looking and Acting the Part

One additional component of preparation involves your appearance and demeanor. For example, avoid distractions in your appearance when dressing for an oral argument, such as elaborate jewelry or loud ties. Dress professionally. In your demeanor, avoid distracting behaviors such as fiddling with your hair, saying "uh," or fidgeting. For a professional appearance, maintain good posture, eye contact with the judges, and a clear, respectful tone of voice.

As part of your demeanor, you need to observe a few particular rules and customs. When addressing judges, use the term "your honor," even if you know the judge personally. When the judge interrupts you, stop talking. You may ask the judge for permission to finish your sentence, but you must then stop immediately. When your time ends, stop talking immediately, even if you are not done. Time limits in oral argument are strict. Remain calm and respectful at all times. Do not allow yourself to become angry or agitated, even if the other attorney or the judge becomes agitated.

— *FIGURE 10-5* —
DO'S AND DON'TS OF COURT ROOM MANNERS

Do	Don't
Address the court as "your honor"	Use the judge's personal name
Stop talking when the court starts talking	Interrupt a judge, even when the judge interrupted you
Keep your voice clear and even	Shout or raise your voice
Remain respectful and calm, even if a judge or opposing attorney becomes hostile	Show anger toward the court
Pause to think	Say "uh" to fill empty space
Breathe	Hyper-ventilate and risk fainting
Stop talking when your time ends	Ignore statements that your time has ended
Remain calm and attentive when asked questions	Appear outraged or defensive in response to hard questions

11

Corresponding with Clients and Lawyers

NOW THAT YOU HAVE LEARNED the basics of writing for legal readers, we return to a more familiar kind of writing: composing letters, e-mail, and other business correspondence to clients and lawyers. When corresponding with non-lawyers, you will again use general vocabulary more than specialized legal terms. You will be concerned about an appealing tone and readability, and you will return to familiar formats for the documents. When writing to lawyers, you will include the technical, legal vocabulary you have gained but will still use the general tone and organization of business correspondence.

Even though correspondence is more familiar, corresponding as a lawyer involves concerns that differ from those you had before studying law. Now you are writing as an attorney. As an attorney, you have a special obligation; you write with the legal profession looking over your shoulder. Your letters blend legal concerns of accuracy and thoroughness with the broader concerns of tone and readability. This blending makes the task of writing correspondence complex and interesting.

The Purpose of Correspondence

Correspondence generally conveys two messages: the actual information and the writer's attitude toward the reader. The purpose of most correspondence is to communicate information. But correspondence is sent from one person to another, so it also conveys the writer's attitude toward the reader. This function is not predominant in other legal documents.

■ Conveying Information

Regarding the information to be conveyed, the legal writer's main concern is communicating that information accurately and clearly. Many of the writing techniques you will use have been covered in the previous chapters on legal research memo organization and revision; you can now apply them to correspondence.

To communicate clearly, organize the content effectively. This effective organization often begins with a list of the information you need to include. Then, when you see all the needed information listed before, decide how to best order that information. Group the content in a way that is logical for your reader. For example, if you are asking a client to provide information needed to prepare a will, you might group the requests by the source of the information, so that your reader can collect the needed information more easily. Thus you might group all the requests that could be answered based on information from an employer, such as life insurance through work, retirement benefits, income continuation benefits, and tax sheltered savings accounts. You might then have other groups for insurance purchased by the client, savings outside of work, accounts with banks, and so on. Although for your purposes you may eventually group this information by the nature of the benefit, grouping it by the information's source may be much more useful to your reader.

After listing the content and determining its order, draft the body of the letter so that it explains that content step by step in language the reader can understand. Avoid using legal terms unnecessarily. If you must use a legal term that your reader will not understand, insert a definition right after the term. Throughout this process, you can rely on the same writing techniques you used to clarify your legal research memo, techniques listed in Chapter 5.

■ Communicating Your Relationship with the Reader

Regarding your attitude toward the reader, your main concern is communicating respect through a business-like yet friendly tone. This tone is somewhat less conversational than face-to-face conversations, but it is more informal than a stand-up presentation to a group of your colleagues.

This tone is created in the opening sentences of the correspondence and reinforced in the concluding paragraph. To create the best tone, avoid extremes of either a chatty tone, which would be too informal, or a cold, impersonal tone, which would be too formal. To appear credible and sincere, make sure the tone of the final paragraph matches the tone of the opening paragraph.

Example, Too Chatty and Informal in Tone

Here's that will you asked for, John. Could you give it a once over right away? Then, if anything bugs you about it or if you have questions, shoot them my way ASAP and I'll get back to you.

Example, Too Cold and Formal in Tone

Enclosed please find a draft revision of your last will and testament, per your request of the tenth of September, 2007. This will and testament should be perused thoroughly at your earliest convenience. Any questions or concerns about this draft should be communicated to my office as soon as reasonably possible so that an answer can be prepared and subsequently provided to you for your use as appropriate.

■■

Example, Business-like Yet Friendly in Tone

> With this letter, I am enclosing a draft of your will, revised as you requested when we met on September 15, 2007. Please review this draft carefully at your earliest convenience and contact me if you have any further questions. After we have resolved any remaining questions, we can then . . . .

Although words create the wrong tone when they are either overly informal or overly formal, using both informal and formal words in the same document creates another problem. When writers shift between levels of formality within a document, readers usually notice the inconsistency and become uneasy. The reader, sensing an inconsistency in the way the writer is relating to the reader, can begin to question the writer's sincerity and trustworthiness. Even if the reader does not question the writer's trustworthiness, he or she will usually see the writer as less skilled, less in control, and therefore less professional. For example, the following sentences exhibit inconsistent tone. Informal language is **bold**; overly formal language is *italicized*.

Example, Inconsistent Tone

> *Pursuant to Florida Statute Xx.x*, Ms. Jascoviak, **you could maybe claim** that the cruise line breached its contract when it denied you the right to *renegotiate the aforesaid contract's* departure time *as per* its promise. Another claim **I came up with** was . . . .

> This memo *is not definitive of* your options. Finding a cause of action *upon which to rest* your claim **could turn out to be a big job** based on my research *thus far*. **I did find some things that seem to be hinting at something feasible.**

Example, Consistent Tone

> Under Florida statutory law, you could claim that the cruise line breached its contract when it denied you the right to change your departure time as promised. You could also claim that . . . .

> You may, however, have other options, such as . . . .

Usually these revisions for even tone also create a more concise text, an added benefit.

The dual messages of content and tone exist in all forms of correspondence, such as letters, e-mail, and inter-office memos. What changes with each form of correspondence is simply the way those purposes are achieved. Even then, the organization of these different forms of correspondence presents several variations on one common organizational theme.

<u>Applying What You Have Learned</u>

Exercise 11-1
Revising a Letter for Tone

The following letter contains language that is both too formal and too informal. Underline the phrases that cause these problems. Then revise the wording to create a consistent tone that is business-like yet friendly.

Blum, Hankley, and Vedvig
Attorneys at Law
June Hankley, Atty.

October 4, 2007

Alden Aspenhoe
Aspenhoe Construction
4514 Caledonia Ave.
Garden City, KS

Dear Mr. Aspenhoe:

Per our agreement, you're going to find copies of Ingerfelder's recent motions attached to this file. You don't need to worry about these motions; they are just part of the usual legal stuff filed in the process of litigation. Subsequent paragraphs in this document elucidate the contents of said motions.

One of the motions enclosed is a Motion to State Particulars. This is just a fishing expedition on the part of the defense, who is attempting to anticipate the strategy of our case. Rest assured that this legerdemain will not be successful, and we will proceed with discovery, the legal fact finding process used by the court to clear up the issues before trial commences.

Another motion is . . . .

Should you have any questions about the contents of this letter, please direct said inquiries to my staff at 555-9492. We are honored to serve you and look forward to sticking it to these deadbeat defendants in the court room.

Very truly yours,

June Hankley, Esq.

Composing Letters

To convey clear information and appropriate attitude in your letters, look first to the letter's organization. When the organization is clear, it is a much easier matter to check the wording and sentence structure and adjust it to achieve an appropriate attitude toward the reader.

For the letter's overall organization, use the same format you would use in any business letter. These business letters usually include a subject line before the salutation. Like most business letters, the paragraphs are usually shorter than those of a more formal document, such as a legal research memo's Discussion. If the letter is several pages long, it may include sub-headings to show how the body of the letter is organized and to help the reader move easily through the letter. The letter's length varies depending on the amount of content, and the letter ends with a closing and signature, as other letters.

Within this format lies the main text of the letter, which has three general parts: the opening paragraph, the body of the letter, and the closing paragraph. The opening paragraph familiarizes the reader with the writer and the purpose of the letter. It usually also states the letter's main point. The body of the letter contains the information the client needs, and it is rather neutral in tone. The closing paragraph closes politely and provides any final information the reader may need to take action, if any is required. The beginning and closing paragraphs, bracketing the body of the letter, communicate the writer's attitude toward the reader. In shorter letters, these opening and closing paragraphs shrink in size, sometimes reducing to a single sentence rather than a paragraph.

— *FIGURE 11-1* —
LETTER TO A CLIENT

EXPLANATION

Weide, Ortiz, and Wehrle
Attorneys at Law
944 Anderson Avenue, West Bend, WI

Atty. Consuela Ortiz

Addresses and Date

January 6, 2008

Ms. Angela Elsmere
458 Stevens Court
West Bend, WI

Subject line

RE: Claim against Aunt Iona's Kitchen Restaurant

Salutation

Dear Ms. Elsmere:

Opening paragraph

As I mentioned in our phone conversation on January 4, I am writing to you to explain the details of the settlement offer Aunt Iona's Kitchen is offering to compensate you for the food poisoning you suffered on November 28, 2007. Although it is a substantial offer,

Main Point

I recommend that you reject the offer for the reasons explained below.

Body of letter

Specifically, Aunt Iona's Kitchen is offering you . . . .

Closing paragraph

In summary, I recommend rejecting the offer at this time. The decision, of course, is yours to make. At your earliest convenience, please contact my office for an appointment. At that meeting, we can discuss the settlement offer, resolve any questions you have, and decide how to proceed.

Closing and Signature

Sincerely,

Consuela Ortiz, Esq.

Added Information

Encl.

If visuals help you understand an overall idea, you may find it helpful to think of letters as having an umbrella structure, as the following diagram illustrates.

— FIGURE 11-2 —

DIAGRAM OF A LETTER'S STRUCTURE

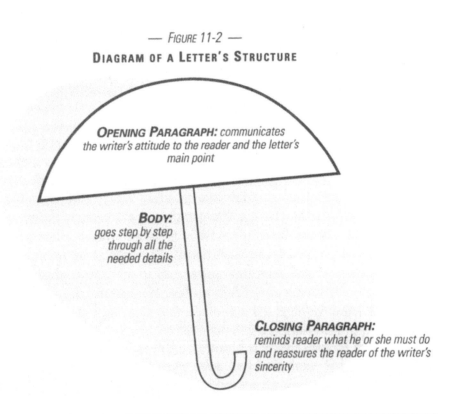

OPENING PARAGRAPH: communicates the writer's attitude to the reader and the letter's main point

BODY: goes step by step through all the needed details

CLOSING PARAGRAPH: reminds reader what he or she must do and reassures the reader of the writer's sincerity

As with other documents, the letter does not need to be written in the order in which the parts finally appear. For example, it may be more efficient to write the body of the letter first, so you can focus on the content before worrying about the details of tone. But for simplicity, the parts are discussed here in the order in which they appear.

The Opening Paragraph

How you structure the opening paragraph depends on the kind of information you are conveying to the reader. When you are conveying good news, the paragraph is easy to write. You can simply start with that news.

Examples, Sentences Introducing Good News

I am pleased to offer you a position as summer law clerk with our firm.

ABC Corporation has accepted our settlement offer of $4 million for your claim against them.

After presenting the basic news, you present the needed explanation in the body of the letter.

If you are requesting information or action from your client, you can begin by focusing on the reasons the client would want to provide the information.

Examples, Sentence Introducing a Request

Before I begin negotiating with ABC Corporation for a settlement to your claim, I want to be sure that I take into account all the losses you have suffered as a result of your injury. To make sure I have all the relevant information, please . . . .

By beginning from the reader's point of view, you communicate to the client that you have his or her interests in mind more than your own, that you are acting as the client's advocate. You also provide the client with motivation to meet your request soon because the client sees how it will be to his or her benefit.

If you are giving the client bad news, you can include a sentence or two that introduces the situation before delivering the bad news itself.

Thank you for taking the time to apply for a clerking position at our firm. We received many strong applications for these positions, and for that reason cannot offer you an interview at this time. . . .

Yesterday we met for two hours with the attorneys for ABC Corporation, attempting to negotiate a suitable settlement for your claim without requiring you to undergo the stress and expense of a trial. However, ...

The client will probably sense that bad news is coming, so do not spend more than a few sentences on this introductory information. Nevertheless, a little introduction can soften the effect of the bad news.

The Body

Most of the time, the body of the letter communicates further explanation of the main point made in the opening paragraph. As described earlier in this chapter, your organization moves through all the needed information, which you may have written in a list as you prepared to write your letter.

Your organization and the sequence of the items on the list should follow the organization that will be clearest and most convenient for the reader. This organization is often different from the first order that occurs to you as you list the points. Thus it is important to take a moment to reorganize the list for the reader's benefit. Taking the time to reorganize this way is the key factor in making the body of the letter appealing to the reader. In the body, organization creates the business-like yet friendly tone that you want in your letter overall.

As you explain all the content on your list, make sure the words you use will be clear to the reader. One of the most frequent complaints clients have about lawyers is that they use words the clients cannot understand. Whenever possible, avoid using unfamiliar legal or other technical terms. When you do need to use legal or other unfamiliar terms, include definitions of those terms.

When you need to include a definition, you can do so without making the letter seem awkward. To accomplish this task, first organize the sentence so that the term to be defined appears toward the end of the sentence.

If necessary, we will file a demurer.

Then add the needed definition as a phrase at the end of the sentence

> *If necessary, we will file a demurer, or* . . . .

If the definition is longer, you can add it in a following sentence.

> *The next step would be asking the court for an Order to Quash. An Order to Quash is* . . . .

The Closing Paragraph

The closing paragraph echoes the tone established in the opening. If the closing paragraph were to shift to a different tone, the reader would become confused about the writer's real attitude. If, however, the tone is consistent, then the reader is reassured that the writer is consistent, sincere, and trustworthy.

The closing paragraph often includes some final, needed information. For example, the closing paragraph usually includes an offer to provide further information.

> *If you have any questions about these recommendations, please feel free to contact me.*

The paragraph may also remind the reader of any action he or she needs to take.

> *Please contact me within a day or two to let me know if you want to accept ABC's offer.*

It may include directions about decisions the reader needs to make or steps the reader needs to take.

> *To complete the settlement process, please contact our office to arrange an appointment. Before we meet, please review the enclosed documents. If you have any questions about any of the information in the documents or about the settlement itself, we can discuss those during our appointment.*

As in the opening paragraph, keep the reader's interest in mind and focus the sentences on that reader. Returning to this focus reminds the client that you have his or her best interests at heart.

This general structure adapts to many different writing situations, as the following chart illustrates.

— FIGURE 11-3 —

HOW THE THREE-PART STRUCTURE APPLIES TO VARIOUS TYPES OF LETTERS

Kind of Letter	1. Orient the Reader	2. Deliver the Message	3. Close Consistently
Giving good news	State the news	Elaborate as needed	Close politely
Answering a request	Refer to request	Answer and explain	Say whom to contact with questions
Making a routine request	Identify self and make request	List what is needed	Thank the reader
Making a special request	Explain why you need this	Make request, with list as needed	Thank the reader and explain how to reach you if there are questions
Giving directions	Overview task	Explain the task step by step	Explain what to do if the reader has problems
Persuading to take action	Refer to background that puts you in a position to recommend	State the recommendation and reasons	Refer to the recommendation and explain the action it would require
Cover letter	Refer to project to which materials relate	List what is enclosed	Close concisely and politely

Kind of Letter	1. *Orient the Reader*	2. *Deliver the Message*	3. *Close Consistently*
Answering a client's complaint	Summarize the complaint	Answer and explain	Explain next step, if appropriate, and close politely
Giving bad news	Establish your role with reader	State the news and explain	Echo the role established in first paragraph

Applying What You Have Learned

Exercise 11-2
Organizing a Letter

Review your most recent legal writing assignment and determine what kind of additional information you might want from your client. Using the organization listed under "making a special request" in the previous chart, draft a letter to the client requesting that information.

— *FIGURE 11-4* —
CHECKLIST FOR WRITING A LETTER

1. List content letter needs to include.

2. Draft the opening paragraph.

– Determine if the letter is conveying good news, requesting information, or conveying bad news.

– If it conveys good news, begin the opening paragraph with that news.

– If it requests information, begin the opening paragraph with an explanation of how providing the information benefits the client.

– If it conveys bad news, begin by introducing the situation in a sentence or two before delivering the bad news.

3. Draft the body of the letter.

- – Order the items on the list in the order most logical to the reader, rather than to you.

- – Especially when writing to non-lawyers, avoid using any terms that would be unfamiliar to the reader.

- – If you must use unfamiliar terms, add a definition after the term.

4. Draft the closing paragraph.

- - Return to the more personal tone of the opening paragraph.

- - Clarify any action the client needs to take.

- - Tell the client how to get answers to any remaining questions.

5. Close politely.

Composing Inter-office Memos

Inter-office memos often function as notes written to a group of people, although they may also be addressed to an individual. These memos usually adopt a more concise, less personal tone than business letters. Nevertheless, they still fulfill the dual purposes of communicating information and attitude toward the reader.

Inter-office memos begin with a standard memo heading, similar to legal research memos. Effective memos get to the main point quickly, either in the first sentence or at least in the first paragraph. The following paragraphs elaborate as needed. In memos running more than one page, sub-headings are often included. The conclusion may be absent or is very brief.

— *Figure 11-5* —
STRUCTURE OF AN INTER-OFFICE MEMO

COMPONENT	EXAMPLE
Heading *Identifies topic and provides basic routing information.*	To: Staff of Kelsey, Parker, & Wyssop From: Peter Parker Date: September 10, 2007 Subject: Staffing Changes
Opening Paragraph *Sets tone and delivers main point*	I am happy to welcome three new paralegals to the firm: Dick Opheim, Jimmy Corneille, and Barbara Stafford. All three will join the support staff pool next Monday. With these three additions, we are back to a full contingent of support staff.
Body *Elaborates as needed on the main point*	Barbara and Jimmy are recent graduates of JACT's paralegal program. Barbara interned with us last summer, while Jimmy interned with the Smallville Public Defender's office. Dick worked previously at Holmes and Moriarty and has four years experience as a paralegal.
Conclusion *Wraps up quickly*	Please join me in welcoming them to our staff.

When writing the opening paragraph, get to your main point quickly but politely. The most common cause of poor inter-office memos is a failure to identify the main point concisely.

Example, Paragraph that does not get to the point concisely

One essential element of a good working team is having plenty of skilled and hard-working support staff. In the last few months, Kelsey, Parker & Wyssop has been lacking in this area, not having adequate staff in terms of paralegal resources. That unfortunate situation, thankfully, will soon be a matter of history. With the addition of three new paralegals to our staff, we should now have support resources that are adequate to meet attorney's needs in terms of both accuracy and efficiency.

Example, Concise Revision

We have just added three new paralegals to our staff: Jimmy Corneille, Dick Opheim, and Barbara Stafford.

Although a concise and appropriate opening often looks obvious and natural to the reader, it usually takes some revision to create. When writing a memo, review your opening paragraph after you have written a complete draft. Spend a few moments cleaning up the opening paragraph, using the same skills you developed for writing effective topic sentences.

In general, the appropriate tone for an inter-office memo is the same as that of a business letter: business-like yet friendly. The memo may be slightly less formal when all the memo's readers know each other well. Nevertheless, it should not become too casual. As in a letter, finding the appropriate tone is a matter of avoiding extremes of being too formal or informal.

Inter-office memos also need to avoid being either too wordy or too cold. When memos take too long to reach the point, they tend to annoy colleagues, even when the memo's tone is warm and friendly. And when a memo sounds cold to the point of seeming rude, it will similarly annoy colleagues, even though the memo communicates the content efficiently and clearly. The following examples illustrate the extremes you want to avoid and the middle path you want to follow.

Example, Too Wordy and Cold in Tone

One essential aspect of efficient office management is the presence of adequate, skilled, and hard-working support staff. Kelsey, Parker & Wyssop has been fortunate in the past to have outstanding legal secretaries, some of whom have been with us for more than a score of years. Recently, however, we have been lacking adequate staff in terms of paralegal resources. That unfortunate situation, thankfully, will soon be a matter of history. With the addition of three new paralegals to our staff, the support resources should now be adequate to meet attorney's needs in terms of both accuracy and efficiency.

Example, Too Wordy and Informal in Tone

Help at last is on the way! You know that we've been looking for some qualified paralegal help for what seems like ages now. Lois, our office manager, has spent hours reviewing hundreds of resumes and interviewing dozens of fresh young faces and experienced pros, and she has finally found three hot prospects for us. Give a warm welcome to Jimmy Corneille, Dick Opheim, and Barbara Stafford.

Example, Concise but Cold Tone

Support staff includes three new paralegals as of Monday: Jimmy Corneille, Dick Opheim, and Barbara Stafford. The staffing should now be adequate to meet your needs.

Example, Concise, Business-like, Yet Friendly in Tone

Please join me in welcoming three new paralegals to the firm: Jimmy Corneille, Dick Opheim, and Barbara Stafford. With these additions to our support staff, we now have adequate personnel to meet your needs.

After you make these edits, you will usually be able to edit the body of the memo for conciseness, and review for technical errors. With those changes, the memo is done and on its way.

Exercise 11-3
Revising an Inter-Office Memo

Revise the following inter-office memo by (1) stating the main point earlier in the memo and (2) revising for an even, appropriate tone.

Blum, Hankley, and Vedvig
Attorneys at Law

TO: All Staff Attorneys
FROM: Marc Vedvig, Managing Partner
DATE: October 10, 2007
SUBJECT: Remodeling Update

Our long awaited remodeling project is well underway, although with the inevitable delays while waiting for subcontractors to complete work or for needed materials to be delivered. Nevertheless, eventually we will have a more efficient and professional looking office and all the inconvenience will have been worth it. The contractor has assured us that the upcoming inconvenience will last no longer than necessary and that all bathrooms will be functioning normally by Oct. 17, one week from today. In the interim, however, we will need to make some adjustments for a few days.

From October 11-14, we will need to shut down one of the office bathrooms while the fixtures are removed and replaced. Therefore, on Monday and Tuesday, the men's bathroom will become a unisex facility. To maintain privacy, we have placed a privacy lock on the inside of the entrance to the bathroom. When you enter the bathroom, you will need to lock the door to insure privacy. As soon as the women's bathroom has been remodeled, that will become a unisex bathroom while the men's bathroom is gutted and remodeled. At that time, you will need to lock the door to the women's bathroom to maintain privacy. As soon as the men's bathroom remodeling is complete, everything will be back to normal.

— *Figure 11-6* —
CHECKLIST FOR WRITING AN INTER-OFFICE MEMO

1. Draft the memo, focusing on including needed content.

2. Put the content in the order most logical to the reader.

3. Determine what the beginning sentences should state and revise or draft those sentences.

   - If the memo is conveying good news or requesting information, state that news or request by the end of the beginning sentence.

   - If the memo conveys bad news, begin by introducing the situation in one sentence, but deliver the bad news by the end of the first paragraph.

4. Draft a subject line that is concise and substantive.

5. Revise the body of the memo for conciseness and accuracy.

6. Check the opening paragraphs in particular for appropriate tone, revising as needed to avoid being too cold or too chatty.

Composing E-mail

E-mail is fundamentally a letter or inter-office memo sent through a different media. The ease of forwarding and speed provided by e-mail, however, creates some special considerations for the legal writer.

E-mail is a relatively new form of correspondence, which creates some risks not present in letters or memos. E-mail does not have as many established traditions of format, organization, or content. That lack of traditions gives the writer more freedom, but also creates more varied expectations from the readers. This variation increases the chance of a writer offending a reader, or at least failing to impress that reader. The chance of problems is also increased because e-mail is extensively used for personal and informal communication. Therefore a writer is more likely to slip into inappropriately informal communication styles, again increasing the chance of offending or failing to impress a reader.

E-mail's speed also creates special risks for the legal writer, particularly when he or she is responding to a previous e-mail. Generally readers expect e-mail to be answered within hours rather than days; lawyers feel more pressure to answer e-mailed legal questions quickly, and sometimes they may send out answers before they have had time to reflect on all the legal aspects of the question. E-mail also reduces the time the legal writer has to get past any emotional responses he or she may have had when reading the original e-mail. As a result, the writer may respond emotionally, losing the more business-like tone needed to sound professional and in control of the situation. Additionally, quick answers may state points too bluntly. If you have ever tried to resolve a personal dispute over e-mail, you have probably encountered some of these pitfalls.

Finally, the ease with which e-mail is sent and forwarded creates substantial risks. Stories abound in the profession of new associates who were fired as a result of inappropriate e-mail sent through work channels. Legal writers have gotten into trouble for sending e-mail that ridiculed employers, included sexual references, or revealed confidential information. Even when the e-mail is sent to an appropriate reader, the e-mail can be forwarded to an inappropriate audience. At a minimum, the writer of such an e-mail can suffer embarrassment and a lessening of his or her professional reputation. Imprudent e-mail messages have also provided the smoking gun in various legal cases or have played a significant part in major public scandals, such as the e-mail made public in the Enron scandal.

Therefore, the first question to consider when composing e-mail is whether the content should be put in writing at all. Perhaps the information is best left uncommunicated, or saved for a time when you talk to your reader face to face. Send information via e-mail only if you are comfortable seeing that information on the world-wide web, because it may well appear there someday.

Also consider your relationship to the reader and choose your general organization accordingly. If the reader is a client, it is more likely that you should organize the e-mail as a letter, minus the information that would appear before the salutation. You can also use a letter's organization when the legal situation is one that would be addressed in a letter if e-mail were not available. If you would use an interoffice memo if e-mail were unavailable, use a memo format.

When choosing your organizational format, consider your reader's expectations about the e-mail's form. You can often determine this by looking at the reader's e-mail to you. For example, if your reader begins e-mail to you with a salutation, you may want to reflect that form by also beginning your e-mail with a salutation. If, however, your reader simply begins by stating the content, you may begin your e-mail the same way without offending the reader.

When using a salutation and organizing e-mail as a letter, take extra care to keep your polite opening concise. While letter readers easily scan down the page, e-mail readers do not always scroll down to the bottom of the message. Therefore, it is best to communicate your main point early in the message.

Use the subject line of the e-mail to communicate key information about the subject, rather than omitting a subject line or using general language. Most e-mail users get many pieces of e-mail every day, and they often decide whether to open an e-mail based on the subject line. If you do not use this line effectively, your reader may never look at your message.

Often the easiest way to craft a good subject line is to write it after you have completed the message. After you have written and revised your message, review it and select one or two key terms from the message. Using those terms in your subject can make it more informative. To keep the subject line short, you may use abbreviations that will be understandable to the reader.

Example, Vague Subject Line

Update

Example, Informative Subject Line

Planning mtg 9/14 at 9:00

In summary, e-mail needs to get to the point quickly without creating an inappropriate tone. To accomplish this dual focus, a writer needs to think about the main point of the e-mail, word that point concisely and clearly, and then place that point within the appropriate e-mail format. For example, see the following sample structures for e-mail.

— *FIGURE 11-7* —
STRUCTURE OF E-MAIL—LETTER FORMAT

COMPONENT   **EXAMPLE**

Subject Line   **Planning mtg 9/14 at 9:00**

Salutation   LRP Members,

    We will hold our next meeting on Wednesday, Sept. 14 at 9:00 a.m. in
    the upstairs conference room. For your reference, I've included the
Body   agenda below.

    [agenda]

STRUCTURE OF E-MAIL—INTEROFFICE MEMO FORMAT

Subject Line   **LR Planning mtg 9/14 at 9:00**

Opening Sentences   The long-range planning committee will meet next Wednesday (9/14)
    from 9:00 until 10:30 in room 9385, with the following agenda

Body   [agenda]

Applying What You Have Learned

Exercise 11-4
Using E-Mail Selectively

With your classmates, make a list of topics you should not discuss in e-mail. Keep a copy of the list for reference in your future legal employment.

— *Figure 11-8* —
CHECKLIST FOR WRITING E-MAIL

1. Determine whether the information is appropriate to communicate in an e-mail.

2. Consider your relationship to the reader and determine whether a letter or memo format would be most appropriate for the e-mail.

3. Draft the e-mail, following the process used for either a letter or a memo.

4. Draft a subject line that is concise and substantive.

12

Writing Other Legal Documents

THROUGHOUT YOUR LEGAL CAREER, you may draft a wide variety of legal documents, and you will move beyond the basic techniques covered in this text. The basics you have learned here, however, will provide a reliable foundation upon which you can build as your experience grows.

The following subsections provide a sampling of three varied kinds of legal writing: pleadings, legislation, and jury instructions. For each of these kinds of writing, this chapter illustrates how the basic principles you have learned apply to those documents. Although the chapter does not cover all of the information you would need, it does provide the basic information you need to begin writing these documents.

Pleadings

Pleadings are documents that lawyers submit to the court during litigation. One kind of pleading is a complaint, which is filed to start a lawsuit. The complaint states the claim a plaintiff is making against a defendant, with the relevant legal theory and enough facts to support the claim. Another kind of pleading, the answer, denies or admits allegations and states defenses. Other kinds of pleadings include counterclaims, answers to counterclaims, third-party complaints, and motions. These pleadings, along with other pretrial documents, help the parties focus the arguments they will address at the trial. They help both parties see the strengths and weaknesses of their cases; they also help the court evaluate cases fairly and efficiently.

Although it requires you to adapt to different format and organizational constraints, drafting a pleading employs many of the writing skills you have already developed. For example, you will use your awareness of the reader: pleadings are read by lawyers, which means you may use legal terms without defining them and you will be concise. You will remember your ethical obligation to be accurate, so you will use legal terms precisely and you will not copy the language from sample pleadings without understanding what the language means. The precise form of a pleading is governed by statutes and court rules, as was true with your brief, so you will follow those rules carefully.

Structure of Pleadings

Pleadings generally have conventional structures.

■ Caption

Pleadings begin with a caption that, like a brief's caption, includes information identifying the court, the parties, the case, and the name of this particular document; the caption must be accurate.

Sample Caption

STATE OF WISCONSIN	CIRCUIT COURT	DANE COUNTY

JEFFREY TOMARO,
    Plaintiff,

v.   Case No. 09999

DAWN RAZENKOV,
    Defendant

COMPLAINT

■ Commencement

The caption is followed by a commencement, or a paragraph stating other needed introductory information. Although you may often revise the wording for conciseness and clarity, be sure to retain all the needed information. For example, the introductory paragraph in a complaint identifies the parties, the attorney drafting the pleading, and the purpose of the pleading.

Plaintiff Jeffery Tomaro, by his attorney Luann Ehle, states the following against Defendant Dawn Razenkov.

■ Body

The body of the pleading includes the supporting information and is often organized in numbered sections. For example, a complaint includes a series of numbered sentences or paragraphs. Each numbered section asserts either a set of facts or the legal conclusion supported by those facts. When all the facts and legal conclusions have been asserted, the complaint alleges that the defendant is liable and states the law that has been met by the previous elements. The body of the complaint ends by listing the damages or losses suffered by the plaintiff.

Sample Body

1. Jeffery S. Tomaro, the plaintiff, is an adult university student residing at 123 Gilmore Street, Apt. 6, Richmond, WI.

2. Dawn Razenkov, the defendant, is an adult residing at 4405 Bellevue Avenue, Richmond, WI.

3. . . . .

4. The defendant offered to sell plaintiff a suite of matching bedroom, dining room, and living room furniture for $2,000 on December 18, 2007. The defendant said that she would bring the furniture to the plaintiff's apartment.

. . . .

7. On December 19, the plaintiff called the defendant to learn exactly when the furniture would arrive at his apartment. The defendant stated that he could come pick up the furniture on the 20th, but that she did not plan to move it for him.

. . . .

■ Demand for Judgment

The conclusion of a pleading, like the commencement, often follows a conventional format. For example, the body of a complaint is followed by the demand for judgment, which asks the court to take particular actions, such as awarding damages. This demand usually begins with "WHEREFORE" instead of a number.

Sample Demand for Judgment

WHEREFORE the plaintiff requests that the court:

(a) declare that the defendant is . . . ,

(b) award the plaintiff damages,

(c) award the plaintiff its costs and attorney's fees, and

(d) grant the plaintiff such other relief as is appropriate.

The signature, which follows, states to the court that the attorney in good faith believes these facts are true and soundly based in law.

— *Figure 12-1* —
SAMPLE COMPLAINT

STATE OF WISCONSIN	CIRCUIT COURT	DANE COUNTY

JEFFREY TOMARO,
    Plaintiff,

       v.   Case No. 09999

DAWN RAZENKOV,
    Defendant

COMPLAINT

Plaintiff Jeffery Tomaro, by his attorney Luann Ehle, states the following against Defendant Dawn Razenkov.

1. Jeffery S. Tomaro, the plaintiff, is an adult university student residing at 123 Gilmore Street, Apt. 6, Richmond, Dane County, WI.

2. Dawn Razenkov, the defendant, is an adult residing at 4405 Bellevue Avenue, Richmond, Dane County, WI.

3. The defendant offered to sell the plaintiff a used suite of matching bedroom, dining room, and living room furniture for $2,000 on December 18, 2007. The defendant said that she would bring the furniture to the plaintiff's apartment.

4. The plaintiff agreed to buy the furniture for the offered price and gave the defendant a check for $2,000 on that same day. The plaintiff also gave the defendant his address and explained that he needed the furniture there by December 20.

5. The plaintiff and the defendant had a valid contract.

6. On December 19, the plaintiff called the defendant to learn exactly when the furniture would arrive at his apartment. The defendant stated that he could come pick up the furniture on the 20th, but that she did not plan to move it for him.

7. During that same conversation, the defendant offered to have the furniture delivered on the 20th for an additional $600. The plaintiff objected to the additional charge, stating that delivery had been included in the original offer and for the payment of $2,000, which he had already made.

8. The defendant denied this and refused to deliver the furniture without further payment.

9. The defendant is liable for breach of contract under the Uniform Commercial Code and Wisconsin law.

10. The plaintiff subsequently rented a truck and hired two college students to help move the furniture.

11. The plaintiff spent a day and a half making the arrangements for moving the furniture.

WHEREFORE the plaintiff requests that the court:

   (a) declare that the defendant is liable for breach of contract,
   (b) award the plaintiff compensatory damages,
   (c) award the plaintiff court costs, and
   (d) grant plaintiff such other relief as is appropriate.

Dated January 14, 2008

Foxgrover, Swedberg, and Xiong

By_____

Luann Ehle, Attorney for Plaintiff
501 North Avenue
Milwaukee, WI

Plaintiff asserts that the facts stated above are true.

_____

Jeffery S. Tomaro

Drafting a Pleading

When drafting a complaint or other pleading, be thorough. Include all appropriate causes of action, so you do not inadvertently waive a claim for your client. To include all the appropriate causes of action, complaints often list more than one legal theory under which the pleader should recover, often labeling each theory as a separate "count." Thoroughness also requires you to state enough facts that show each element of your claim, so the claim can survive any Motion to Dismiss.

The first task when writing a complaint or other pleading is identifying the legally required content. For example, to write a complaint, you would research the law and facts enough to choose the cause of action and identify the relief available for the client. To make certain that you do not miss any needed points, try working backwards from the relief you want for the client to the legal theory that will provide that relief.

— *FIGURE 12-2* —
STEPS TO IDENTIFY POSSIBLE CAUSES OF ACTION

1. Identify the relief your client wants, including alternatives the court might provide.

2. Identify the causes of action for which the law provides that kind of relief.

3. Identify the relevant law for each cause of action.

4. Identify the elements required by the law used for each cause of action.

5. Research your facts and choose the facts that show that each of the required elements is met.

This process should provide the content needed in the complaint.

When writing a pleading, make sure all the information is accurate. In the caption, make sure both parties are identified accurately. Include all the defendants you intend to sue and be sure their names are correct and correctly spelled. Use the jurisdiction's procedure to get a file number for your case, and double check that number in the caption. Below the caption, insert a commencement sentence that identifies the parties and the filing attorney. When writing the complaint, state the needed facts with enough precision to provide adequate notice to the opponent and to survive a Motion to Dismiss. But keep the content flexible enough to allow you to include information later at trial or in another subsequent proceeding.

The next step in drafting a pleading involves organizing the content to increase clarity. Most pleadings follow a standard organization, so this step is easier than organizing a research memo or brief to a court. For example, when organizing a complaint, you essentially file the needed information into the appropriate places in the document. To make it easier to maintain clarity, divide the facts in a complaint into separate groups when you believe the defendant will deny some of the facts but will not deny others. This approach makes it more likely that you will be able to determine, based on the defendant's answer to your complaint, precisely what the opponent's claims and arguments will be.

After you have divided your facts for clarity, present them in a logical order. Complaints often present information in a step-by-step, inductive order, which differs from the deductive order used in Discussions or the sequential order used in Statements of Fact. Using inductive order means that the complaint first alleges facts and then alleges the conclusion that those facts prove. For example, the body of the complaint begins with facts about the parties and where they live, information needed to establish jurisdiction. After those facts, the complaint in federal court alleges the legal conclusion those facts support. (In state court, this is assumed rather than stated in a separate paragraph.)

The complaint lists the facts pertinent to each element of the claim and asserts that each element has been established. The complaint must allege facts sufficient to show all the elements of the cause of action. When all the elements have been alleged, the complaint then alleges the claim, identifying the relevant law. For example, if the complaint alleges a cause of action based on a statute of other enacted rule, that complaint cites the statute or rule in one of the paragraphs.

— *Figure 12-3* —
SAMPLE ORGANIZATION FOR BODY OF A COMPLAINT

Plaintiff _____, by his/her attorney _____, states the following against Defendant _____.

1. Plaintiff's name, address, and general identification.
2. Defendant's name, address, and general identification.
3. Other facts needed to establish subject matter jurisdiction.
4. *If in a federal court, an allegation that this court has jurisdiction.*

COUNT 1
5. Facts related to first element of claim that are not likely to be debated.
6. Facts related to first element that are likely to be debated, if any.
7. *Allegation that first element is met.*
8. Facts related to second element of claim that are not likely to be debated.
9. Facts related to second element that are likely to be debated, if any.
10. *Allegation that second element is met.*

....

11. *Allegation that defendant is liable under relevant law.*

COUNT 2

Plaintiff realleges facts in paragraphs 1-10, and additionally alleges the following.

12. Additional undebatable facts needed and related to first element of second theory.

13. Additional debatable and needed facts.

14. *Allegation that first element of second theory is met.*

15. Additional undebatable facts needed and related to second element of second theory.

16. Additional debatable and needed facts.

17. *Allegation that defendant is liable under relevant law for second theory.*

. . . .

21. As a result of [defendant's action or inaction], plaintiff suffered [list 17. damages, such as physical injuries and medical bills incurred].

22. Plaintiff also suffered [list damages Plaintiff suffered].

After the body of the complaint is completed, add the request for relief, date the document, and add closing signatures. The request for relief begins with a standard opening phrase and then lists the actions that the plaintiff wants the court to take. It ends with a standard phrase that allows the court to provide other damages that were not listed. The signatures, like signatures on other documents, identify the people who created the document and establish that these people stand by the content of the document.

Applying What You Have Learned

Exercise 12-1
Analyzing a Complaint

Review a complaint you were given as part of an assignment. Identify all the parts, just as they were identified in the previous example. Also identify possible improvements or corrections needed in that document.

— *Figure 12-4* —

Checklist for Writing Complaints

When researching and analyzing

1. Identify the relief your client wants, including any alternatives the court might provide.

2. Identify all the causes of action that would allow that relief given your facts.

3. Identify the relevant law for each cause of action.

4. Identify the elements required by that law used for each cause of action.

5. Research your facts and choose those facts that establish each of the required elements.

When drafting

6. Set up the standard components (caption, commencement, signature, and verification) to be accurate and conform to all relevant court rules.

7. Identify the plaintiff(s) and defendant(s) in the first two paragraphs, including all the information needed to establish jurisdiction.

8. Establish the elements of the cause of action.
   • State facts that establish an element.
   • State that the elements of the cause of action have been met.

9. Allege that the defendant is liable under the specific statute or common law establishing your cause of action.

10. List the damages your client has suffered.

11. Request relief from the court, including
   • all the damages the court could provide.
   • a catchall phrase such as "and any other relief the court finds equitable."

Legislation: Statutes and Regulations

As you learned in Chapter 2, statutes and regulations are often not drafted with readability in mind, although they should be. Well written legislation is more likely to achieve its actual intent, minimize the need for judicial interpretation, and be easier for citizens to follow. Readers of legislation include the attorneys and judges who will interpret the rule technically, but they also include journalists, government officials, and the general public. All are trying to understand and obey the rule.

Although clarity is desirable in a rule, precision is a must. Legislation drafters are sometimes intentionally general about some terms, but they avoid accidental ambiguity. They know that some lawyer at some point is likely to scrutinize every word in the legislation looking for a loophole. Good drafters scrutinize their own words and remove those loopholes before the rule is enacted.

Drafting Legislation

Drafting legislation requires maximizing readability without losing precision. To achieve this, you will use the same writing techniques you have used in your previous legal writing tasks. For example, you will use the same analysis skills. As when reading statutes, you will

- organize the legislation's information into "if . . . then" clauses,
- identify the major parts,
- outline your lists within lists,
- identify terms that are key in this legislation,
- check the existing statutes to see if those terms are already defined, and
- research case law to see if common law exists in this area.

After you have assembled your content, you will use some of the writing techniques you learned in Chapter 5 when revising legal research memos for clarity. For example, you will

- repeat key terms to avoid ambiguity,
- avoid over-loading sentences for readability, and
- use structural terms to clarify the relationship of different ideas in the statute.

When drafting legislation, consider how the law would apply to widely varied facts. Legislation must cover a wide range of circumstances with equal effectiveness. Even the simplest legislation requires thorough testing against hypotheticals. Think about many different hypothetical situations and test the legislation for workability in those situations. When working through this testing process, you will apply the skill you developed to explain and apply a legal standard in your legal research memo (See Chapter 4). Now, rather than having one set of facts to which you apply the law, you will create various sets of facts and mentally see how the law applies. You can become more effective in this process by identifying the "middle term" because that middle term will help you determine which facts would or would not fall under the statute.

In summary, drafting legislation employs all the techniques you learned regarding accurate wording and clear sentence structure. You may apply these techniques differently, but this is a variation rather than a fundamental change. For example, you may vary your use of precision to allow for occasional intentional ambiguity. You may reapply your principles of clear sentence structure to deal with complicated lists and complex subjects. You may insert more definitions as you address a wider, more varied audience. After you have drafted your legislation, you will test it extensively against all sorts of hypothetical situations until you are sure your language will address all those situations effectively.

Applying What You Have Learned

Exercise 12-2
Drafting Legislation

Assume that you work for a state legislator who wants to create a law to prevent reoccurrences of the following events, which happened to his constituents. You have researched the statutes and found no statute covering this point.[1]

1. A three-year-old child had an asthma attack after receiving a teddy bear from his grandmother because the teddy bear was filled with crushed peanut shells, and the child is allergic to peanuts. The grandmother had purchased the teddy bear at a garage sale. She knew of the allergy and had checked the tag on the bear, but that tag did not list what the stuffing included.

2. A six-year old contracted encephalitis after sleeping with a stuffed toy that his father had purchased from a local resale store. Doctors later determined

---

1. It is unlikely that there would be no relevant legislation, but assume this to keep the exercise as simple as possible.

that the toy had been the source of the encephalitis and that the toy must have been already contaminated with the disease when the father purchased it.

3. A teenager who is allergic to feathers purchased a large stuffed teddy bear with a head that could turn. She checked the tag on the toy before purchasing it, which was located on the back of the bear's head. It listed the contents, which did not include feathers. This was accurate as far as the head of the teddy bear was concerned, but the body did include feathers in the stuffing. There was no other label on the teddy bear, other than the one attached to the head.

He gives you the following sentences as a start for the legislation he wants.

Every stuffed toy, whether it is new or used, must have a label that accurately lists all of the contents. Every stuffed toy also has to be sanitary when it is sold.

Identify the problems with this preliminary language, asking yourself the question included in Figure 12-5. As you do this, create a list of the things that need to be done to turn this preliminary draft into a workable piece of legislation.

After you have completed your analysis of the statute, you can begin drafting the actual wording in earnest, using all the techniques you have learned to make sure the wording is precise and the overall statute is as readable as possible.

— *Figure 12-5* —
CHECKLIST FOR DRAFTING LEGISLATION

1. Identify the problem being solved.

2. Research case law to see if common law exists in this area.

3. Draft a preliminary statement of the legislation that would address that problem.

4. Critique the preliminary draft to identify all information needed by asking the following questions.

 • Will this cover the situations contemplated?

- Will it apply to situations that the legislator would not want covered?

- What terms need to be defined to avoid confusion?

- Is this legislation enforceable? If not, what requirements could be enforceable?

- Are the requirements of the legislation clear? For example, could a prosecutor read the statute and determine what elements need to be proven to charge someone with a violation?

- Does the statute include "if" and "then" components, so the reader knows what is required and what happens if the requirements are or are not met?

5. Revise the draft to include the needed information and phrasing.

6. Organize this draft.

   - Organize the information into "if . . . then" clauses.

   - Identify the major parts.

   - Outline your lists within lists.

   - Identify terms that are key in this legislation.

   - Check the existing statutes to see if those terms are already defined.

7. Revise for clarity.

   - Repeat key terms to avoid ambiguity.

   - Avoid over-loading sentences for readability.

   - Use structural terms to clarify the relationship of different ideas in the statute.

Jury Instructions

Jury instructions explain the law to the jury so they can apply it to the facts and reach a verdict. There are many instructions on individual points of law, and the judge selects the instructions needed for a particular trial. Generally speaking, jury instructions explain how the trial will proceed, what the jury must decide, what factors the jury must consider in making its decisions, and how the jury must proceed. Some instructions are given before the trial, when potential jury members enter the courtroom. These instructions generally inform jurors about the parts of the trial to come and their conduct during the trial. Some are read during the trial, as when the judge instructs a jury to disregard a statement from a lawyer or witness. The judge gives the most significant instructions at the end of the trial, either after the evidence or, more commonly, after each side has finished closing arguments.

Although the judge is responsible for the jury instructions, lawyers for each side often draft the instructions they want and submit them to the judge. The judge reviews each individual instruction submitted by the attorneys and may use either attorney's version, use his or her own instruction, or decide not to give an instruction on that point. The judge takes this responsibility seriously, because an error in the instructions can lead to an appellate court finding error in the trial. The judge will not read instructions that seem biased toward one side or the other. Therefore the instructions, even when written by advocates for the parties, must be objectively stated. When giving the instructions, the judge generally reads aloud to the jury from a written text. Because the jury will hear the instructions only once, the instructions have to be extremely clear.

Balancing this need for accuracy with the need for clarity is key when drafting instructions. The instructions must provide an objective and accurate statement of the law, or the judge will not accept them. The instructions must be clear, or the jury will not remember and apply them.

Drafting Jury Instructions

Drafting jury instructions may be a matter of revision or may require starting from scratch. Most jurisdictions have pattern jury instructions that can be used as is or can be modified to fit your case. Sometimes, however, you may need an instruction for which pattern instruction exists. For example, you may need an instruction that explains a city ordinance that a defendant has violated, and there may be no pattern instruction for that particular ordinance.

Whether revising a pattern instruction or revising one you drafted, use the same revision techniques you have previously used to make the text clearer. Divide sentences and focus subjects and verbs, as you learned when revising your legal research memo for clarity. Use the same repetition of key terms and logical links. You will use the same techniques for explaining a statute that you used when analyzing a statute as part of your research. Use short sentences and active verbs to add emphasis, just as you did when revising your brief.

One critical step in revising jury instructions is to make sure each sentence focuses on one main idea, as you learned when revising your legal research memo. Often an instruction can be more readable if it is divided into smaller sentences. Consider, for example, how the second version of the following jury instruction is easier to understand than the original.

Original version: all one sentence

Negligence, either on the part of the plaintiff or on the part of the defendant, is the failure to do what a reasonably careful and prudent person would do under the same or like circumstances, or the doing of something that a reasonably careful and prudent person would not do under the same or like circumstances.[2]

Improved version: divided into three sentences,
each focused on one main idea

Negligence is the failure to do what a reasonably careful and prudent person would do under the same or like circumstances. Negligence can also be the act of doing something that a reasonably careful and prudent person would not do under the same or like circumstances. Negligence can apply to either the plaintiff or the defendant.

The second version divides three ideas into separate sentences: (1) negligence is failure to act, (2) negligence is acting wrongly, and (3) negligence can apply to either party. The first version packs all that information into one sentence. The first jury instruction may be concise, but it is not easily understood. In contrast, the second version presents one idea at a time, and the content is more manageable.

2. Jury instructions used as samples are typical examples, but not copied verbatim from any one source.

To make a jury instruction clearer, you can also use the revision technique of keeping the subject and verb together. In the following example, which illustrates this point, the subject, verbs, and direct objects are marked with italics

Original version: subjects, verbs, and objects divided

The party must prove his contentions by the greater weight of the evidence. A greater *number* of witnesses testifying to a fact on one side or a greater *quantity* of evidence introduced on one side *is* not necessarily of the greater *weight*. The *evidence* given upon any fact that convinces you most strongly of its truthfulness *is* of the greater *weight*.

Improved version: subjects, verbs, and objects kept together

The party must prove his contentions by the greater weight of the evidence. One *side has* not necessarily *provided* the greater *weight* just because that *side produced* a greater number of witnesses testifying to a fact. Nor has one *side* necessarily *provided* the greater *weight* just because that *side introduced* a greater quantity of evidence about a fact. A *side provides* a greater *weight* of evidence on a fact by providing evidence that convinces you most strongly of its truthfulness.

Part of this process is deciding which terms you need to keep and which to omit. Often you will naturally identify many of these essential terms as you identify the elements of the law. However, watch for other essential terms. For example, you may have wording that represents the evidentiary standard, such as "beyond a reasonable doubt" or "by a preponderance of the evidence." These phrases, although sometimes cumbersome, may be legally required. After you have identified the words you must use, you can feel more confident in eliminating other complicated wording. You can then read through the instruction to check the wording, specifically checking for any word that an average high school graduate would have difficulty understanding. If that reader would have to stop and think a while to understand the term, replace it with a more familiar word or phrase.

Exercise 12-3
Revising Jury Instructions

Working in pairs, review the following sentences, which are excerpted from a larger jury instruction. Read the sentences aloud and notice where and how they are hard to understand. Then revise the sentences for clarity. Experiment with the techniques you have just learned to see how they improve the sentences. Specifically, divide the content of the first sentence into several shorter sentences. Then revise the second sentence to get the subject and verb closer to each other. To accomplish this, you may want to choose a different subject and verb so that you can avoid using a list as the subject. As you experiment, periodically read your revised sentences aloud to see how the revisions are working.

"Consortium" involves the love and affection, the companionship and society, the comfort, aid, advice and solace, the rendering of material services, the right of support, and any other elements that normally arise in a close, intimate, and harmonious marriage relationship. A wrongful invasion, impairment, or deprivation of any of these rights, resulting from a disabling injury to a spouse, is a legal loss and a basis for damages to the other spouse harmed or deprived.

Another technique that can make jury instructions clearer is to use the same word for the same idea. You learned about this technique's usefulness for revising legal research memos, but it becomes even more important in jury instructions. If a concept is worded in slightly different terms in a jury instruction, then the jury has to stop and think about the term to determine if it represents a new concept or is just a previous concept worded differently. This takes time, and while the jury is sorting this out the judge is continuing with the instruction. The jury cannot keep up, and some content is inevitably lost. In contrast, when the writer uses the same wording for the same legal concept, the jury recognizes that concept immediately when it hears the same word. The jury is more likely to remember it and more likely to keep up with the speaker's content. For example, the following instruction is confusing because of the wording in the first version. The second version, however, fixes this problem by removing unnecessary terms.

Original version: unneeded terms included

> When deciding this case, you must determine the facts, basing your interpretation on a consideration of all the evidence in light of the law as contained in these instructions. All the relevant law in this case is not embodied in any single instruction, but rather in all my explanations of the law to you. Therefore, you must consider these instructions as a whole and construe them in harmony with each other.

Improved version: unneeded terms omitted

> When deciding this case, you must first determine what the facts are. To determine these facts, consider all the evidence and all the law in these instructions. My instructions explain the law to you, but no one instruction contains all the law. To understand the law, you must consider all of my instructions. You must interpret these instructions in a way that makes them fit together as a whole.

The second version is easier to understand because it repeats the same words for the same idea. It clarifies key ideas by this consistent repetition of words, such as the use of "all" and "as a whole." This repetition of key terms makes it more likely that those terms will stick in a juror's mind.

If a word is an essential legal term that will not be clear to the jury, then you need to introduce those words in sentences that provide the jury an opportunity to understand the term. Sometimes a term is intuitively clear, as the term "reasonable person." Sometimes a term cannot be defined and is not intuitively clear. When that occurs, try to use the term in a context that makes its meaning as clear as possible. Sometimes, however, the law provides a definition of the term. If so, you can insert the definition right after the first use of the term being defined, as you did in other documents. That is the point where the jury is wondering "what does _____ mean?", so that is the useful place to define that term.

Example, well-placed definition

If you decide that the defendant was negligent, then you must then decide whether the defendant's negligence was the *proximate cause* of the damages that the plaintiff has claimed. A *"proximate cause"* is a cause that produced the injury that the plaintiff has complained of, producing that injury in a natural and continuous sequence, unbroken by any intervening cause.

A final technique for making jury instructions clear is to put the information in a logical sequence and present that sequence clearly. If you have ever tried to follow poorly organized instructions for assembling something, you have experienced the problems that occur when instructions are not carefully sequenced. Poor instructions ask you to do something before they identify the parts you are supposed to use. Similarly, poorly sequenced jury instructions either tell the jury to do something they do not know how to do or give the jury information without telling them why they need it. To work well, instructions need to give the jury information when it fits logically with the task at hand.

To provide this logical sequence, you can use the umbrella structure you learned to use when writing correspondence: provide an overview of the task, list the steps involved separately in a logical order, and then remind the reader that the task has been completed. For example, if you were dealing with a statute that included three elements of a crime, you would begin by stating that the jury needs to find all three elements of the crime to find the defendant guilty. Then you would list the elements. If the elements were complicated or involved sub-steps, you would explain everything needed to determine whether the first element was met first before going into the requirements of the second element. For a clear sequence, present the sub-steps of any instructions in the same order in which the jury needs to use them.

Excerpt of Jury Instruction using this umbrella structure

To make its case, the plaintiff has the burden of proving all three of the following propositions by a preponderance of the evidence:

(1) that the defendant was negligent,

(2) that the defendant's negligence was the proximate cause of the damages that the plaintiff has claimed, and

(3) that the plaintiff suffered damages.

To determine that first proposition, whether the defendant was negligent, you must first decide . . . .

Also clarify the sequence of the conditions and results. For example, to explain a condition necessary for the sentence to be true, place it in an "if" phrase at the beginning of a sentence. In the following example revision, the use of these two techniques improves the clarity substantially in comparison to the original version.

Original version: stating an exception without sequenced steps

In asserting the amount of pecuniary damages suffered by the plaintiff, you may consider whether the defendant made an unconditional offer of reinstatement. You are instructed that the rejection of an employer's unconditional job offer ends the accrual of potential back pay liability, absent special circumstances. Determine financial damages by. . . .

Improved version with clearer sequence of steps

If you decide the defendant is liable for financial damages, then you must determine the amount of the financial damages suffered by the plaintiff. To do this, you must. . . .

When you determine the amount of financial damages, consider whether the defendant offered to unconditionally reinstate the plaintiff. If you determine that the defendant did offer to unconditionally reinstate the plaintiff and that the plaintiff rejected the offer, then you may use the date of the rejection in your calculations of back pay liability. If no other special circumstances existed, then you may use the date of that rejection as the ending date for your calculation of the back pay liability. But if . . . .

Although the second version is longer than the first, it is much clearer. The extra length here is needed because several exceptions must be explained. When possible, keep your instructions concise, but never sacrifice clarity for conciseness alone. Resist the urge to skip or combine separate, logically essential steps.

Exercise 12-4
Revising a Jury Instruction

Apply the techniques you have just learned to the following instruction, which includes the definition you revised previously. Specifically,

- divide sentences where needed,
- remove any unneeded terms,
- use legal terms consistently,
- place the definitions where the jury needs them,
- place the information in a logical sequence, and
- use the umbrella structure for the overall instruction.

You may use your previous revisions, although you probably also want to place it in a different location in the instruction. As you did in the previous exercise, read your revision aloud to see how it is working.

INJURY TO SPOUSE: LOSS OF CONSORTIUM

"Consortium" involves the love and affection, the companionship and society, the comfort, aid, advice and solace, the rendering of material services, the right of support, and any other elements that normally arise in a close, intimate, and harmonious marriage relationship. A wrongful invasion, impairment, or deprivation of any of these rights, resulting from a disabling injury to a spouse, is a legal loss and a basis for damages to the other spouse harmed or deprived. In answering this question of whether the plaintiff should receive damages for loss of consortium, you should consider the nature, the form, and the quality of the relationship that existed between the spouses up to the time of the injury. Based on that relationship, determine what sum will represent fair and reasonable compensation for any loss of consortium that was sustained by the deprived spouse as a result of the injury. If you find that the loss will continue in the future, include in your answer damages for the period you are convinced it will continue to exist. Compensation for loss of consortium, except as it relates to material services, is not measured by any rule of market value. Instead, it is measured on the basis of what you find is fair and reasonable compensation for the loss sustained by the deprived spouse.

Compensation for material services is to be measured by what it would reasonably cost in the market for like services. So as not to duplicate damages, do not include in your answer any allowance for loss of earnings or loss of earning capacity of the injured spouse. Those damages are dealt with in another question.

— *FIGURE 12-6* —
CHECKLIST FOR DRAFTING JURY INSTRUCTIONS

1. Begin with a model instruction or draft your own instruction if needed.

2. Use the same words or phrase for the same idea throughout the instructions.

3. Divide the information into separate sentences, with one idea in each sentence.

4. Revise sentences so that the subject and verb are close together. If the verb has a direct object, also keep that direct object near the verb.

5. Sequence the sentences so they present the ideas in the same order in which the jury will use them.

6. Identify critical terms and then remove any other, unneeded terms.

7. Add definitions where needed. When adding a definition, include that definition immediately after the sentence where the term is introduced.

8. When explaining conditions, consider using an "if . . . then" structure in a separate sentence.

— *Figure 12-7* —
SAMPLE JURY INSTRUCTION

COMMENTARY

SAMPLE INSTRUCTION

1. *This paragraph uses the umbrella structure by first stating the general point and then listing the three conditions that can create that situation. The wording at the beginning of the list, "any of the following three things," prepares the reader for the list's structure.*

1 Sometimes the expansion of a park will increase a lot's market value, even though that expansion took some of the lot's land. This can happen if any of the following three things occur:

(1) if the expansion improved the physical condition of the lot,

(2) if the lot is more valuable because it is close to the park's expansion, or

(3) if an owner can now put the lot to a different and more profitable use.

2. *The second paragraph then introduces the next logical step, which is what the jury must decide if they find that one of the three previous conditions existed. Presenting the instructions in a logical order, just like instructions to construct something, is important. Although the jury as a group actually decides the questions later in deliberation, they have to remember the instructions now, as they hear them read. To help the jury do this, the instructions need to follow the order in which the jury will complete the tasks.*

2 If you find that the market value of the Plaintiff's lot has or will increase because of the park's expansion, then you should subtract that increase from the damages you determined. If you find that this increase in market value is greater than the damages you determined, then you should decide that the damages are zero.

3. *The opening of the third paragraph, "but even if," provides a clear signal of how the following information relates to the previous information.*

3 But even if the increase in market value is greater than the damages you determined, you should not subtract anything from the value of the land actually taken from the Plaintiff's lot for the park's expansion.

Conclusion

This chapter has introduced a variety of legal documents you may be writing in the future. For each of these sample documents, it explained how you can apply the techniques you learned in previous chapters to these new documents. Although the writing tasks you face may differ from these examples, you also will be able to apply the basic techniques learned in this book to those tasks.

The techniques you have learned are basic not because they are simple but because they are fundamental. Although you will add more techniques to your repertoire, you will use these fundamentals throughout your legal career. As your expertise with these fundamentals grows, you will find it easier to adapt your writing to the particular demands of any new task, and you will be able to rise to the challenge of all the legal writing tasks you undertake.

Index

E

Editing: Chapters 5, 9 passim, 231-33, 267, 269-70.

E-mail: 247-51.

Emphasis: Chapter 9 passim.

F

Facts:

   Background: 166, 183

   Choice of: 26, 27, 28, 36, 37, 75-77, 94, 95, 100, 106, 166, 168, 171, 183, 184, 187, 191, 198-99.

   Legally significant: 27, 34, 35, 36, 67, 68, 71-73, 75-77, 92, 94, 100.

   Organization of: 75-77, 94, 100, 106, 168.

   Wording of: 198-201.

Feedback: 146-47.

Finding tools: 24, 55-57.

Formality, see Tone.

Format: 7, 8, 9, 11, 182, 190, 248-49.

G

Good law: 48, 53.

H

Handling questions: Chapters 6, 10 passim.

Headings: 27, 64, 67, 78-80, 91, 92, 105, 117-19.

Headnotes: 22-24.

Historical approach: see Organization.

I

Informing and persuading contrasted: 156-57.

Inter-office memos: 242-47.

Introductions: 64, 67, 87, 106, 162, 190.

Introductory phrases, see Phrases, Introductory.

Intrusive phrases, see Phrases.

Issues:

   In opinions: 28, 33, 35-37.

   Objective: 12, 64-65, 67, 70-75, 89-90, 92, 99, 107.

   Persuasive: 162, 164-65, 182, 191, 206-07, 218.

J/K

Judge's point of view, see Readers.

Jurisdiction: 26, 48, 50-53.

Jury instructions: 55, 268-70.

L

Large-scale organization, see Organization.

Legal authority: see Authority and Relevant legal standard.

Legal opinions: see Opinions, legal.

Legal Research Memos: 12-16, 92-113, Chapters 4, 5 passim.

Legal standard: see Relevant legal standard.

Legal Terms: 25, 37. See also Word choice.

Legally significant facts, see Facts.

Legislation drafting: 264-67. See also Statutes.

Letters: see Correspondence.

Listening: 146-47.

Lists in statutes: 39-42.

M

Memorandum of points and authorities: see Briefs to a trial court.

Memos: see Legal research memos or Inter-office memos

Mandatory authority: see Authority, mandatory.

Manners: Chapters 6, 10 passim.

Middle terms in reasoning: 83-84.

N

Note-taking: 35-37, 50-52.
Notice: 11.

O

Opinions:
   Legal: 6, 22-37, 68.
   Dissenting: 31-32.
Oral arguments: Chapter 10 passim.
Oral presentations: Chapters 6, 10 passim.
Organization:
   For clarity: Chapter 5 passim.
   In briefs to a trial court: 156, 172-74, 198-200.
   In correspondence: 234-41.
   In legal research memos: Chapter 4 passim.
   In opinion: 30-34.
   In oral argument: 225-27.
   Large-scale: 26, 31, 117-22, 156, 172-74.
Paragraph: 30, 31, 124-31, 156, 187, 230-31, 236-39.
Overview paragraph: 65-66, 69, 95, 102, 109, 184.

P

Paragraph organization: see Organization, Paragraph.
Parallel structure: 98, 110, 111, 117, 119, 186.
Passive voice: 199, 201.
Persuasion: Chapters 7, 8, 9, 10 passim.
Persuasive authority: see Authority.
Phrases and clauses:
   Introductory: 121-22, 130-31.
   Intrusive: 135, 187, 195.
   Placement of: 130-31, 134-35.
Pleadings: 5, 259-63.
Point headings: 184, 185.
Point of view: see Readers.
Precedent: 53-54. See also Authority.

Precision: 13, 31, 63. See also Accuracy.
Primary authority: see Authority.
Procedural information: 27, 184-85, 192.
Process, see Writing process.
Professional responsibility: 5-6, 17, 48, 50, 62-63, 160, 226-228.
Purpose: 4, 28, 62-63, 160-61, 220-21.

Q

Questions: Chapters 6, 10 passim.
Questions Presented: 12, 64-65, 67, 70-74, 89-92, 99, 107.
Quotations, use of: 68, 84, 93, 103.

R

Readability: 98, 102, Chapter 5 passim.
Readers:
   Adjustments for: 3-4, 7-10, 17-19, 24-25, 143, 152, 237-38, 247-49.
   Legal: 7-10, 62-63, 95, 102, 116, 117, 140, 152-55, 160, 165-66, 185, 254.
   Nonlegal: 152, 230-33, 268-69.
Reading: Chapter 2 passim.
   Cases: 22-37.
   Statutes: 38-45.
Reasoning: 30, 31, 32, 33-34, 35, 36, 37, 81, 83, 96-98, 103, 104, 112, 187-88.
Relevant legal standard: 25, 29, 34-37, 48, 65-68, 69, 78, 81-86, 99, 103, 109, 155, 184, 194, 209.
Regulations: 51, 52. See also Statutes.
Repetition: 16, 64, 98, 104, 109, 130-31, 207, 218.
Research:
   Generally: Chapter 3 passim.
   Process: 57-59.
Research memos, see legal research memos.
Revision
   For clarity: Chapter 5 passim.
   For persuasiveness: Chapter 9 passim.
Rules: see Relevant Legal Standard.